Praise for *Financial Savvy for the Self-Employed*

"A unique single-source reference on financial topics vital to one's success as a self-employed individual."
—Barbara Brabec, publisher of *Barbara Brabec's Self-Employment Survival Letter*

"Busy entrepreneurs can overlook the important ways their personal finances intersect with their business finances. This valuable and crisply written guide will clear up confusion, set you on the right track, and keep you there."
—Theodore J. Miller, editor of *Kiplinger's Personal Finance*

"When you're self-employed, there's no corporation looking out for you, and the government certainly isn't, but Grace Weinstein is—with practical and useful advice."
—Paul and Sarah Edwards, authors of *Working from Home*

"Grace Weinstein's book is punchy, with enough advice to present any small-business person with a huge return on the investment."
—Lewis Altfest, CFP, author of *Lew Altfest Answers Almost All Your Questions About Money*

"An authoritative book for anyone considering or already on the path of self-employment. Grace Weinstein provides a comprehensive and insightful guide that gives the reader the necessary tools to create his or her own success. A reference that belongs on the entrepreneur's bookshelf."
—Katharine A. McGee, CFP, director of the National Association of Personal Financial Advisors

GRACE W. WEINSTEIN

Financial Savvy
for the
Self-Employed

HENRY HOLT AND COMPANY
NEW YORK

Henry Holt and Company, Inc.
Publishers since 1866
115 West 18th Street
New York, New York 10011

Henry Holt® is a registered
trademark of Henry Holt and Company, Inc.

Published in Canada by Fitzhenry & Whiteside Ltd.,
195 Allstate Parkway, Markham, Ontario L3R 4T8.

Library of Congress Cataloging-in-Publication Data
Weinstein, Grace W.
Financial savvy for the self-employed / Grace W. Weinstein.
p.   cm.
Includes bibliographical references and index.
1. Finance, Personal—United States.   2. Self-employed—United
States.   3. Self-employed—Pensions—United States.   I. Title.
HG179.W4387   1995   94-34155
332.024—dc20   CIP

ISBN 0-8050-2537-5
ISBN 0-8050-2539-1 (An Owl Book: pbk.)

Henry Holt books are available for special promotions and
premiums. For details contact: Director, Special Markets.

First published in hardcover in 1995 by
Henry Holt and Company, Inc.

First Owl Book Edition—1996

Designed by Kate Nichols

Printed in the United States of America
All first editions are printed on acid-free paper.∞

10   9   8   7   6   5   4   3   2   1
10   9   8   7   6   5   4   3   2   1   pbk.

For Lee, Samantha, and Rachel—

a joy forever

Contents

Acknowledgments

Appreciative thanks go to a great many people and organizations, too many to list. In addition to all of the self-employed men and women, both struggling and successful, who shared their stories with me, I would like to single out the following, with special thanks for their special help: Barbara Brabec, publisher, *Self-Employment Survival Letter*; John Clark, Social Security Administration; Howard Golden, Kwasha Lipton; Stuart Kessler, CPA, Goldstein Golub Kessler & Company; Lawrence E. Kraus, CPA; Diahann Lassus, CFP, Lassus Wherley & Associates; Jerome Manning and Anita Rosenbloom, Stroock & Stroock & Lavan; Adelina Martorelli, American Society of CLU and ChFC; Sean Mooney, Insurance Information Institute; Steven Norwitz, T. Rowe Price; Chris Petersen, Health Insurance Association of America; Ray Silva, the Guardian Life Insurance Company; David Wasserstrum, CPA, Richard A. Eisner & Company; and Don White, Group Health Association of America.

Introduction

If you work for yourself—whether you incorporate or remain a sole proprietor, whether you work at home or rent office space elsewhere, whether you remain a one-person band or expand your operations—you have special concerns when it comes to managing your money.

- You probably find it difficult to separate personal and business finances.
- You may need to draw on outside resources to supplement your own funding.
- You must manage on an erratic income, finding ways to level the peaks and valleys that go with generating your own paycheck.
- You may be uncertain about matters of record keeping, credit, insurance, taxes, estate planning, even marriage and divorce planning, where personal and business lives intersect.

You are far from alone. For more than a decade the ranks of the self-employed have included at least 8.5 percent of the American work force. Today, following an era of corporate restructuring and downsizing, there are at least twenty million men and women working for themselves. Not surprisingly, perhaps, the 1990s have been called the decade of small business.

You may have started a business because you had an idea that needed pursuing, because you were "excessed" from a salaried job, or because you were bored in retirement. You may have been a recent college graduate unable to find a career position, a midlife manager who was suddenly redundant, a physically challenged man or woman unable to commute to a workplace yet fully able to run a business.

Whatever your reasons for getting started, whatever type of business you run, and however great the demand for your product or service, small business can be a perilous undertaking. You probably know that the failure rate of start-up ventures is high, but are you also aware that one of the biggest problems lies in inadequate financial planning?

Solo entrepreneurs, caught up in the excitement of creating and marketing a new idea, frequently fail to understand just how essential it is to do personal financial planning as well as business financial planning and to separate the two. Knowing where business stops and personal life starts is difficult for the entrepreneur in terms of time; it is equally difficult—and may be even more important—in terms of money.

The successful entrepreneur integrates business and personal finances, for purposes of planning, but separates the mechanics. When you're a one-person show, in other words, your business goals and your personal goals must form a unified picture. But your checkbooks, your record keeping, and your finances in general should be separate. This book is designed to provide a road map to help you achieve that goal.

As an overview: Part I deals with the mechanics of getting started—how to structure your business, how to manage on an erratic income, where and how to raise money. Part II focuses on all-important fringe benefits, on the health and disability insurance you must provide for yourself and on the special property and liability protection you need for your business.

Part III gives you the ins and outs of dealing with taxes, including vital information on the office at home and on avoiding the pitfalls that go with being an independent contractor or using independent contractors to expand your productivity. Part IV stresses the importance of planning ahead—retirement planning, investment strategy, and estate planning. And part V deals with expanding your business in a variety of ways. You will also find a useful listing of additional resources at the end of the book.

In each chapter, the personal and business sides of finance are interwoven in ways that should be helpful whether you are just getting started or you have been self-employed for years. You will find out how—and how not—to use family money to launch or expand your business. You will see how important it is to diversify investments outside your business and how to protect both your family and your business through insurance. You will learn how to integrate business and personal estate planning, and how marriage and divorce can affect your business for better—and for worse.

I wish you good luck!

Part I

In the Beginning

1 Getting Started

- In Sacramento a young college graduate opens a catering business when she realizes that her psychology degree isn't going to land her a salaried job.
- A midlevel manager at IBM, now an ex-manager, opens a bookstore while a colleague, in anticipation of a layoff, buys a franchised printing business.
- A sixty-nine-year-old in Annapolis, a retired real estate broker, starts a referral service to help older homeowners find contractors for small home-improvement jobs.

From one end of the age spectrum to the other, from one coast to the other, small business is flourishing. Whether you are a recent recruit or are just considering joining the twenty million or so Americans who are self-employed, you face two fundamental decisions: what form your business should take, and whether to work at home or to rent space. Each decision has a significant impact on your personal finances.

Structuring Your Business

There are five basic organizational formats to consider: the sole proprietorship, partnership, regular C corporation, S corporation, and the new hybrid called a limited liability company. Some entrepreneurs focus on tax considerations in deciding which structure to adopt, but you shouldn't overlook the importance of personal liability and personal control.

In addition, according to Larchmont, New York, attorney Julian Block, a key factor is the projected income stream over the life of the business. If you expect losses, at least in the early years, you need to decide whether it will be best to save those losses to offset future earnings (which means forming a regular C corporation) or to take those losses immediately on your personal income tax returns (which means selecting any of the other four business structures).

Sole Proprietorships

Most self-employed people, especially one-person operations, start out as sole proprietorships simply because it's easiest. You own the business yourself, make all of the decisions, collect any profits, deduct all of your expenses (subject, of course, to IRS regulations), and report any income (or loss) on your personal income tax return (using Schedule C to report profit and loss from the business). There is little paperwork and little cost involved in setting up shop as a sole proprietor: if you go into business and are not either a partnership or a corporation, then you are a sole proprietor. Put your name on the door, secure whatever local licenses you need, and get going.

On the downside (pros and cons of sole proprietorships are spelled out in table 1.1), you *are* your business. Even if you keep totally separate records, as you should, business losses are personal losses. If you are sued, your personal assets as well as your business assets are at risk. "If you get your business into legal trouble or too far into debt," CPA Bernard Kamoroff notes in

Table 1.1: Sole Proprietorship

ADVANTAGES	DISADVANTAGES
Ease of formation. Less formality, fewer legal restrictions	**Unlimited liability**. Sole proprietor fully responsible for debts.
Sole ownership of profits. Owner need not share with anyone	**Unstable business life**. The enterprise may be crippled or terminated upon illness or death of the owner
Control and decision making vested in one owner. Lends flexibility, ability to respond quickly to business needs	**Less available capital**. Long-term financing harder to secure
Relative freedom from government control and special taxation.	**Relatively limited viewpoint and experience.**

SOURCE: Adapted from Antonio M. Olmi, *Selecting the Legal Structure for Your Firm,* Washington, D.C.: Small Business Administration, undated.

Small-Time Operator, "not only could you lose your business, you could lose your shirt."

What's more, as a sole proprietor, no taxes will be withheld; instead you must pay estimated taxes based on what you expect to earn (see chapter 6 for more information on taxes). You may find it difficult to borrow money from banks and other "official" lenders; financing may have to come from friends and family, which can make it even more difficult to sort out your personal and business finances (see chapter 3). Fringe benefits cost you more because they are not fully tax deductible. And a sole proprietorship is harder to leave behind as a thriving entity; for more information on estate planning see chapter 9.

Nonetheless, many solo providers of services—photographers, computer consultants, copywriters, florists, caterers, and so on—choose to operate as sole proprietors. If you do so, be sure you understand the financial implications. You may operate at a loss, or a very modest profit, before finally making money from your business. When you do, regardless of whether or not you've made money in the past, that income is taxable.

For example: A New Jersey newsletter publisher had borrowed money to get started. When her newsletter finally started turning a profit after three years, she repaid the start-up loan. But the money she used to repay the loan, even though she wasn't able to use it herself, was still taxable income to her. "People have a tough time with this," says Diahann Lassus, a certified financial planner with Lassus Wherley & Associates in New Providence, New Jersey. "They don't see the draw as net profit. This is one of the big differences between a sole proprietorship and a corporation. If you have a corporation, even a one-person corporation, you're paid a salary, have withholding, know exactly what your net profit is. With a sole proprietorship, anything the owner takes out is part of net profit because the owner doesn't get a salary." But this doesn't mean that incorporating is right for you. Read on.

Partnerships

If you are going into business with others, you may want to establish a partnership. A partnership has many of the advantages of the sole proprietorship. It's easy to establish, income can be distributed according to any formula you determine among the partners, and that income is reported on each partner's personal income tax return. Deductions for business expenses, too, can be taken by each partner on his or her personal income tax return. A partnership also has similar disadvantages, notably the fact that each partner is personally liable for debts of the partnership. One partner can make commitments binding on all partners. It also carries the potential for a falling-out among partners, a situation that can cripple an otherwise successful business and often has all of the emotional ramifications of a divorce. The pros and cons of partnerships are itemized in table 1.2.

Problems can be forestalled, at least to some extent, by a carefully drawn partnership agreement, a document that accountant Stuart Kessler calls "a prenuptial for a business." You don't technically need a formal agreement; a handshake will do.

Table 1.2: Partnership

ADVANTAGES	DISADVANTAGES
Ease of formation. Less formality and expense than forming a corporation	**Unstable life.** Elimination of one partner automatically dissolves the partnership, although the partnership can be reorganized
Direct rewards. Partners motivated by sharing in profits	**Long-term financing harder to obtain than for a corporation.** May be easier than for sole proprietorship
Flexibility. More flexible in decision-making process than a corporation. May be less so than a sole proprietorship	**Firm bound by the acts of just one partner.** Partnership is legally responsible for acts by each partner.
Relative freedom from government control and taxation.	**Difficulty of disposing of partnership interest.** Buying out a partner may be difficult unless specifically arranged for in the written agreement

SOURCE: Adapted from Antonio M. Olmi, *Selecting the Legal Structure for Your Firm*, Washington, D.C.: Small Business Administration, undated.

But informal partnerships are not a good idea. The Uniform Partnership Act, which has been adopted in every state but Louisiana, defines a partnership, with or without a formal agreement, as "an association of two or more persons to carry on as co-owners of a business." If you don't sign a partnership agreement but act as partners, in other words, you will still have all of the responsibilities of a partnership but you won't have any of the protection against misunderstanding and conflict that a formal agreement can provide. And if you don't sign an agreement providing for continuation of the partnership when one partner leaves, the partnership will automatically dissolve.

Such an agreement may include whatever details you like, but it should cover the crucial elements of partnership responsibilities and duties ("I'll deal with clients; you handle the finances"), the method for admitting new partners, the length of the partnership (if it is not intended to be indefinite), the method of assigning profits and losses, how to resolve disputes, and what happens if one partner should leave, become incapacitated, or die. A competent attorney can help, but be sure to use one who has worked with small-business partnerships (see chapter 10, on selecting advisers). Each partner may also want to consult a separate attorney, just to be sure that the agreement protects each individual.

Be sure to talk about everything in advance, so that you know whether you and your partners have similar goals and expectations. As Stephen G. Thomas, a former partner of an environmental consulting firm in North Dakota, wrote in *Inc.* magazine, "Partners may have different opinions on what risk is justifiable, how money should be managed, and what the work ethic really means." You and your partners may have different strengths—that may be what makes you a good team—but in a start-up business, when you and your partners may be the entire staff and therefore responsible for everything from management decisions to making coffee, you won't be comfortable unless each partner feels that everyone is pulling his or her own weight. Feelings that one partner is not contributing equally, well-founded or not, inevitably lead to friction.

One point to work out up front is who earns how much. Do you want to consider how much income each of you brings in during the year and then distribute profits on a proportionate basis? Or do you simply want to assume that each of you will be working just as hard, regardless of the volume of work brought in, and that therefore you will split the income fifty-fifty (or, of course, in thirds or fourths; the fraction depends on the number of partners)? There is no single right answer to this question, although the fifty-fifty arrangement is simpler; the important thing is to spell out your arrangement, in writing, in advance. Remember, too, that partnership income is flow-through income; that is, it flows right through the partnership to each of you as individuals and is reported on your individual income tax forms.

TIP

If you and two pals start a printing business together, you will each be a "general partner" with full rights and responsibilities. If Uncle Joe kicks in some bucks to help you get started, he may be designated a "limited partner," one who risks only the amount of his investment in the business so long as he does not participate in active management.

Regular C Corporations

Instead of either a sole proprietorship or a partnership, you may decide to form a corporation. You can incorporate all by yourself or with partners, but carefully think through your reasons for doing so.

Joni and Dale Warner own Two Country Crafters in South Florida, Florida, makers of ceramic and wood crafts for the home. The Warners incorporated because they were "concerned about product liability." Says Dale, "The main reason was to keep the business separate from us personally."

Protection against liability—whether lawsuits about defective products or angry creditors—is the main reason small businesses incorporate. It's a way of protecting your personal assets—your bank accounts, your kids' college funds, and your home—from being wiped out along with your business. But this isn't true for every type of business, and you should consult a competent adviser before incorporating. It won't help, for example, if you're a writer and are accused of libel. It won't help if you're a doctor defending a claim of malpractice. In such situations, personal assets are not shielded by incorporation.

But there can be other benefits to incorporation (see table 1.3). The owner of a regular C corporation, for example, can deduct the family's entire cost of health insurance and deductible health care as well as premiums for disability insurance and up to $50,000 of life insurance. Deducting the cost of these fringe benefits also results in a lower net income on which Medicare tax is due.

Table 1.3: Corporation

ADVANTAGES	DISADVANTAGES
Limited liability for owners/stockholders.	Extensive government regulation and required local, state, and federal reports.
Ownership readily transferrable.	Expense and legal formalities in forming a corporation.
Separate legal existence. Corporation continues to exist and do business if a principal owner is disabled or dies	Double tax. Income tax on corporate net income (profit) and on individual salary and dividends. Double tax can be eliminated by forming an S corporation
Relative ease of securing capital. Assets of corporation can be used to secure long-term financing	Personal guarantees may be required by lenders.

SOURCE: Adapted from Antonio M. Olmi, *Selecting the Legal Structure for Your Firm*, Washington, D.C.: Small Business Administration, undated.

Of course, there are other financial implications of incorporating your business. First, it will cost you money to do so: there are fees to be paid, books to be kept, regular board meetings to be held and documented, and annual tax returns to be filed for both your corporation and yourself. You can do all of this yourself, but it may not be advisable to do so.

The regular corporation is the only form of business that is a legal entity in and of itself. Your corporation must pay taxes on its profits, therefore, even as you pay personal income taxes on the income you derive from the corporation. Corporate tax rates may be lower than individual tax rates (although this is not always the case), but there is effectively double taxation on the corporate level. This double taxation may be avoided if you are a small, one-person service business, however, because you can probably take all of your profits as salary. Just be sure you get good legal and accounting advice.

S Corporations

A hybrid form of incorporation, available in most states, mitigates some of the tax problems of the C corporation: the S corporation, formerly called subchapter S corporation. With an S corp, elected by filing Form 2553 with the Internal Revenue Service, you have protection against liability. You also avoid double taxation because profits are reported on your personal income tax return and are taxable at your personal income tax rate. There is no tax payable by the corporation as such; instead profits "pass through" to the shareholders.

What's more, with an S corp you have added flexibility. You can choose to use the cash basis method of accounting rather than the accrual basis that regular corporations generally must use. The cash method allows you to minimize taxes by judiciously accelerating and deferring income and deductions.

Moreover, Diahann Lassus, whose financial-planning practice is organized as an S corp, notes that you can lower your "salary" while taking additional money out of the business as flow-through income. You have to pay income taxes on all of the money you take out of the business, whatever you call it, but the separation can be beneficial, for example, in lowering the amount of Social Security tax that is due—no FICA tax is paid on flow-through income—or in lowering self-employment income so that you qualify for business subsidies that may be enacted in

---

TIP

Choose competent advisers in structuring your business, but don't rely on them exclusively. One newly minted consultant discovered, after receiving delinquency notices and penalties from both federal and state taxing authorities, that setting up an S corporation required filing for this special tax status with the IRS as well as filing incorporation papers with the state. Advisers had neglected to point this out. Advisers don't pay the penalties.

the future. One caveat, however: you can't take less salary than the IRS considers reasonable for your industry and your level of profit, or you may wind up facing tax penalties.

S corporations became very popular after the Tax Reform Act of 1986 set top corporate tax rates higher than the top individual rate. They are likely to be far less popular now that the 1993 tax act has reversed the situation, pushing top individual tax rates higher than top corporate rates. In 1995, if your adjusted gross income tops $117,950 as a single or $143,660 as a married couple filing jointly, you are taxed at a 36 percent rate; at higher levels of income the rates are even higher. By contrast, the corporate tax rate (on regular C corporations) is still 34 percent for businesses with taxable income of up to $10 million—a level most self-employed people don't reach.

You still avoid double taxation with an S corp, but it's more important than ever to get skillful advice from an attorney or an accountant before structuring your business or considering a change. Be particularly cautious if you do business in a state that has not enacted S corporation provisions similar to the federal provisions.

Remember, too, that taxes are only one part of the story. According to the accounting firm of Price Waterhouse, S corporations are at a disadvantage compared with regular C corporations in providing fringe benefits. Amounts you pay toward accident and health insurance, medical expense reimbursement, and group term life insurance are deductible by your S corporation but are also, for the most part, taxable income. Table 1.4 provides a comparison of business structures; limited liability companies, described in the next section but not addressed in the table, are similar to partnerships but with the limited liability of corporations.

Limited Liability Companies

Still another organizational structure is rapidly becoming available; by mid-summer 1995, almost every state had adopted enabling legislation. Called the limited liability company, this for-

Table 1.4: Choosing the Right Structure for Your Business

	SOLE	PARTNERSHIP	C CORP	S CORP
Liability of Owner	Unlimited	Unlimited (except for limited partners)	Limited	Limited
Taxation of Income	Passed through to individual tax return	Each partner is taxed on allocated share of income whether or not distributed	Corporation is taxed	Same as partnership
Federal Tax Rate	Individual rate	Individual partners' rates	Graduated, up to 34 percent	Same as partnership
Administrative Costs	Minimal	Minimal, but should develop written partnership agreement; separate tax return	Incorporation filing and separate tax return fees; additional payroll costs	Same as C corp plus filing for S corp status
Life of Entity	Dissolved at death of sole proprietor	May be dissolved at death or withdrawal of a partner	Legal continuity unaffected by death or withdrawal of key employee/shareholder	Continuity unaffected; death of shareholder will terminate S corp election if shares pass to an ineligible shareholder
Management	Proprietor has direct control	Usually ruled by committee and majority vote	More centralized and organized management	Same as C corp

SOURCE: Weber Lipshie & Company, *Trendlines,* August–September 1992.

mat has some of the advantages of partnerships along with some of the advantages of corporations.

Limited liability companies (LLCs) have the flexibility and tax treatment of partnerships along with the limited liability of corporations. This limited liability has made the structure very attractive to professional service firms traditionally organized as partnerships. In the wake of multimillion-dollar charges against the assets of large accounting firms and the personal assets of their partners, many large firms reorganized as limited liability companies. The same principle applies to far smaller firms.

LLCs, like partnerships, are pass-through entities with profits and losses reported on the individual tax returns of the "members." Note, though, that state laws differ dramatically; in some states a one-person business may take the LLC form while in others this isn't possible. In the latter case an S corporation might be the best choice. One other potential drawback is simply that the LLC concept is new; since lenders are generally unfamiliar with this business structure, you may have difficulty securing loans.

CHECKLIST FOR STARTING A SMALL BUSINESS

- Consult an attorney regarding legal requirements.
- Consult an accountant regarding financial and tax requirements.
- Decide on the organizational structure best suited to your business.
- Register the name of the business with your state.
- Make appropriate applications for state licenses to operate.
- Apply for a local business license, if applicable.
- Obtain a federal employer identification number by filing Form SS-4.
- Consult an insurance agent about necessary protection.

SOURCE: Adapted from Arthur Andersen, *An Entrepreneur's Guide to Starting a Business*, Chicago: Arthur Andersen & Co., 1991, p. 5.

Working at Home

Both the catering business and the referral service described at the beginning of this chapter can be run from home. So can many other small businesses, from word-processing services to graphic arts studios, accounting firms to custom sign production. Before you decide whether to work at home or to rent space, however, consider the trade-offs.

On the plus side, working at home gives you total flexibility to plan your workday and your workweek. You can burn the midnight oil if that's when you are most productive. You can reduce your tax bill through taking deductions for your home office (see chapter 6). You can go to work in jeans, make time for your family, and save the time and money normally expended on commuting.

On the downside, that total flexibility may mean that you either become distracted by household chores, and find it hard to focus on work, or that you never take time off from work because it's always there. It takes considerable self-discipline to keep from going to either extreme. You must set your own deadlines and adhere to them, trying not to go overboard toward all work and no play. You have to make a deliberate effort to separate work and leisure, and business finances from personal finances. You may feel isolated, and you may find it difficult to combat that isolation or even to hire help when you need it, because others may be reluctant to come into a home office. You may also find it difficult to maintain a businesslike, professional image.

Some work-at-home businesspeople feel so strongly that they are not taken seriously because they work at home that they go to great lengths to conceal the fact. A few years back an entrepreneur marketed an audiotape of the background noises you would typically hear in an office—ringing phones, clicking computer keys, and so on—to make clients and customers on the other end of a telephone line believe they were calling a "real" office.

But at least twelve million Americans have found working at

home to be desirable. You can, too, if you set your own ground rules in advance. For example, Annie Moldafsky, a writer-turned-marketing-communications-consultant in Chicago, says, "When I had a home office, it was a professional office. I got dressed in the morning to walk across the hall. Doing so put me in the proper frame of mind and helped me to separate my responsibilities to my household and my responsibilities to my clients."

If you work at home, be professional—in managing time, answering the phone, getting dressed, dealing with family members, and managing your money. Install a separate business telephone line; it documents your tax deduction for telephone calls (the basic cost of a home line is not deductible, even if you use it partly for business; see chapter 6) and keeps family members from interrupting business conversations. Have an answering machine, voice mail, or answering service to pick up calls during hours when your business is closed. And do close your business when the workday is over. Set limits on the hours you work; tell others you are unavailable during those hours but then make a point of being available to them at other times. A big problem for many home-based workers is knowing when to stop.

Another problem for many is the blurring of business and personal bills and record keeping. If you rent an outside office, you're more likely to keep your finances separate. If you work at home, it's just as important to be meticulous about doing so. Have a separate checking account for your business, and maintain careful records documenting income and outgo; chapter 2 describes this process in more detail.

Find out what the local rules are, too, so you don't unknowingly run afoul of the law. Steve Jobs may have started Apple Computer from his garage, but he couldn't have done so legally in many locations. Unfortunately, some localities continue to frown on home-based businesses. This is especially true if your business brings people to your home and added traffic to your neighborhood, but it also can be true even if no one comes to your home office; there are many cities and towns where archaic zoning rules either restrict all home-based businesses or specify which are OK and which are not.

Talk about archaic: New Rochelle, New York, is one of a number of municipalities with a laundry list of permitted home businesses. It is OK to be a milliner at home, according to this list, but not a management consultant. The case is in the courts at this writing, but similar laws are on the books all over the country—including New York City, which permits home offices for doctors and lawyers but specifically prohibits them for public relations and advertising agencies, interior decorators, and stockbrokers. Of course, many people in New York City, as elsewhere, operate home businesses with no one the wiser; according to the American Home Business Association, New York City actually has more home-based businesses than anywhere else in the country.

What to do if you run afoul of zoning regulations? Consider filing for a variance if your home-based business does not conform. If the only problem is that you might have employees come to your home, consider using contract workers who can work on their own premises (see chapter 10 for more on using outside help). If noise is an issue, see what you can do about soundproofing.

Operating outside the law, even if you're comfortable doing so, always entails the risk of being caught. But time and social trends are on your side. As Lynne Waymon writes in *Starting and Managing a Business from Your Home,* an SBA booklet that is currently out of print, "Cultural and national trends point in the direction of zoning regulations that allow quiet, nonpolluting, low-traffic kinds of home businesses. More and more corporations are employing people to work at home. Most neighborhoods will adopt a 'live and let live' attitude if you keep your premises neat and quiet and don't create traffic and parking problems."

Municipal rules, however, may not be your only worry. If you live in a condominium or cooperative bound by bylaws and a board of directors, you may find yourself in hot water with a home-based business. Doctors are almost always permitted to have offices in their homes, according to municipal zoning regulations, but a psychiatrist in Chicago was told recently that he was violating his condominium development's no-business provision and must move his practice.

All that said, you can probably run a home-based business without interference so long as you don't bother your neighbors. If you don't have a commercial sign out front, generate traffic and parking problems, or hire several in help, it's likely that no one will know and no one will complain about your home-based business.

Just don't keep yourself too much of a secret. Customers and clients must know where to find you. This may mean taking a business listing in the telephone book—not only more expensive than a residential listing, but a tip-off to anyone who cares that you are running a business at home. If you earn money from your business, you must pay estimated and annual income taxes. If you hire help you must file the appropriate tax forms for them. If you start a retirement plan other than a simple individual retirement account (IRA), you will need a federal identification number in addition to your Social Security number. There are lots of ways in which any home-based business can become known—all of which may be to the good if you want potential customers and clients to know where to find you.

Moving On

Some self-employed people work out of their homes forever. Others find, after a while, that it's time to move on. For Annie Moldafsky, the moment of truth came when her family sold one house and bought another. "We were going to be renovating our new house, and I realized it would be impossible to work at home during the construction. Then, too, my accountant felt it looked much better on my income tax to have a separate office. So I moved, and I do find it easier now to separate my work life and my personal life. It's easier to leave the office, and work, behind at the end of the day."

Moldafsky is still a one-woman business. Others move their offices when the need for staff outgrows the space at home. You'll know when, and if, the time is right for you to move.

Outside Space

The choice isn't simply between running a business from your kitchen table and renting a full-fledged office. The home office itself can take many forms, from a bridge table set up in the family room (not a good idea if you want to claim a tax deduction for a home office) to a separate room dedicated to an office to a separate suite or adjacent structure. The outside office, similarly, can run the gamut from shared space in a business "incubator" or professional suite to your own private offices.

Business incubators, designed as shared space with support services for start-up ventures, can be particularly helpful. For information on business incubators, contact the National Business Incubation Association, One President Street, Athens, OH 45701; 614-593-4331.

A New York consultant on work and family issues moved out of her home office into incubator space last year and finds it the best of all possible worlds. She and her partner share a one-room office with a reasonable rent and have access to a receptionist, fax and copy machines, a conference room, a coffee machine, and a microwave. Mail is collected, the telephone is answered with a personal touch, and clerical services are available at an hourly rate.

"It keeps us from being totally isolated," she comments, "and we've had marvelous brainstorming sessions with others on the floor." Among the tenants, some well-established and some start-up ventures, but all self-employed, are an attorney, an accountant, a speaker's bureau, and a couple of placement firms. Similar incubator space exists in many cities; in the Manhattan Yellow Pages the listing is under "office and desk space rental service."

If you are ready to lease commercial office space, start by identifying your needs and your budget, then talk to a commercial real estate agent. In determining your budget, don't forget what it will cost to move and to furnish your new quarters, to hook up utilities, and to print new stationery. And be prepared to put down at least one month's rent as a security deposit; some landlords will require more because small businesses are poor credit risks.

Then negotiate the lease carefully, and be sure that it spells everything out without any ambiguity. Find out:

- How long the lease will run, from beginning to end.
- What adjustment will be made if the space isn't ready by your scheduled move-in date.
- The amount of the rent, and exactly how much usable space you are renting. Commercial leases in some cities allocate a portion of each tenant's rent to common spaces such as hallways, elevator shafts, and bathrooms.
- Who pays for improvements and, if you do, whether you may take those improvements with you when you move on.
- What services are provided. If you like to work at night or on weekends, for example, be sure the building will be heated or cooled during these off hours.
- Whether you can renew the lease at expiration, at a given rate, and whether you can sublease the space to others if you move out in advance of expiration. You might need more space if your business succeeds beyond your current expectations, or, conversely, you might have to retrench and move back to a home office if things don't go well.

Wherever You Work

Whether you remain at home or take business space elsewhere, remember the following guidelines.

Separate Bank Accounts

Draw lines between your personal and business finances. Maintain a separate checking account for your business and funnel all business income and outgo through that checking account. This paper trail will enable you to have an accurate picture of how your business is doing. It will also satisfy the IRS in case you are audited. If you maintain a home office, where some of your expenses are inevitably intermingled, write a business check to yourself for the applicable portion of your homeowners insurance, heating bill, and other office-in-the-home deductibles.

Insurance

Be sure you have adequate insurance coverage. If you have computer equipment, you may need special insurance. If people come to your office—whether clients, customers, or just the occasional computer technician—you need liability insurance. If you produce a product, you'll need product liability coverage. If you hire help, you'll need workers' compensation coverage. If you use your car for business, be sure your automobile insurer is aware of the fact; you don't want an unpleasant surprise after you file a claim. (You'll find more information on insurance in chapter 5.)

Leasing Equipment

Consider keeping costs down by leasing equipment instead of buying, thereby eliminating the large cash outlay associated with either an outright purchase or a sizable down payment on a financing arrangement. Virtually every kind of equipment, from a copying machine to an automobile, can be leased. When you lease, you don't need to worry about equipment becoming obsolete; at the end of the lease you can upgrade. Lease payments are deductible as operating expenses, although you may do better on the tax front with a purchase.

The downside of leasing, in addition to fewer tax benefits, is that it usually costs more. When you're finished with a lease, all you own is a piece of paper; when you finish paying off an auto loan, by contrast, you own a physical asset that can be sold. Furthermore, because a lease is a contractual obligation, you can't just walk away; if you no longer need the equipment, for any reason, you will probably have to continue making payments until the lease is up.

TIP

If you will rely on your own automobile insurance when leasing a car, ask the dealer or leasing company for gap insurance. This will supplement your personal policy and make up the difference between the car's depreciated market value (the amount your policy will pay) and the amount you owe on the lease (which you must continue to pay if the car is stolen or totaled in an accident).

Before you sign a lease, check into the leasing company's reputation. And don't assume that the terms of a lease are fixed; you can and should negotiate to get the best deal you can. Then be sure that the contract spells out:

- the term of the agreement and any renewal options;
- the value of the equipment, for insurance purposes;
- what happens to the equipment at the end of the lease period;
- the payment amount; and
- cancellation penalties.

Utilizing Resources

Take advantage of every resource available. The SBA publishes a lot of useful information. Most community colleges offer inexpensive, practical courses designed specifically for small business and the self-employed. Trade or professional associations in your specific area of business and national and regional associations of small-business owners can offer opportunities for networking and sharing experience.

Electronic bulletin boards are a boon to the computer literate, allowing the self-employed to benefit from one another's advice and experience without ever leaving the office. Many bulletin boards are local; others are national. The CompuServe Information Service's Working from Home Forum, as one example, has linked small businesses all over the country in a network that can provide information, practical tips, and help with specific problems. In the latter category, using Working from Home's bulletin board for public relations and advertising, a public relations practitioner in upstate New York quickly located a photographer to cover an event in Raleigh, North Carolina. The Small Business Administration itself has started SBA On-Line; response was so strong that the number of phone lines was doubled by the end of the first week.

Sharing Resources

To save both money and time, pool your resources with other entrepreneurs rather than going it alone. The business incubators described earlier are one way to pool resources but you can also do so on your own, with one or more colleagues. For example, find a colleague, preferably in a related business, and rent office space together. A photographer and an illustrator did exactly this, in Fort Worth, Texas, and got far more space than either could have afforded alone. Two formerly home-based interior designers teamed up to rent space in Deerfield, Illinois; because their customers came from different areas, the two decorators didn't step on each other's toes. In fact, in similar circumstances, you could make an arrangement where you would help each other out if faced with assignment overload.

According to a survey conducted in late 1992 by the Kessler Exchange, a small-business research and membership organization based in Northridge, California, one-third of the more than five hundred small-business owners surveyed shared resources on a regular basis. Beyond sharing information, the most common form of cooperation, many reported sharing equipment and supplies; office, manufacturing, or warehouse space; advertising space; or promotional material. Some even shared employees. Table 1.5 demonstrates the positive results.

Another way of sharing resources involves joining an association designed for that purpose. For example, as a member of Support Services Alliance, either individually or through a trade association, you can tap accounting, tax, and record-keeping

Table 1.5: Sharing Resources

SHORT-TERM RESULTS	OF THOSE SURVEYED
Money saved	36%
Sales increased	31
Time saved	30
Acquired an otherwise unobtainable product or service	22

LONG-TERM RESULTS	
Improved profits	33%
Increased clientele	33
Improved image	27
Lower overhead	23
Business deals with the sharing business	22

SOURCE: Northridge, Calif.: Kessler Exchange, 1992.
NOTE: Numbers do not add up to 100 percent because some business owners reported multiple results.

services; you can also (in many states) secure medical, dental, life, and disability insurance. SSA, formed in 1977 to enable small businesses to secure the volume discounts available to large companies (other examples are long-distance telephone services, car rentals, and a mail-order prescription drug program), is located in Schoharie, New York; 800-322-3920.

Record Keeping

Keep accurate and up-to-date records of both personal and business finances. Start now. Don't wait until tax time or until you are totally confused. Good records will be needed to prepare tax returns, to make both personal and business decisions, and to apply for credit. Maintaining good records, as time consuming as it may seem, will save you money in the long run.

But good records needn't mean excessive records. Many of us are drowning in a sea of paper, unable to determine what must be kept and what can be thrown away. As a result, we keep too much. Here are some guidelines that should help:

On the Personal Side

Keep the papers you will need to document facts for as long as those facts might be questioned.

Some things have to be kept almost forever: records on a home purchase and home improvements (to document—and reduce—your "cost basis" when you sell); buy and sell documents on securities, paintings, rare coins (for the same reason); old tax returns (to give you a detailed record of your affairs over the years). Insurance policies should be retained for several years after the expiration date, in case a delayed claim is filed. And you'll want to keep your budget sheets and net worth statements (described in chapter 2) to measure your progress over the years.

Other records need to be kept for shorter periods of time. Any papers that document a tax deduction (other than those related to long-term capital gains or losses, such as on a house or securities) should be kept for a minimum of three years after the filing of that return; that's the usual audit period for federal income tax returns, although some states have different rules. For deductions claimed for the 1995 tax year, on a return filed in 1996, this means keeping related documents until 1999. Tax records to be kept for at least three years after filing include bills substantiating home office deductions or deductible business travel, bills for medical services, records of casualty or theft losses, and so on. (You'll find more information on tax requirements in chapter 6.)

Other bits and pieces of the paper storm that drifts through your life may be discarded almost immediately. Bills from automobile service stations and department stores, for instance, may be disposed of as soon as your payment is accurately credited, as can any expired warranty on a product or service.

Keep documents that are difficult or impossible to replace (birth certificates, house deeds, securities) in a bank vault or, as a definite second best, in a fireproof strong box at home. For current records try an accordion file, with a pocket for each category: insurance policies, bank statements, bills and receipts, warranties, and so forth. Don't forget a list of what's in your safe-deposit box.

> ### TIP
> Instead of filing canceled checks by month and year and winding up with decades of checks filling old shoeboxes, try this: As you reconcile each month's bank statement, sort canceled checks by category. Then store them in files labeled by tax-related category—home improvements, medical and dental bills, and so on. Keep the rest, filed by month, for a year or until you're sure you won't need to prove that you've paid a bill, then discard. This method reduces paper clutter; it also keeps your tax records properly filed and readily available.

On the Business Side

Beyond documenting tax deductions, your records should tell you how much cash you owe, how much cash is owed to you, and how much cash you have on hand.

Specifically, according to Paul and Sarah Edwards, authors of *Working from Home* (and gurus on the subject), you may need to track (depending on your specific business):

- banking transactions
- bills, so that you know which bills are due and pay them on schedule
- time and expenses, so that you can bill customers and clients where possible or, at least, track your own expenditures on a project
- billing or invoicing, so that you know how much you are owed and can send prompt statements to get paid for the goods or services you've delivered (this is crucial; if you don't bill on time, you won't be paid on time)
- inventories, if you must maintain them, so that you know just what you have on hand at any given time
- sales records, so that you know exactly what you've sold and any sales tax you've collected

To accomplish all of this the SBA suggests keeping five basic journals:

1. A check register, with the purpose of each check noted (remember, this is a separate checking account for your business).
2. Cash receipts, if you have a cash-based business, showing the amount of money received, from whom, and for what.
3. A sales journal showing the business transaction, date, for whom it was performed, the amount of the invoice, and the sales tax, if applicable.
4. A voucher register providing a record of bills, money owed, to whom it is owed, the amount, and the service.
5. A general journal to track the other four.

If your business is a sole proprietorship providing a service (rather than products), you may need only a checkbook and a general ledger with separate pages for income and outgo. For example, I use a six-column ledger book with pages set aside at the beginning of each year to record invoices out ("receivables"), by client, amount, the date sent, and the date received. The next twelve pages are then used to record income for each month, with columns devoted to each regular client and to catch-all categories (corporate assignments, magazine articles, books); specific receipts are annotated in the left-hand column by date, with amounts entered in the appropriate column. Another set of twelve pages is devoted to month-by-month expenses. Again, dates and payees are listed in the wide left-hand column, with the other six columns devoted to categories (postage and supplies, periodicals, travel, telephone, and so on). Columns on both the income and outgo side are added month by month, and yearly totals (buttressed by a file folder full of receipts and the 1099 forms received from clients) are then available for income tax preparation.

This record keeping is especially important if you have a small home-based business in an area that could be considered a

> **TIP**
>
> Business financial records that you may want to keep indef-
> initely include (1) profit-and-loss statements, which will
> help you analyze your business or put a value on it when it's
> time to sell; (2) canceled checks—all of them, since they
> are business related; (3) copies of income tax returns and
> related material; and (4) pension records.

hobby. Perhaps you sew doll clothes or do custom woodworking.
The IRS may decide that what you are doing is only a hobby, and
it will disallow expense deductions. Records of all income and
outgo will be very helpful if this should happen.

If your business is either a partnership or a corporation, if
you have employees or if you maintain an inventory, your bookkeeping must be a bit more complicated. First of all, while
many self-employed individuals have the option of choosing
either the cash or accrual method of accounting (that is, of
recording income and outgo when actually received or when
the transaction occurs), businesses with inventory must use the
accrual method. This may become a significant factor only in
accounting for year-end transactions, where a sale may be made
in one calendar year and cash received in the next, according
to CPA Bernard Kamoroff, but you should definitely seek the
advice of an accountant in setting up your record-keeping
system.

Your business checkbook is an essential part of your business
record keeping, but it should not stand alone. A ledger book will
allow you to summarize transactions, post cash purchases (if you
pick up a pad of paper at the stationery store, you're not likely to
pay by check), and have a complete record of your business's
cash flow. A ledger book also allows you to note reimbursements
that your business makes to you for cash expenses.

Annie Moldafsky posts expenses in her ledger book every day.
Then once a month she submits records to her bookkeeper, who
cuts a check to cover expenses. As an example, Moldafsky notes,
she ran short when returning from New York to Chicago on a

business trip and had to pay her airport limousine by personal check; she was then reimbursed from the business. More typically, she records automobile expenses (gasoline, tolls, and the like) in a notebook kept in her car. Then every month she prepares an expense sheet and the business reimburses her for these out-of-pocket expenses.

Similarly, Barbara Brabec, publisher of *Self-Employment Survival Letter*, uses a spindle to collect receipts for all of the "nickel-and-dime purchases, such as Wite-out and photocopying and postage due," she makes each month, then at the end of the month writes a business check to herself as reimbursement. "A lot of people take the little receipts to their accountant at the end of the year," she says, "which is dumb—and expensive." (*Self-Employment Survival Letter* is a very useful quarterly publication for the home-based businessperson. Write to P.O. Box 2137, Naperville, IL 60567.)

Be sure, by the way, that you do have a business checking account. A great many self-employed people start out (and too many continue) using a personal checking account for their business. "Many," says Brabec, "simply don't have enough funds to split between two checking accounts." But she feels it's better to pay personal bills from a business account, designating them as personal (with an accounting code of your choice), than to pay business bills from a personal account. "Only hobby-type businesses," according to Brabec, "use personal checking." If you want the Internal Revenue Service to take you seriously as a business—and believe me, you do—you want a separate business checking account.

If you feel that a business checking account is too expensive (minimum balances and fees do tend to be higher on business checking accounts), consider one of the following:

• If you're a sole proprietor, not a partnership or a corporation, open a second personal checking account to use exclusively as your business account. The checks may not have your business name printed on them, but so long as you use the account solely for business, it should satisfy the IRS.

• Establish a personal checking account, then order checks from a private check printer with the correct account number and your business name. An accountant suggested this tactic, one he implemented by ordering separate checks with a different series of check numbers and his wife's business's name on them, on the couple's personal account. (She should, of course, have had her own account for her business.)

• Use a savings and loan or thrift instead of a commercial bank for your business account, as Brabec does. A credit union might also work for you. "Banks don't pay interest on commercial accounts, but S and Ls do," she points out. "And there are no checking fees." There is a drawback, however: you can't tap an S and L if you need a business loan, but it may help you secure a loan from a commercial bank (see chapter 3) if you are a customer before you apply.

Chapter Highlights

• Sole proprietorships, partnerships, and S corporations report business earnings as personal earnings; if the business is sued or goes under, personal assets are vulnerable.

• Owners of regular C corporations can pay themselves salaries and protect personal assets from business obligations but may be subject to double taxation.

• Limited liability companies enjoy the tax status of partnerships and the limited liability of corporations.

• Self-employed people who work at home must be particularly careful about separating personal and business life, personal and business finances.

• Sharing resources can make it financially feasible to work outside the home.

• Adequate and well-maintained records, both personal and business, will help you track the progress of your business, prepare yearly tax returns, and stay on good terms with the IRS.

2 Managing on an Erratic Income

Traveling the peaks and valleys of an up-and-down income can trip up the most savvy entrepreneur. One month you're buoyant, as receivables are actually received; the next you're in despair as past-due accounts pile up. Yet, good month or bad, the mortgage must be paid and your family must eat.

What to do?

Right now, preferably before signing up your first client or selling the first widget (although after is OK too; later is better than never), think through your objectives, develop both personal and business budgets, get a handle on your net worth, and be sure you have adequate reserves to tide you over.

Defining your goals is an essential first step. You have to know where you're going, both personally and professionally, before you can get there. Plunging ahead without thinking through your objectives is like setting out on a vacation trip in unfamiliar territory without a road map.

Break down goal setting into three parts: goals, objectives, and action. *Goals* are an expression of your values, a long-range look ahead at what is most important to you. As you start a business, is your primary goal to make enough money for a secure retirement? To form the foundation for business expansion? Or simply (or not so simply) to earn enough to support time with your family? Do you want to do something you love, even if you might make less money than you could by taking a job? Or is it important to you to make a lot of money?

Objectives are a step-by-step path to your goal. Once you've clarified a long-term goal, a goal that may take many years to attain, you can break it down into specific objectives. *Action*, the hard core of your financial program, is the here-and-now, day-to-day behavior that will make both objectives and goals possible.

For example: You are in your forties, planning to leave a corporate job running a data-processing department to open your own word-processing business. Your primary goal is to generate sufficient profits to ensure a worry-free retirement. That's a worthy goal, but it's both vague and long-term. It needs to be reduced to manageable objectives. Your specific objectives might include the establishment of a cash reserve adequate to support you during the first year of a start-up business plus developing marketing strategies to build profits over the long haul. The action you take to meet those objectives, and therefore your long-term goals, might include reducing expenses to build your cash reserve, seeking help from professional advisers in developing a business plan, and learning all you can about potential clients for the business you plan to start.

It's important to be flexible: If your research indicates that a word-processing service won't yield more than modest profits, you'll have to either adjust your goals or get into a different business. If you're farther down the road and realize that your business won't produce the profits you need, think about enhanced marketing strategies and/or branching out into new arenas.

Annie Moldafsky, a successful writer in Chicago, decided a few years ago that her abilities to make real money as a writer seemed somewhat limited. Since she was being called on to do consulting assignments—and had a background in retailing and communications, strengths that could be packaged in a new way—Moldafsky decided there was more to be made as a marketing communications consultant than as a freelance writer. But she built on her prior experience: "The credits I had as a freelance writer were crucial in developing my presence as a consultant.

The fact that I had written on these subjects, studied different areas, made me an expert."

If you have a salaried spouse, you may be able to start a one-person business with your spouse's salary as temporary backup. If you're on your own you don't have that luxury. Either way, even if your primary goal is doing something you love, you want your business to be self-supporting as quickly as possible. To make it self-supporting, you need to plan. And your planning should be realistic. Financial planner Diahann Lassus notes that "most people starting their own business lose touch with reality when doing their economic forecasts." On paper it all seems so easy. But having a much-needed product or service and actually finding the customers who need that product or service are two different things. Sending bills and collecting the cash are two different things as well.

Many small-business owners overstate anticipated revenue and understate actual expenses. Remember this rule of thumb,

---

TIP

Use the outline format you learned in elementary school to structure your goals, objectives, and actions. For example:

   I. My long-term goal is to make enough money for a comfortable retirement.

  II. My short-term objectives, designed to help me reach that goal, are:

    A. To establish a cash reserve to cover one year's expenses

    B. To develop marketing strategies to build my business

 III. The action steps I will take to achieve these objectives include:

    A. Reducing debt

    B. Finding competent professional advisers

    C. Conducting marketing studies to identify my customer base often applied by venture capitalists applying a cold, objective eye to hopeful start-ups: divide revenues by two, multiply expenses by two, and if the business can still make it, you're OK. And be prepared for violent swings in income; very few self-employed people can count on a steady flow of cash.

On a day-to-day basis, managing your cash flow, both personal and business, is the most important thing you can do. Managing cash flow on the personal side includes monitoring income and outgo on a regular basis. It's the same on the business side, although a tad more complicated, since you must manage getting paid on time, think about things like depreciation, and satisfy Uncle Sam by keeping additional tax-related records.

The big issue, across the board, is understanding your own needs. Look at what you can realistically expect in terms of revenue and cash flow, and then look at your ongoing expenses. Consider the total picture in terms of best case–worst case scenarios and build in some margin for error. If your expenses total $2,000 in a given month and you're going to bill $2,000 that same month (but may not receive part or even all of the money for another month), you've got to figure out another way to live in the interim.

The key: tracking income over an entire year, then spending no more than the average earned in any one month. Any excess

---

UNDERSTAND YOURSELF

1. Why are you going into business for yourself? Rethink it if your only reason is an inability to find a job. Go right ahead if you are utilizing specific skills, fulfilling personal interests, or have other positive reasons.

2. Where do you want to be in one year? In five years? In ten? Will making "enough" money leave you wanting to retire? To explore new interests? To expand your business?

3. How much money is "enough?" Have you set a target?

4. Does being a one-person business satisfy you? Or do you hope to expand, to hire employees and move into larger quarters?

should be held in a reserve fund to cover inevitable shortfalls in income. Don't rush out to spend a nice big fee, in other words, until you are very sure about when the next check will arrive. And don't permanently upgrade your lifestyle on the basis of a temporary surge in income; selling your dream house after a couple of years because income declines can be tough, both financially and emotionally.

Preparing a Budget: No Pain, All Gain

"Budget" isn't a four-letter word. And a budget isn't a static document offering silent rebukes for failed efforts at money management. It *is* a working tool that helps you control expenses. Lassus calls it "expense planning."

Many self-employed men and women focus so intently on business plans and a business budget that they ignore personal financial planning. But you need parallel budgets, one for the business side of your life and one for the personal, if you are to achieve your objectives. Each budget should consist of two parts: an income-outgo (or profit-and-loss) calculation and a net worth statement (called a balance sheet in business).

What Goes Out Must Come In

The first part of your budget consists of an income-outgo statement for your personal life and a profit-and-loss statement for your business. Do both. In the end, the money may all flow in and out of a single pocket, but it's important to draw a line between your personal funds and your business funds. You need to keep them separate to satisfy the IRS. You also need to keep them separate so that you know whether or not your business is actually turning a profit. Blurring the lines only confuses the issue.

Personal Budget

Start by identifying your predictable current income. On a single sheet of paper list all of your definite sources of income: salary (your spouse's, perhaps, or your own from a part-time job), business income (if you've reached the point where you can count on some income), interest, dividends, alimony, royalties, commissions, rents—anything you know you'll have in hand in the course of the year. Put down the annual totals. You can break them down to a monthly basis later on.

On a separate sheet (or on the same sheet, in a parallel column) identify your projected income a year from now. Don't count uncertain income (that includes income from your business, until it's well established) in either column.

Then, on another sheet of paper, identify your current outgo, by category, on an annual basis. Pull together current figures from your checkbook and charge account records. Then identify anticipated expenditures in the same areas a year from now. Convert your annual figures to monthly ones, so that you can allocate funds ahead of time for an annual insurance premium or a semiannual tuition bill. Round all figures to the nearest five dollars, too, to make the task easier.

This outgo worksheet will be a tool you'll use to control expenses while you build your business income. So set up your outgo categories in descending order, from necessities to luxuries. Start with those expenses that are both fixed and absolutely essential: housing (rent or mortgage payments), insurance, taxes. Then list those that are essential but variable: food, housing repair and maintenance, utilities, clothing, transportation—all the things you have to have but that can be cut back if necessary. Last come the things you may have to pare to a minimum, at least for the time being: entertainment, recreation, travel, gifts, hobbies. Use the following worksheet as a guide, adjusting categories to suit your personal needs and wants:

INCOME-OUTGO WORKSHEET

Monthly Income	This Year	Next Year
Salary		
Your own		
Your spouse's		
Business income		
Your own		
Your spouse's		
Interest		
Dividends		
Rental income		
Royalties		
Social Security		
Pension benefits		
Annuities		
Bonuses		
Commissions		
Tips		
TOTAL		

Monthly Outgo	This Year	Next Year
Fixed Expenses		
Housing (mortgage or rent)		
Household insurance		
Other insurance		
Taxes		
Installment purchases		

(*continued on next page*)

INCOME-OUTGO WORKSHEET (*continued*)

Monthly Outgo	This Year	Next Year
Variable Expenses		
Food (at home and out)		
Home maintenance and repairs		
Utilities and fuel		
Telephone		
Clothing		
Transportation		
Entertainment, recreation		
Clubs, organizations		
Gifts, contributions		
Optional Expenses		
Hobbies		
Travel, vacations		
Housing (a second home or major home improvement)		
Second car		
Other (boat, RV)		
TOTAL:		

More budget tips:

• Remember taxes. The self-employed don't have taxes withheld from paychecks, but that doesn't mean taxes aren't due. You will have to pay quarterly estimated taxes as well as have cash on hand to pay income and self-employment taxes each spring (see chapter 6).

• Remember benefits. When you have no employer to contribute all or part of the cost, you must provide your own vacation time, sick leave, health insurance, and retirement income (see

---

TIP

When income is erratic, you need an extra dose of self-discipline to make a budget work. Chart your income for at least six months, preferably for a year, then build up your savings by spending an amount no more than midway between your lowest monthly income and your average monthly income. Try to set aside some money from each check you receive, no matter how difficult it may be, to cover the times when there may be no checks at all.

---

chapters 4 and 7). While it's tempting to put every spare penny back into your business, it would be shortsighted to ignore the need for health insurance and retirement income.

• Remember inflation. Put an inflation factor in your budget. When inflation is at 4 percent, you'll need 4 percent more income to live the same lifestyle a year from now. Put another way, if you can live on $30,000 today you'll need $36,600 five years from now to provide the equivalent of today's $30,000. In ten years you'll need $44,400 (see table 2.1)—and will have to either beef up income or curtail spending. With luck and hard work your business will grow by more than the rate of inflation, but do your projections carefully.

Use table 2.1 to help determine how much you'll need in future years. For example, if you get along on $45,000 today, expect the rate of inflation to be 4 percent, and want to know how much you'll need in five years, look at the intersection of year five and 4 percent in the table, then multiply $45,000 by 1.22. The result: $54,900.

Business Budget

Business profit-and-loss statements are similar to personal income-outgo statements. The purpose is the same—to track income and outgo—but the categories are different. Just as your

Table 2.1: Coping with Inflation

	RATE OF INFLATION					
YEAR	4%	5%	6%	7%	8%	9%
5	1.22	1.28	1.34	1.40	1.47	1.54
6	1.27	1.34	1.42	1.50	1.59	1.68
7	1.32	1.41	1.50	1.61	1.71	1.83
8	1.37	1.48	1.59	1.72	1.85	1.99
9	1.42	1.55	1.69	1.84	2.00	2.17
10	1.48	1.63	1.79	1.97	2.16	2.37
11	1.54	1.71	1.90	2.10	2.33	2.58
12	1.60	1.80	2.01	2.25	2.52	2.81
13	1.67	1.89	2.13	2.41	2.72	3.07
14	1.73	1.98	2.26	2.58	2.94	3.34
15	1.80	2.08	2.40	2.76	3.17	3.64
16	1.87	2.18	2.54	2.95	3.43	3.97
17	1.95	2.29	2.69	3.16	3.70	4.33
18	2.03	2.41	2.85	3.38	4.00	4.72
19	2.11	2.53	3.03	3.62	4.32	5.15
20	2.19	2.65	3.21	3.87	4.66	5.60
21	2.28	2.79	3.40	4.14	5.03	6.11
22	2.37	2.93	3.60	4.43	5.44	6.66
23	2.46	3.07	3.82	4.74	5.87	7.26
24	2.56	3.23	4.05	5.07	6.34	7.91
25	2.67	3.39	4.29	5.43	6.85	8.62
26	2.77	3.56	4.55	5.81	7.40	9.40
27	2.88	3.73	4.82	6.21	7.99	10.25
28	3.00	3.92	5.11	6.65	8.63	11.17
29	3.12	4.12	5.42	7.11	9.32	12.17
30	3.24	4.32	5.74	7.61	10.06	13.27

SOURCE: Washington, D.C.: Department of Agriculture.

personal income-outgo statement contains basic categories (such as interest and commissions on the income side, fixed and variable expenses on the outgo), your business statement contains four categories of specific information: (1) sales, (2) direct expenses (labor and materials), (3) indirect expenses (rent, utilities, depreciation, office supplies—the costs you have even if the product is not produced or the service is not delivered), and (4) net income (or profit).

Business income may consist entirely of sales receipts (until they are actually received, these are receivables) plus some interest on cash reserves. Business outgo will include rent (if you lease an outside facility rather than work out of your home), utilities, insurance, taxes, supplies, inventory (if your business requires one), income for yourself (a "draw"), and anything else pertinent to your particular business.

You may update your personal income-outgo statement once a year, but you'll want to prepare a business profit-and-loss statement monthly or quarterly as well as on a year-end basis so that you can track your progress and make appropriate projections. The statement will be relatively simple if you conduct a straightforward personal service business, more complicated if you produce a product or must maintain an inventory. Table 2.2 shows an income statement for a small flower shop.

Managing Cash Flow

Your business profit-and-loss statement indicates when sales take place, which is not necessarily when the money is actually received. To show how cash is really moving through your business account you need a *cash flow statement*. A cash flow statement identifies when cash should be received and when it must be spent, how much cash will be needed and when it will be needed. Keeping cash flow statements up-to-date and preparing periodic projections let you schedule purchases and payments as efficiently as possible and know in advance whether you will run short of cash. If you have this early warning system and see that you will have a cash shortfall, you can arrange for short-term money as needed (see chapter 3).

As Linda Howarth Mackay puts it in a useful booklet written for the SBA, *Financial Management: How to Make a Go of Your Business*, "Because all sales are not cash sales, management must be able to forecast when accounts receivable will become 'cash in the bank' and when expenses—whether regular or seasonal—must be paid so cash shortfalls will not interrupt normal business operations."

Table 2.2: Sample Profit-and-Loss Statement for ABC Flowers

Net Sales:		$68,116
Cost of Goods Sold:		$47,696
Gross Profit on Sales:		$20,420
Expenses		
Wages	$6,948	
Delivery Expenses	954	
Bad Debts Allowances	409	
Communications	204	
Depreciation Allowance	409	
Insurance	613	
Taxes	1,021	
Advertising	1,566	
Interest	409	
Other Charges	749	
TOTAL	$13,282	
Net Profit (net sales − total indirect sales):		$7,138
Other Income:		$886
TOTAL NET INCOME:		$8,024

SOURCE: Linda Howarth Mackay, *Financial Management: How to Make a Go of Your Business,* Washington, D.C.: Small Business Administration, 1986, p. 11.

The cash flow statement, along with the profit-and-loss statement, make up your business budget. But both work for you only if you use them as management tools. Even the smallest one-person business can benefit by measuring actual receipts and disbursements against projections. Moldafsky, for example, prepares a spreadsheet once a year and updates it as she tallies each month's income and outgo. "When it's time to renegotiate my lease each year," she says, "I can see what percentage of my income is going to rent, to telephone, et cetera. I can see how long my letterhead lasts, and so on."

Moldafsky prepares her spreadsheets by hand, but many small-business owners prefer computer spreadsheets. There are also a wide variety of money management and accounting programs you may want to investigate. They range from simple checkbook management (all you may need if you run a cash-based service business) to bookkeeping, accounting, and tax

---

TIP

The answer to a cash shortfall is not necessarily greater sales volume. It costs money to make sales. Instead consider:

1. Beefing up margins, so that you make a larger profit on each sale;
2. Making serious efforts to collect receivables on time;
3. Depositing money immediately, so that it starts working for you without delay; and
4. Using a money market mutual fund to earn a bit more interest than you would with a bank account.

It will help if you track net profits on a monthly basis so that you can make adjustments, if necessary, to meet your annual goals.

---

preparation. *Home Office Computing* magazine is a useful source of information on software as well as all aspects of home office (and small-business) management.

Managing cash flow so that it works for you is essential. Here are some key elements:

Charge Enough for Your Services

How much is enough? Enough to cover all of your expenses and yield a reasonable profit. You may feel that you must keep your prices down if you are trying to establish a new business, but it won't do you any good in the long run if you get customers used to below-market pricing on which you can't subsist. In fact, it's not unusual for small-business owners to be so busy that they think business *must* be good—only to go out of business because prices or fees are set too low to make money.

If you are producing a product, whether T-shirts or flower baskets or whatever, find out how profit margins are set in your field; typically markups double the cost of production, but there are variations you may need to consider. If you are conducting a personal service business, whether as a graphic designer or a bookkeeper or whatever, you don't have production costs to consider but you do have to value your time properly and consider overhead costs realistically.

Here's one formula for calculating fees:

1. Determine what you could be earning in a salaried job (let's use $52,000 as an example).
2. Divide that salary by fifty-two weeks ($1,000 a week).
3. Divide that figure by the forty hours in a workweek ($25 an hour).
4. Multiply that hourly rate by 2.5, to cover both overhead and profit (some consultants use a multiplier of 2.8 or 3.0; at 2.5 an hourly rate of $25 becomes an hourly fee of $62.50). To charge by the day multiply by eight (your per diem fee is $500).

Although this method is frequently recommended, it may result in artificially low numbers. The following method of determining overhead and profit may be more realistic:

1. Find your daily rate, once again, by calculating how much you would be paid if you were a salaried employee. Let's use the same example of $52,000. This time, though, divide by 261, the average number of working days in a year, and you get $199 (which we'll round off to $200, for simplicity's sake).
2. Determine your overhead. Either calculate your actual overhead and divide by 261 working days or take 70 percent to 85 percent of your daily rate (less if you work at home, more if you maintain work space outside your home). In this example your overhead would range from $140 to $170.
3. Add in your profit. If your targeted profit is 5 percent over the prime rate and the prime is 6 percent, to continue our example, then 11 percent of your combined daily rate and overhead ($200 plus $140, conservatively) would be $37.40.

4. Add the three (daily rate, overhead, and profit) together (rounded to $377) and multiply by two. Your per
diem fee in this example would be $754 (or, if you must
calculate higher overhead costs for an outside office,
$821).

A third set of guidelines goes like this:

1. Determine how much you actually need to live on each
month, including things like health insurance premiums and Social Security taxes that may previously
have been picked up, at least in part, by an employer.
Then add in all of your business-related expenses; if
your office is in your home, this includes a portion of
household cleaning expenses as well as all supplies,
telephone bills, advertising, and the like.
2. Divide the total by the number of hours you can bill
each month (not the number of hours you can work;
remember that marketing and managing your business
take considerable time) and you'll see what your per-
hour fee must be in order to cover costs. Then, after
ascertaining what similar businesses in your area are
charging, add a profit margin that will bring your fees
into the middle range of what appears to be acceptable
for your business and your area. If your product or
service is worthwhile, you shouldn't have any trouble
convincing customers that a middle-range fee is fair.
Then, as your reputation grows and your service or
product is increasingly in demand, you can increase
your fees.

Try to Be Paid on Time

Too many small-business owners are less than businesslike
when it comes to pressing for payment. The result, too often, is a
business that goes under while appearing (on paper) to show a
profit. When Dun and Bradstreet surveyed small-business
owners, it found that nine out of ten never sent a bill the day they

> ### TIP
> **Know your customer. Nonprofit organizations typically are short of funds and can be expected to pay at the low end of a sliding scale. Large corporations, on the other hand, expect to pay for quality service; underpricing can actually lose you a corporate assignment.**

provided a service or shipped goods. Some waited as long as thirty to forty-five days before sending the first bill, then failed to follow up in a timely fashion. Service-based businesses, including professional practitioners such as attorneys and CPAs (who should know better!) are the worst.

Think about it. If you were employed and drawing a steady salary, would you wait indefinitely before inquiring about a delayed paycheck? Well, your business is your source of income and it's up to you to make that income as steady as possible.

Many service providers face collection problems because they complete the work before any money changes hands. If you're in a line of work where this is standard operating procedure, and you can't get an advance, try to protect yourself by choosing your clients carefully. If nothing else, stick to those with a track record. Many writers I know who've been burned by nonpaying publications have dealt with start-up publications that never quite got off the ground—at least not enough to pay their writers.

The first rule of cash flow, says Larry Winters of Dun and Bradstreet's Small Business Services division: even before you provide the service or ship the goods, send an invoice with a note asking, Is this correct? Is this our agreement? Should there be any changes? Will you pay on terms? Then, after you've done what you contracted to do, follow up. Call or write on day fifteen, asking, Is everything OK? Can I expect payment by such-and-such a date? This may be labor-intensive, but it's not as labor-intensive as letting things go, then following up a couple of months down the road. By that time your customer may have forgotten exactly what you did, and the buck may be passed from person to person before the invoice even begins its way through the processing chain.

It also helps to indicate "due on receipt" on your invoices, to offer a discount for quick payment, or to charge interest or a flat late-payment fee (you might call it a "rebilling fee"), and to follow up on a regular basis. If you're working on a major project, try to arrange payments in installments tied to target dates; some consultants, for example, ask for one-third payment up front, one-third on completion of a specific portion of the work, and the final third on completion of the entire project.

It may also be wise to put a "no later than" clause in any agreement, particularly with respect to corporate assignments that may be subject to approval by a number of people. Agreements that I make with corporate clients always state that the final one-third or one-quarter of the fee will be paid either "upon submission" or "upon approval, but no later than [a specific date, typically three weeks after submission]." Agreements for work assigned through a third party, such as an advertising agency representing a corporate client, specify that I'm to be paid on time regardless of when (or if) the agency receives its fee from the client.

Keep Expenses in Line

Writing down your expenses is only the first step in keeping them under control. Use your expense records to analyze what you're doing. Are you spending too much on postage, for example, because you haven't bought a postage scale? Have you stuck with the same print shop when you could save money on printing

---

TIP

Send invoices that look professional—and call them invoices. An energy consultant in Lenexa, Kansas, told *Home Office Computing*, with some incredulity, that a major client wasn't paying his bills because he called them bills. Once they were labeled invoices, he was promptly paid.

costs by shopping around or by asking your current printer for a new bid? Have you put off taking advantage of the competition among long-distance telephone carriers? Are you spending a great deal on equipment repairs because you thought you couldn't afford new equipment? Perhaps a new copier would pay for itself if your old one keeps breaking down. Or maybe you should consider leasing a new copier instead of buying one (see page 21).

Your overhead will be less if you work at home, but you still shouldn't spend a penny more than necessary. This may mean working at a beat-up old desk, but that doesn't matter if you're the only one who sees the desk. It may mean missing discounts for buying supplies in bulk, but better to miss out on a discount than to tie up cash you need to buy groceries.

When cash is tight, too, be selective about which bills you pay. Start with those that otherwise will incur interest. If you're using credit cards or cash advances to pay for business-related items, these are the bills to pay first. Credit card interest rates have come down (finally) from the 19 percent average they held for a decade, but credit card interest at 13 percent or 14 percent is still too much to pay. Your local office supply store, on the other hand, may be willing to let you extend payment by a month or two, at least occasionally, without any interest charges.

Even when cash isn't particularly tight, adopt the habit of paying bills as they come due and not before. Barbara Brabec, publisher of *Self-Employment Survival Letter*, has adopted a system of maintaining two sets of nine-by-twelve-inch envelopes, one for business bills and the other for personal bills. As they come in, bills are filed in the appropriate envelope and a calendar entry is made for the due date. Reviewing the calendar, which contains both the due date and the amount, helps Brabec see how much cash must be on hand by the end of each week to pay bills. If there isn't enough she knows some juggling must be done.

There are also specific techniques that can keep costs down. For instance, you might join a *buying group* to secure volume discounts on everything from office supplies to health insurance. Look for discounts through a trade association or a coop-

---

TIP

One of the best ways to keep expenses down is to steer clear of fraudulent schemes targeting small business. Examples, collected by the Better Business Bureau and Call for Action, include:

- **Office products.** Telemarketers pose as service reps selling paper, toner cartridges, and other supplies. The prices are inflated and ordered products rarely arrive.
- **Phone service scams.** You're supposed to consent to a switch of long-distance carriers, but tricksters sometimes succeed in catching telephone customers unawares.
- **Phony invoices.** Entrepreneurs failing to keep careful records may mistakenly pay bills for classified ads or directory listings that they never ordered.

---

erative or form an informal buying network with allied businesses. If you join an existing group, be sure you understand membership costs and what your own commitment will be, then evaluate the trade-off in time and money.

You also might do well to consider *swapping services* or, more formally, *barter*. That's what the owner of a bicycle shop in Roanoke, Virginia, did when he wanted to install a shower; Rob bought the raw materials, then traded a bicycle for a plumber's labor.

Rob isn't alone. A Chicago-based cleaning firm exchanges cleaning services for rental cars, catering, and income tax preparation. A newspaper publisher in Cleveland trades advertising space for computers, office equipment, and supplies. And Karen Houle, owner of University Language Center in Minneapolis, has swapped language lessons for printing, advertising, legal assistance, accounting services, graphic design, and even, according to the Kessler Exchange, haircuts.

Barter has become big business—so big that the International Reciprocal Trade Association notes over $6 billion worth of barter deals in 1992. Be aware, though, that the IRS does expect income tax to be paid on the value of bartered goods and services.

Swaps can be made directly, which is great if your plumber wants a bicycle, or they can be made through one of about four hundred organized barter groups or exchanges, both national and regional, that offer more flexibility. Some three hundred barter exchanges act as a clearinghouse for the exchange of products and services among their clients, typically charging a commission on each transaction. About a hundred reciprocal trade companies work a little differently, exchanging trade credits for goods and services.

Under a reciprocal arrangement, typically, you would pay a fee to join a barter group, then receive scrip or credits for the full retail value of goods or services you provide to other members. The scrip can then be used to purchase goods and services from other members. You might write a marketing brochure for a local dentistry clinic, then use the scrip you earn not to get your teeth fixed, although you could, but to have your stationery printed. With a scrip- or credit-based system, no single trade has to be an even swap. If your marketing brochure is worth $600, you might use part of your $600 in scrip to purchase stationery and the rest to repair the muffler on your car. You can even use cash to fill out a purchase. And you don't have to do the complex record keeping required. The group keeps track and reports the transactions to the IRS; you receive a year-end 1099-B form (the same form used for miscellaneous income, such as that reported by stockbrokers).

An added dividend: do a good job for a barter client and you may wind up with a cash-paying client. After all, a key tenet of marketing is making your name and abilities known. For more information on barter and a list of barter exchanges near you, write to the International Reciprocal Trade Association at 9513 Beach Mill Road, Great Falls, VA 22066.

Leasing office equipment and vehicles can keep more cash in your pocket too. With small-business loans tough to get (see chapter 3), it can be much faster and easier to make a leasing arrangement. Leasing also has other advantages: clear-cut tax write-offs (although you may do better by taking advantage of the $17,500-per-year direct write-off described in chapter 6), little up-front cash (compared to the down payment on an automobile, for example), and protection against technological change (upgrading computer equipment at the end of a lease is a lot easier than selling old equipment and buying new). But do be sure you understand the terms of the lease, including the interest rate and any penalties for breaking the agreement early.

Have Adequate Cash Reserves

An emergency fund keeps the wolf from the door when income slows to a trickle. A rule of thumb for a personal safety net is that you should keep three to six months' income in a readily available liquid form, just in case you need a new roof or a major car repair. For the self-employed, a year's worth of living expenses is a better guide. It will probably take at least that long for your business income to become at all reliable.

Dave Diesslin, a Certified Financial Planner in Fort Worth, Texas, calls this the "spare tire" concept. You need to ascertain, before you see cash on hand as investable cash, just how much you would need to pay living expenses and keep your business going during a downturn. You need more cash reserves if you have an inventory-dependent business than if you're running a business based on personal service. But either way you should anticipate a year to a year and a half when you may need to draw on cash reserves to stay afloat. Many businesses start out with

---

TIP

Having trouble keeping costs down? An outsider may help. Just as office organizers have cleared up clutter for many small-business people, independent consultants can review your bills, shop around, and save you money on everything from copying paper to overnight delivery services. Some charge a fee, but others charge a percentage of the amount they save their customers. Your local chamber of commerce or Small Business Development Center may be able to help you locate a consultant.

enough cash to open the doors but not enough to survive the first year. Some business owners think a temporary cash surplus is money that can be invested for the long term.

Figure out how much you'll need for living expenses for a year, then double the number to be on the safe side. When cash builds up during the good times, restrain the urge to invest that cash without thinking through the answers to two basic questions: If I need the money, can I get it? What will it cost me to get it?

You can put your hands on money in the stock market, but you run the risk of equities being down in value just when you need the cash. Think of the poor souls who had to tap their equity investments in late October 1987. Yes, equities typically yield the best investment results over the long term. But the key is long term. The stock market is not the place for money you may need, and need very badly, within the next couple of years. The biggest mistake many self-employed individuals make is in not realizing that the business itself is part of their total investment picture. As Diesslin notes, "The entrepreneur should think of his own business as investment in a high-risk small-capitalization company." Other investments, when you are able to make them, should be tailored to provide both liquidity and diversification (see chapter 8 on investment strategy).

Beyond actual cash on hand, cash reserves can also consist of an emergency line of credit, such as a home equity loan (best arranged when your income is up, not down) or a personal loan based on your spouse's salary. When it comes down to the wire, you may also seek help from friends and relatives. (All of these sources of financing are discussed in detail in chapter 3.)

Net Worth

As a small-business owner, your personal and business net worth may be totally intertwined. Yet it's important, here as elsewhere, to separate the personal and business sides of your life. Start by preparing separate net worth statements for yourself and for your business.

Net worth, the total of all of your assets minus all of your liabilities (everything you own minus everything you owe), is more than a static snapshot. It is—or should be—a tool to help you measure your financial progress. Calculated periodically, it represents the success with which you are converting income into assets. And it measures the success of your business.

Assets

Start to calculate your personal net worth by listing all of your liquid assets: cash on hand, savings and checking accounts, money market funds, the cash value of life insurance, the market value of securities—anything that either is cash or can be quickly converted to cash. Then add in the current value of your business (if you were to sell it today), of illiquid investments, and of personal property. Don't forget that having to sell your home or car in a hurry probably means realizing less cash than you might otherwise expect. Selling a business, especially a one-person service business, is even more difficult (you'll find more details on valuing a business, selling it, and passing it on in chapter 9).

Liabilities

Then list everything you owe: mortgages, outstanding loan balances, charge account balances, taxes due, tuition payments, and so on. Don't forget yet-to-be-paid medical bills or charitable pledges. Subtract your total liabilities from your total assets and you'll have your net worth.

Below is a sample net worth worksheet to use as a guide in assessing your personal financial situation. (Note that the value of your business is part of your personal net worth.)

Will your available net worth—the money you can put your hands on without jeopardizing your family—be sufficient to bankroll your business? Before you turn to your business balance sheet calculations, you may want to build up your personal net

NET WORTH WORKSHEET

Current Assets		Current Liabilities	
Checking, savings, money market accounts:	_____	Mortgage (balance due):	_____
Certificates of deposit:	_____	Taxes:	_____
Business (current value):	_____	Business loans:	_____
Savings bonds (current value):	_____	Installment debt:	_____
Life insurance (cash value):	_____	Charge account balances:	_____
Securities (market value):	_____	Insurance premiums:	_____
Annuities (surrender value):	_____	Charitable pledges:	_____
Pension (vested interest):	_____	Other:	
Real estate (market value):	_____	TOTAL LIABILITIES:	_____
Personal property (market value):	_____		
Other:	_____		
TOTAL ASSETS:	_____		

TOTAL ASSETS − TOTAL LIABILITIES = NET WORTH

worth through increasing income (perhaps you can moonlight, or work part time at your start-up business while holding down a salaried job) and decreasing outgo (cut your expenses to the bone, at least until money starts to come in from the business in a reliable way).

Balance Sheets

Your personal net worth, and the way it changes from year to year, provides a picture of your financial well-being. Your business net worth, shown on your balance sheet, provides the same information about your business. Each balance sheet portrays the financial health of your business at a given moment, typically the end of an accounting period, by measuring what your business owns and what it owes; the difference is its net worth or your equity interest in the business.

The simplicity or complexity of your business balance sheet will be dictated by the type of business you own. A one-person service business with no inventory can have a very simple balance sheet; a retail or manufacturing business will have more assets and liabilities to show. You may have your accountant draw up your balance sheet, especially if you are running a retail or manufacturing business, but it's still a good idea for you to fully understand and evaluate the numbers so that you can use them as a tool in measuring progress.

Assets include not only cash, equipment, furniture, trademarks, inventory (if any), and the like, but also money due from individuals or other businesses (known as accounts or notes receivable). Liabilities are funds acquired for your business through loans or the sale of property or services to the

Table 2.3: Sample Balance Sheet for ABC Flowers

Cash	$ 1,896	Notes payable	$ 2,000
Accounts receivable	1,456	Accounts Payable	2,240
Inventory	6,822	Accruals	940
Total current Assets	$10,174	Total current liabilities	$ 5,180
Equipment and fixtures	1,168	Total liabilities	5,180
Prepaid expenses	1,278	Net worth*	7,440
Total assets	$12,620	Total liabilities	$12,620

* Assets − liabilities = net worth
SOURCE: Linda Howarth Mackay, *Financial Management: How to Make a Go of Your Business*, Washington, D.C.: Small Business Administration, p. 11.

business on credit. If you owe more money to creditors than you own in assets, your net worth will be a negative number.

In preparing a balance sheet, list assets in decreasing order of how quickly they can be turned into cash, and list liabilities in order of how soon they must be repaid. (See table 2.3.)

Record Keeping

Are you of the shoe box school of record keeping? If you are—if your personal financial records consist of a box full of receipts and canceled checks that you dump on your accountant's desk each spring—you'd better think twice before opening a business. (You also should rethink your personal habits; you're probably missing some legitimate tax deductions, and you're almost

---

GIVE YOUR BUSINESS A CHECKUP

Columnist Jane Applegate, author of *Succeeding in Small Business* (Plume, 1992), suggests periodically taking the pulse of your business. Here is a quiz based on part 1 of her business checkup, questions to ask yourself:

- Is my business doing better or worse financially than it was at this time last year?
- Have I gained any new clients or customers in the last three months?
- Have I lost any clients or customers in the last three months?
- When was the last time I called on any prospective clients or customers?
- What would happen to my business if my major client or customer went bankrupt, died, or took his or her business elsewhere?
- What have I done recently to attract attention to my business? Have I advertised? Sent out a newsletter?
- Do any customers owe me more than $1,000? Five thousand dollars? Ten thousand?
- What am I doing to collect the money I'm owed?

---

definitely paying more in accountant's fees by not organizing your records yourself.)

A business needs business records. Even if you are a one-person business relying on personal talent—with no outside office, no employees, no inventory—you need records both to satisfy the IRS and to document your own progress. Refer back to chapter 1 for tips on both personal and business record keeping.

Chapter Highlights

- Determine your goals and objectives and the action steps you will take to meet those goals and objectives.
- Do two budgets: an income-outgo statement for your personal finances, a profit-and-loss statement for your business.
- Remember taxes, benefits, and inflation as you look ahead.
- Prepare periodic cash flow statements to see how cash is actually moving through your business.
- Improve cash flow by charging enough for your products or services, staying on top of customer payments, keeping expenses in line, and having adequate cash reserves.
- Net worth statements for your personal finances and balance sheets for your business will help you measure progress over time.

3 Borrowing Money

It may not take much money to start or run a business if you work at home, have a service-oriented business, and can use your old college typewriter on the kitchen table. More than two-thirds of all new firms begin with less than $10,000 in total assets, according to the SBA, while almost half begin with less than $5,000. Sooner or later, however, any successful business will need money—for computers and copiers, advertising and marketing, stationery and supplies, and so on.

Where will you get that money?

Study after study has shown what you probably already know: it's tough for a small business to get money from "official" sources—the banks and venture capitalists and other institutional lenders, who are more interested in well-established businesses with well-cushioned bottom lines. As a not-so-funny one-liner has it, "Bankers only want to lend money to people who don't need it." To be fair to lenders, I have to say that it costs them as much to make a small loan as it does to make a large one, and large loans are clearly more profitable. The result, however, especially during the credit squeeze of the early 1990s, is that it's much easier to obtain money after you already have some, when you don't need it quite so badly.

A great many self-employed women and men, therefore, are

forced to rely on their own resources: credit cards, personal loans, home equity lines of credit, family, and friends. This chapter will discuss all of these sources of financing your business, along with ways of keeping personal loans businesslike, and then turn to official sources of small-business credit.

Establishing Personal Credit

If you're leaving the security of a salaried job (insofar as jobs have any security these days) for the self-employment marketplace, it's a good idea to establish a solid credit identity in advance. If you've been living close to the edge, running up credit card debt that you find hard to repay, you'll have to pay off that debt and build a solid credit record before you can rely on those same credit cards for business financing. And if you own your own home and you expect your income to drop precipitously, as it very well may in the start-up phase of your business, establish a home equity line of credit in advance. In other words, get all your ducks in a row—personal credit, home equity lines, even margin loans from your stockbrokerage firm—as early as possible.

There are several avenues to explore:

Overdraft Lines on Checking Accounts

Overdraft or reserve checking, a line of credit offered by banks, is activated as an automatic loan if you overdraw your checking account. You must apply for overdraft checking just as you would apply for a credit card or an installment loan. The service is free until you use it; then interest charges kick in.

An overdraft provision can keep you from bouncing checks and incurring sometimes-hefty charges for doing so. Before you sign up, however, compare provisions at different banks. Interest charges can vary considerably. In addition, some banks activate the overdraft only in increments of fifty or a hundred dollars, so that you may end up owing interest on one hundred dollars when you've actually borrowed only ten. Some institutions credit only a small portion of subsequent deposits to paying off the overdraft, so that the loan is extended over time. And some won't repay your loan from your next deposit at all unless you specifically request that they do so.

Credit Cards

Many entrepreneurs run up massive credit card debt to finance their businesses. Since minority and female business owners often find it more difficult to secure conventional financing (more on this later), they tend to rely heavily on credit cards. A 1992 study by the National Foundation for Women Business Owners reports that more than half of female-owned firms used credit cards for short-term financing, compared with 18 percent of all small to medium-size firms. The smaller the firm, in fact, the more likely the use of credit cards.

As reported in the *Wall Street Journal,* for example, Darryl Robinson founded Robotica Automation Consultants in Boston in 1987 "with $1,000 in savings and seven bank credit cards." Robinson was able to steer clear of high-cost cash advances but did use the credit lines as needed, to augment working capital.

The big problem with credit cards, of course, is the rate of interest they typically carry. In an era when interest rates of all kinds dropped steadily (mortgage interest rates in 1993 were at their lowest level in twenty years; a thirty-year fixed-rate mort-

---

TIP

Qualifying for a loan, personal or business, means meeting the test of the five Cs:

- **Character**
- **Cash flow**
- **Capital**
- **Collateral**
- **Economic Conditions**

TIP

Consider a business or corporate credit card for the additional perks it offers. The MasterCard Business Card program, for example, lets small businesses take advantage of
hotel room rates (like corporate rates) up to 60 percent off
regular room rates. American Express offers small-
business perks as well.

---

gage loan was available, for a while, at under 7 percent), credit
card interest rates held all too firm. True, the average rate finally
inched downward from almost 20 percent to about 16 percent in
1995, but this is still a very high-cost way to finance a business.

Still, credit cards can provide an essential business backup. If
you think you might want to have them available for this purpose, be sure to:

• Maintain a good credit record, repaying promptly. This will
make it possible to qualify for a low-interest-rate credit card. But
you'll have to shop around to find the best deal. Many issuers
have cards at 12 percent to 15 percent, while some offer interest
rates (to people with rock-solid credit histories) as low as 8
percent and 9 percent. Some of these very low rates are come-
ons, however, designed to go up sharply after a short time.

• Check your credit record periodically to make sure it is
accurate. Credit-reporting agencies (credit bureaus) have frequently been criticized for inaccuracies in their records, inaccuracies that can make it impossible for you to secure credit of
any kind. (If you plan to apply for a business loan, too—see page
73—make sure your personal credit record is accurate and up-
to-date; banks are screening prospective borrowers very carefully and will certainly look at your personal credit record.)

If you are denied credit based on information in your credit
record, you are entitled to a free look at that record. At other
times it may cost a few dollars. TRW, one of the "big three"
credit-reporting agencies, now provides consumers with one
free copy a year, but Equifax and Trans Union charge up to eight

CONTACTING CREDIT BUREAUS

To secure a copy of your credit report, check your local tele-phone book under "credit-reporting agencies" or contact:

Equifax Credit Information Services
P.O. Box 740241
Atlanta, GA 30374-0241
Phone: 800-685-1111

TRW Complimentary Credit Report Request
P.O. Box 2350
Chatsworth, CA 91313-2350
800-682-7654

Trans Union National Consumer Relations
P.O. Box 7000
North Olmsted, OH 44070
(Trans Union prefers written communication.)

dollars per credit report. It can be money well worth spending, however, if you detect an error before it derails an important loan application.

Home Equity Loans

Home equity loans or lines of credit, frequently used by the self-employed, have two big advantages over both overdraft checking and credit cards: they usually provide a larger pool of money, and they cost far less. The disadvantage: in borrowing against your home equity, you are putting your home on the line. If your business fails, you may lose your home as well.

Nonetheless, you may want to tap the accumulated equity in your home to finance your business. If so, here's what you need to know:

• A home equity loan is akin to an old-fashioned second mortgage; it provides a fixed sum of money that must be repaid over a fixed term. A home equity line of credit is a revolving line of credit; you establish a credit line, then write checks against that amount as needed. Home equity lines of credit are more widely available and more popular than second mortgages.

• Typically you can borrow up to 80 percent of the appraised value of your home minus any amount you still owe on your first mortgage. But this is a maximum. The actual amount you can borrow is governed by the factors that go into any application for credit: your income and how much other debt you have outstanding. The income limitation, in particular, makes it wise to apply for a home equity line of credit while you have a steady salary and before you start your own business.

• Because a home equity loan or line of credit is secured by your home, you will usually face the same closing costs you have when you take a first mortgage: application fee, lawyer's fees, title search, appraisal, and, sometimes, points. But this is a highly competitive market and many lenders are offering no-point, no-cost home equity loans. Be sure to shop around and compare costs before taking any loan.

• Interest rates on home equity lines of credit are usually variable—if the interest rate goes up, so does your monthly payment. Find out how often the rate is adjusted (most are adjusted monthly, but some change quarterly or even semiannually) and what limitations there are on how much the payment may rise (federal law requires that home equity lines of credit issued since December 8, 1987, have a cap on interest rates). Many lenders offer introductory "discount" or "teaser" rates. Be sure to find out exactly what happens to the interest rate after the introductory period.

• Some lenders charge transaction fees every time you access the account. Before you apply, find out whether your lender makes these charges and how much they are.

Life Insurance Loans

If you own a whole-life insurance policy, you can borrow against the policy's cash value to provide financing for your business. The interest rate on older policies may be as low as 5 percent to 8 percent; newer policies generally charge variable

---

TIP

Want to buy a house? If possible, you may want to do so before you go out on a self-employment limb. By law, mortgage lenders may not discriminate against the self-employed. In practice, however, many are leery of the self-employed, particularly of those in seasonal businesses with up-and-down income. When you apply for a mortgage as a self-employed individual:

• Be prepared to provide two years of federal income tax returns, a year-to-date profit-and-loss statement, balance sheet, and business credit report. If you have been self-employed for less than two years, you may have to supply a previous salary history. The alternative to all of this documentation is a no-income-verification loan with asset verification, which typically requires a higher down payment and has a higher interest rate. A variation on this is a no-income-verification, no-asset-verification loan; as you might suspect, down payment requirements and interest rates are extremely high.

• Shop around among banks, thrifts, credit unions, and mortgage bankers. A mortgage broker may also prove useful in scouting sources of loans.

---

rates, which may be higher at any given time. An advantage of a life insurance loan is that it need never be repaid, although the death benefit will be reduced by the amount of any outstanding loan. If you borrow against life insurance you should also know that:

• The true cost may be higher than the stated interest rate because, as the National Insurance Consumer Organization points out, the dividend rate is usually adjusted downward when a loan is taken. Ask your company about its dividend rate with and without a policy loan.

• You should pay the interest each year, whether or not you ever intend to repay the loan. If you don't pay the interest on the loan as it comes due, the company will deduct the interest from the policy's remaining cash value, adding it to the principal of the loan, so you'll end up paying interest on the interest.

Margin Loans

If you maintain a stockbrokerage account but prefer not to sell your securities, you may be able to obtain financing through a margin loan. Investing on margin means buying securities with less than the purchase price, borrowing the rest from your broker. It's a way of leveraging the purchase so that greater profits can be made; of course, if the securities decline in value, greater losses are possible as well.

But margin loans aren't restricted to buying securities. Brokers are touting these loans, in fact, as a low-cost alternative to credit cards. Margin loans use your securities as collateral, much as a home equity loan is secured by your house. Typically you can borrow up to 50 percent of the value of common stocks, 75 percent or more on bonds and Treasuries.

But a home equity line of credit, assuming that you have sufficient equity in your home to borrow against, may make more sense than a margin loan. Here's why:

• Interest on home equity loans of up to $100,000 is tax deductible; interest on margin loans is deductible only if the proceeds are used for a taxable investment.

• Although a home equity loan may be more expensive in the short run because of closing costs, a margin loan is very costly over the long haul, especially if the value of the underlying securities should decline. Also, if the value of your securities does decline, you may receive a "margin call" and have to either come up with the cash or lose your securities.

Securities may instead be used as collateral for a bank loan, which also puts the securities at some risk if your business should fail and you are unable to repay the loan.

Loans from Retirement Plans

If you are starting a business part time while you're still employed, you may look longingly at the cash in your 401(k) plan. Rather than withdraw funds outright—you'll have to prove "hardship," pay income taxes, and, if you're under age fifty-nine and a half, pay a 10 percent tax penalty—many plans permit you to take a loan from the plan. The amount of the loan can range from a minimum of $10,000 (on an account of at least that amount) to a maximum of $50,000 (on an account of $100,000 or more). You pay market interest rates (but the repayment goes back into your own account, so you're paying yourself) and generally must repay the loan within five years. Meanwhile, the interest you pay may be tax-deductible if you've borrowed your own contributions *and* if you use the money toward your small business or another investment.

Loans against 401(k) plans usually must be repaid if you leave your job, so if you're leaving a salaried job to start your business, a loan won't work. But you can still tap the accumulated money in your 401(k) plan by taking it out and not rolling it over into another tax-qualified plan. The problem here, of course, is that you'll pay taxes on the money, both ordinary income taxes and, if you're under age fifty-nine and a half, Uncle Sam's 10 percent tax penalty. In addition, you'll lose the tax-deferred compounding that will make a big difference in your retirement lifestyle later on. Try not to use tax-qualified retirement money for your business unless you really have no other options.

Loans from Family and Friends

Once you've exhausted your savings and taken the kind of personal loans described above, you may want to turn to family and friends. Many self-employed women and men find start-up and expansion capital through such personal loans, but be aware that unless structured carefully to remain businesslike (and even, sometimes, if they are), loans from family and friends can undermine relationships and cause long-lasting conflict. They may also lead to unintended tax consequences.

Keep a loan from family or friends businesslike by providing the same kind of business plan and other information that you would provide to any investor and *by putting the arrangement in writing*. This holds true whether you are talking about large amounts or relatively small ones. Joel Isaacson, a financial planner in New York City, speaks of his own experience: "I was going to lease a copier, and lease rates were at 12 percent to 14 percent. At the same time, my father-in-law had money in CDs, with 8 percent CDs being renewed at 3 percent to 4 percent. I borrowed money from him to buy the copier, paying him 7 percent. It was a win-win situation. I got a better rate, and so did he." Isaacson prepared a written agreement with repayment terms spelled out.

Here are some additional suggestions by the accounting firm of KPMG Peat Marwick:

• Pay interest on the loan, in an amount at least equal to the applicable federal rate (AFR). The rate changes monthly. In September 1995 the AFR for a loan of up to three years was 5.91 percent, for a loan of three to nine years was 6.38 percent, and for a loan of more than nine years was 6.91 percent. If you don't pay interest at all, the loan may be considered a gift and your cooperative relative or friend may be saddled with gift tax. If you don't pay interest at the AFR, your lender may also have to pay income tax on the "imputed" income, the amount he or she should have received in interest but didn't.

• To satisfy the IRS, in addition to paying applicable federal rates of interest, include in your written agreement the date payment is due and what collateral backs the loan in the event you can't pay up.

It's also a good idea to spell out just what role your "angel" will play in the business. Just as Mom and Dad may expect to be invited to dinner every Sunday if they help you with the money to buy a house, investors who put up sizable sums may expect to participate in management decisions; if that isn't your intent, make it clear from the outset. But do keep investors informed about your progress and do repay your loans on schedule. If not, you'll be in over your head emotionally as well as financially.

LOAN CRITERIA

Whether you borrow from friends and family or from outside lenders, you need to be able to answer these questions:

- What will the money be used for? Is this a long-term need or a short-term one?
- How much do you need? Have you built in a sufficient cushion for the unexpected?
- When and how will the debt be repaid?
- What collateral do you have to back the loan? Are you relying on business collateral (such as the value of your equipment or inventory) or personal collateral (such as securities or your home)?

The Business Plan

Whether you will borrow from family and friends, from banks, or from venture capitalists, you will need a business plan. Don't underestimate its importance. A business plan is a formal document to present when you're seeking financing. But it also is more: it can help you define your goals and determine how to reach them, and it can be a strategic tool to help you measure progress and redefine objectives as you go along. As the accounting firm of Arthur Andersen puts it, "An effective business plan serves at least four useful purposes:

- It helps an entrepreneur crystallize and focus ideas.
- It creates a track for management to follow in the early years of a business.

- By identifying and quantifying specific business objectives, it creates benchmarks against which the entrepreneur and the management team can measure progress.
- It provides a persuasive vehicle for attracting capital to help finance the business."

These words may be aimed at larger start-up operations, but they can be adapted to your needs as a self-employed entrepreneur. When your business needs money for either start-up or expansion, lenders will require a business plan.

Business plans can be complicated and lengthy documents. For the self-employed, however, it's possible to take a simpler approach. The key elements are:

- Your business idea, defined as narrowly as possible. As Janet Attard asks in *The Home Office and Small Business Answer Book* (Henry Holt, 1993), "Are you in the business of selling dried floral arrangements or decorative home accessories? Do you have a word-processing business, a resume service, or a secretarial service?" Unless you focus your concept, you won't be able to sell it to anyone else—lenders or customers.

- Your background, experience, contacts—the things that can make the idea work. Management is vitally important to most investors, so you want to bring in everything about your own personal background that can make a favorable impression.

- Where your business will be located and why it will work in that location. If you're opening a retail business, for example, you should know the traffic patterns and demographics in the area you've selected.

- How you'll find and keep customers. Your marketing plans should be carefully described.

- The competition. Will you be the only photographer in the neighborhood? The only one who concentrates on corporate promotional pieces? If not, what will you do differently or better than your competitors? How will you respond to their efforts to compete with you?

BUSINESS PLAN OUTLINE

I: The Business
    A. Description
    B. Product/service
    C. Market
    D. Location
    E. Competition
    F. Management
    G. Personnel
    H. Application and expected effect of investment
    I. Summary
II: Financial Data
    A. Sources and applications of funding
    B. Capital equipment list
    C. Balance sheet
    D. Break-even analysis
    E. Projected income statement
    F. Cash flow projection
    G. Historical financial reports
    H. Summary
III: The Financing Proposal
IV: Supporting Documents

SOURCE: Washington, D.C.: American Bankers Association.

• How much it will cost to get started and to run your business. Be sure you include all conceivable costs and include a cushion for the unforeseen, or your business could be in trouble right from the outset. (If you're borrowing money, be realistic in your estimates of how much you'll need; if you underestimate your needs and then have to return to the lender for more, you won't appear financially competent and well organized.)

• How much of your own money you plan to commit to the business and where you will get that money. Investors and lenders have a right to know whether you are depleting your savings, putting your home on the line, or going to relatives; they will also tend to look more favorably on requests from entrepreneurs who have committed their own funds to the venture. You have to share the risk, in other words, just as you must do when you make a down payment on a house.

• How much money you want to borrow, exactly what it will be used for, when you need it (if not all at once), and when you expect to be able to repay the loan.

• How much you plan to pay yourself, or draw from the business.

• Financial projections for the next three to five years, putting your goals in terms of an attainable time frame. Back up your forecasts with as much detail as possible.

Bear in mind that you may have to rewrite your plan, shifting the emphasis to appeal to different lenders. Bankers are usually more interested in cash flow and collateral, for example, while venture capitalists may be more interested in your long-term prospects (see table 3.1).

You can get help in developing your business plan by working with your accountant or financial planner. Or you can find help at little or no cost by contacting one of the seven hundred or so Small Business Development Centers (SBDCs) around the country, many at community colleges, or by contacting the Service Corps of Retired Executives (SCORE), a nationwide volunteer organization (800-634-0245). Both SBDCs and SCORE are funded by the Small Business Administration.

"Official" Sources of Money

The availability of small-business credit (or lack thereof) has been a hot topic among policy makers. After the bad loans that undermined the thrift industry in the 1980s and threatened to do in insurance companies and banks in the 1990s, lenders became extraordinarily averse to risk. Since little is riskier than lending money to a small new venture, small-business credit virtually dried up. Even with efforts to remedy the situation, and some evidence in mid-1994 that financing is becoming somewhat more available,

Table 3.1: The Most Important Factors Influencing Lenders, on a Scale from 1 to 3

SOURCE	MANAGEMENT (CHARACTER)	COLLATERAL	CASH FLOW	EARNINGS CAPACITY	MARKETABILITY OF PRODUCT
Banks	3	2	1	—	—
Finance companies	3	1	2	—	—
Investment bankers	1	—	—	3	2
Insurance companies	3	1	1	2	—
Institutional funds and syndicators	3	1	1	2	—
Entrepreneur's friends and relatives	1	—	—	—	2

SOURCE: Arthur Andersen, "An Entrepreneur's Guide to Starting a Business," Chicago, Ill., Arthur Andersen & Co., 1991, p. 9.

the best bet for the self-employed is still money close to home—money from yourself, from family, from friends.

Bank financing may be even harder to secure if you are a woman or a member of a minority group. It's hard to prove—although the Federal Reserve Board is looking into allegations—but many minority and female small-business owners perceive discrimination on the part of banks. Some studies have confirmed the perception.

A 1988 study by the New School for Social Research in New York City found that 32 percent of white-owned firms received bank loans, compared with 25 percent of black-owned firms. In addition, the average loan was $51,630 for whites and $20,604 for blacks. More recently, a 1993 study by the Kessler Exchange found that minority small-business owners, particularly African-Americans, have a hard time raising money. Of those who sought a bank loan within the past three years, success rates were close to 80 percent for Caucasian, 62 percent for African-American, and about 72 percent each for Asian and Hispanic applicants.

And a 1992 study by the National Foundation for Women Business Owners reports that female business owners are 22 percent more likely to report problems dealing with banks than are businesses at large. Women appear to be asked for more assets and greater collateral (as much as 300 percent of the loan has been reported), and an astonishing one in five of female business owners reported that their loan officer insisted on their spouse's signature on loan documents in addition to their own, even when the spouse had nothing to do with the business.

In mid-summer 1994, acknowledging that its loan-guarantee program was not adequately serving the needs of women and members of minority groups, the SBA launched a campaign to at least double the number of loans made to these groups by the fall of 1995. Rather than waiting for banks to approach the agency with small-business loans, as had been the practice, local SBA officials are being encouraged to seek out potential borrowers. Part of this effort includes a new simple one-page application form for loans of up to $50,000. Another pilot program aimed specifically at female business owners allows them to be pre-qualified for an SBA-guaranteed loan before approaching a lender.

Different lenders stress different factors. Here's what you need to know about official sources of capital—banks, federal and state programs, and venture capitalists.

Banks

While it may be almost impossible to secure start-up financing from a bank, at least for the very small business, the National Federation of Independent Business (NFIB) reports that about 85 percent of loans to up-and-running small businesses come from banks. Table 3.2 indicates the success rate of established businesses in securing bank financing.

Some institutions, dedicated to the needs of the local community, set money aside for small-business loans; Vermont National Bank, as one example, has a "socially responsible banking fund" designated for loans to local small businesses as well as afford-

Table 3.2: Success Rates of Small-Business Owners Who Attempted to Obtain Financing from a Bank or S and L for an Established Business

TYPE OF FINANCING	PERCENTAGE OF APPLICANTS WHO RECEIVED A LOAN
Business loan	74%
Personal loan	78
Line of credit	72
SBA-backed loan	44

SOURCE: Kessler Exchange, 1993. A survey of 520 small-business owners.

able housing, environmental, and educational projects. Ask around to see if any institution in your community has a similar program. It may not be difficult; a 1993 survey by the Community Bankers Association, a trade association of retail banks and thrifts, indicates that banks are making a big effort to beef up their commitment to small business. Three-quarters planned to increase SBA lending, while almost seven out of ten planned to offer more products and services for small businesses.

Banks offer different types of loans to meet different needs. Before you apply for any loan, even for a personal loan collateralized (for example) by your car, you need to determine how much you need, how long you will need the money, and how you will generate sufficient cash flow to repay the loan. In addition to your business plan, you may also need to submit information about the collateral available to back the loan, together with appraisals of current value, a personal financial statement, and a written breakdown of how you will use the loan funds.

Commercial loans may be short-term or long. They may be collateralized by specific personal or business assets such as equipment you already own or are purchasing with the loan, securities, CDs, and your own personal guarantee or that of a cosigner. The value of the collateral usually must be somewhat greater than the amount of the loan; it should also be somewhat liquid, so that the bank can recover its money if necessary. Even then you may have to provide a personal guarantee, at least until you reach certain earning projections for a specified period of time. Typically you'll also need to provide financial statements, a twelve-month projection of business income and expenses, and your personal income tax returns for the past three years.

A very good summary is found in *Steps to Small Business Financing*, a booklet jointly published by the American Bankers Association and the National Federation of Independent Business; ask your local bank for a copy. Another good resource is *The Credit Process: A Guide for Small Business Owners*. Published by the Federal Reserve Bank of New York, it is available by writing to the Public Information Department, 33 Liberty Street, New York, NY 10045.

A *line of credit* at a bank can be a good vehicle for short-term financing because it allows you to borrow repeatedly, up to a specified amount. You repay and reborrow as funds are needed in the course of a year, then apply to renew the line of credit for another year if necessary. These loans, which often must be secured by collateral, let you maintain an even cash flow; they can be very helpful if you operate a seasonal business, need to take advantage of special supplier discounts, are waiting for a big customer to pay a bill, or want to gear up for a special sales effort. Typically you would repay a line of credit in monthly installments consisting of both principal and interest; some lenders, however, will let you pay only interest for a period of time, then repay the principal.

At most banks your only cost for a line of credit is interest on the amounts you access. Some institutions, however, will want you to maintain anywhere from 10 to 20 percent of your available credit in a business account.

A *term loan* may run up to three years (an intermediate term) or more (a long-term loan); any loan over five years or so may have to be linked to specific business purposes, such as the purchase of a building. Both are usually repaid monthly or quarterly from the business's profits. Term loans may be appropriate when you need to finance equipment, improve or acquire real estate, or expand your business.

Interest rates on loans may be variable or fixed. A variable or floating rate changes when an underlying index—typically the prime rate—changes; a fixed rate remains the same throughout the life of the loan. In addition to the interest rate, which may vary from lender to lender, you will probably pay application and commitment fees. Always find out in advance just what costs are associated with borrowing money.

As you compare costs and terms at different institutions bear in mind that you'll do better approaching a bank, hat in hand, if

---

TIP

While the wave of financial institution failures and mergers seems to have ebbed, be careful as you pick a lender. A 1992 survey by the Kessler Exchange found that 14 percent of the small-business owners surveyed had a relationship with a bank or S and L that failed. Thirty-one percent of those business owners said the failure caused them to lose a line of credit. More than half said they had not been able to reestablish credit elsewhere.

Before you take a loan, check the stability of the lending institution. Look at (or ask your accountant to look at) the bank's "statement of condition" or, if it's publicly owned, its annual report to stockholders. A key number: the institution's ratio of equity capital to assets, which should be at least 5 percent. Or place a toll-free call to Veribanc (800-442-2657), a bank-rating service that will give you instant ratings of specific institutions, by telephone, at a nominal charge billed to your credit card.

Even after you have obtained a loan, be alert to reported changes at your lender. Small-business owners with perfect repayment records have had loans called when lenders needed to beef up revenues. You'd be wise to have alternative financing options lined up, just in case.

you've developed an ongoing relationship with that bank. In a 1993 survey by the Kessler Exchange, 70 percent of those who obtained credit reported having had a prior business relationship with the institution; 45 percent had done personal business with the institution that lent them money.

Small Business Administration Programs

If you're having trouble obtaining a conventional loan for your business, consider the guaranteed loan programs of the Small Business Administration. After a period in the doldrums, the SBA has been beefing up its loan programs and now offers several programs you may want to consider.

Under its *7(a) program*, the SBA guarantees repayment of up to 80 percent of the loan amount if the borrower defaults. Under a new addition to the 7(a) program, called *CapLine* loans, the SBA guarantees up to 75 percent of a credit line.

These loans, available at private lenders, are made at favorable interest rates of 2¼ to 2¾ percent over the prime rate, but repayment usually stretches over a longer period than loans from conventional lenders. The loans carry a graduated guarantee fee, starting at 2 percent for loans up to $100,000 and ending at 3.875 percent for loans over $500,000.

And they can be hard to get. Although the SBA had about $8 billion to hand out in fiscal 1994, and was able to do so, it can run out of money. In 1993 the program ran short of funds in April, just six months into its fiscal year. Moral: apply early, because loans are granted on a first-come, first-served basis.

But the SBA program is well worth investigating. George Klopfer started Polk Audio in 1971 when he was twenty-one years old, with $200 in cash, one partner, and work space in a dirt-floored garage. The two "hippies," as Klopfer told a small-business lending conference sponsored by the American Bankers Association in 1993, couldn't convince a bank lending officer to extend a loan of $7,500. Under an SBA loan with a 90 percent guarantee they obtained $75,000—and the bank was still at risk for only $7,500.

TIP

Having trouble raising money? Watch out for the scam artists known as advance-fee loan brokers. They advertise that, in exchange for a fee, they will act as an intermediary and find a lender. Too often, however, they take the fees and run, leaving you holding the bag.

Common sense indicates that you're not likely to receive money from faraway sources when local sources have turned you down. If you do want to explore loan opportunities through a broker, the Council of Better Business Bureaus suggests that you find out if the broker is known to local established lending institutions. And the Federal Trade Commission urges you to check out the company with your local consumer protection agency and the state attorney general's office. (That there are no complaints on file is not necessarily proof of an honest operation, however; many scam operators move from place to place, operating under different names.)

Then secure the following information, in writing, before you sign an agreement or pay any fee:

The SBA *Microloan* program started in mid-1992 as a five-year pilot program designed to help the smallest of small businesses, particularly those run by women, minorities, and low-income entrepreneurs, who have the most difficulty raising capital. Microloans are in amounts of up to about $25,000 but may be for as little as $200; the average is $10,000. Repayment periods vary, up to a maximum of six years.

Microloans are granted through nonprofit community organizations, typically on the basis of character rather than collateral. Some are made directly to individuals, while others work through peer groups and recycle the money throughout the group. Either way, the money is provided by the SBA to the organizations, which, in turn, set up revolving funds for the loans.

- **The name and address of the broker, in addition to the length of time the broker has been in business.**
- **The total number of contracts the broker has signed in the last year, the number of successful contracts, and the number of actual loans closed.**
- **The percent of company income derived from fees paid by clients *before* and *after* obtaining funding.**
- **The possible sources of the loan money. (Confirm this information with the alleged sources, law enforcement agencies, and the Better Business Bureau.)**
- **A complete description of services provided by the broker and of what is covered by the advance fee.**
- **A full description of the broker's refund policy. (But keep in mind that a refund guarantee is only as good as the company itself.)**
- **A copy of the broker's agreement. (If possible, have this agreement reviewed by both an attorney and a local lending institution before signing.)**

SOURCE: "Advance Fee" Loans, Arlington, Va.: Council of Better Business Bureaus, 1990.

To find a Microloan program near you, contact the closest SBA office.

A new SBA LowDoc program offers loans of up to $100,000 with a simple, one-page application. These loans are available through commercial lenders, including banks, who are guaranteed repayment of up to 80 percent of the loan amount if the borrower defaults. The best way to find most SBA loans (with the exception of Microloans, available through nonprofit community organizations) is through your own bank.

Although most SBA loans are in the form of guarantees to banks, the agency also makes direct loans to some veterans and to handicapped persons.

Information about SBA loans, counseling for applicants, and general business advice are available at little or no cost through Small Business Development Centers, and through SCORE. If you need help with a specific business problem, contact a Small Business Institute. If your problem is chosen, it will be the subject of a class assignment and you will benefit by receiving the collective wisdom of professor and students. Often, in fact, these campus-based institutes assign problems to graduate students. To locate one of these helpful sources call the SBA Answer Desk, toll-free, at 800-827-5722 or SCORE, at 800-634-0245.

One of the things you'll learn through these information sources is that you don't want to go to just any bank for an SBA loan. Although about half of the nation's banks participate in the SBA loan program, along with some nonbank lenders, fewer than seven hundred lenders have been granted the "certified" lender status that lets them guarantee a three-day turnaround on loan requests, so long as those requests are accompanied by all the necessary documentation. And fewer than two hundred of these lenders have the status the SBA calls "preferred," a designation that allows them to approve SBA-guaranteed loans in-house, without waiting for word from Washington. Whether certified or preferred, special-status lenders can eliminate much of the hassle associated with government red tape; your nearest SBA office can give you names of preferred or certified lenders in your area.

Don't overlook SBA training when you're focusing on SBA money. A variety of SBA-sponsored workshops, seminars, and programs is available around the country. In addition to programs open to all, SBA's Office of Women's Business Ownership focuses on the needs of female business owners, while SBA's Women's Network for Entrepreneurial Training links female volunteers in a mentoring program for fledgling business owners. All SBA programs, including these, are delivered through offices on the district level. To find your nearest district office, look in your telephone directory or call 800-8-ASK-SBA.

One more SBA service: with a personal computer equipped with a modem, you can call SBA On-Line, talk to other business owners, and get answers to specific questions, in addition to getting SBA loan information and applications. To gain access to the SBA bulletin board toll-free, call 800-697-4636. For a broader range of information at a nominal charge, call 900-463-4636. In the District of Columbia, the number is 202-401-9600.

State Programs

With the enormous growth of small business, there appears to be parallel growth in state and local programs designed to help. Many receive funding from a combination of public (federal and state) and private sources. Some are aimed specifically at minorities or women, some target those with low income, others will help any small business.

Rhode Island topped the list of states providing financial support for small businesses, according to a 1994 report by the Corporation for Enterprise Development in Washington, D.C. Over a three-year period, a Rhode Island small-business loan fund lent needed cash to almost ninety companies that had previously been rejected by at least two commercial banks. Other states making outstanding efforts to help small businesses include Massachusetts, Minnesota, and Illinois.

In Chicago alone, loans made by banks may be guaranteed in part by a raft of agencies and programs, including the State of Illinois Department of Commerce, the City of Chicago Department of Planning and Development, the Illinois Development

---

TIP

The SBA also makes disaster loans to small businesses struck by floods, earthquakes, and other natural disasters. The loans can cover physical and financial losses in designated disaster areas and are applied for through the Federal Emergency Management Agency.

Finance Authority, the Illinois State Treasurer's Women's Finance Initiative, the City Treasurer's Linked Deposit Program, the City of Chicago MicroLoan, the Women's Self-Employment Project, and the Neighborhood Institute Microloan Program—all in addition to SBA programs.

Other states and communities have similar wide-ranging programs. One source for a reasonably complete list (up-to-date as of 1992, in the 1993 edition): *The States and Small Business*, a directory of programs and activities published by the Office of Advocacy of the SBA. To obtain a copy, send twenty-one dollars to the Superintendent of Documents, P.O. Box 371954, Pittsburgh, PA 15250-7954.

Venture Capital

Few self-employed people can attract venture capital, especially in the start-up stage, but the subject is worth a mention. The major difference between banks and venture capitalists is this: Banks are creditors; they want to be sure that your cash flow is sufficient to repay the loan and, if it is not, that there is sufficient collateral to make good. Venture capitalists are investors and, often, owners; they want a superior return on their money and they also, as a rule, want an ownership position in the company. Venture capitalists also tend to be more interested in advanced technology and to show little if any interest in small service businesses. This latter point may change with the introduction of some venture capital funds, targeted solely at women, that focus on industries where women play major roles: retailing, health care, and the media.

Right now, for the most part, banks and venture capitalists are alike in one significant way: neither is particularly interested in small companies or small loans. Because it costs just as much to investigate the prospects of a small company as it does to investigate a large one, and as much to administer a small loan as a big one, most self-employed people and most start-up ventures secure financing from personal resources—their own savings and the investments of relatives and friends.

If you are interested in exploring the world of venture capital, however, look at *Pratt's Directory of Venture Capital*; issued yearly, *Pratt's* is considered the bible of the field. Then attend a venture fair in your region or join a local group that brings entrepreneurs and venture capitalists together. An example is the New Jersey Entrepreneurial Network. At regular luncheon meetings, fledgling companies have a chance to describe their needs and prospects to potential investors.

When the Going Gets Tough

With personal bankruptcy filings at an all-time high—partly as a result of the high living of the 1980s combined with the new economic realities of the 1990s—both you and your business may be at risk if you can't pay back borrowed money.

If you should run into a cash crunch, take a deep breath, sit back, and see what steps you can take before filing for bankruptcy. It may be easy to file, but the results are long-lasting and not particularly pleasant. Bankruptcy can remain on your credit record for ten long years; during that period it can be very difficult if not impossible to secure credit, take out a mortgage loan, or start another business requiring start-up financing.

But sometimes bankruptcy seems inevitable. Before you file, here's what you need to know:

There are two types of personal bankruptcy. A *Chapter 7* bankruptcy is a straight liquidation, under which your assets (except for specified exempt assets) are sold to repay as much of your debt as possible. A *Chapter 13* bankruptcy is a debt repayment plan; you get to keep most of your property but must agree to a court-ordered schedule of debt repayment out of current income.

Whichever way you file for personal bankruptcy, the slate can never be wiped completely clean. Debts linked to property, such as a home or an automobile, must be paid in full or you will lose the property. Under Chapter 7 (less so under Chapter 13, which is more lenient) some legally enforceable debts, including taxes and alimony, are never forgiven.

Business bankruptcies are generally filed under *Chapter 11*, which permits debt restructuring, although they may also be filed under the liquidation plan of Chapter 7. Under Chapter 11, creditors have a say in the process, which can slow things down tremendously. But that isn't necessarily the biggest problem. Where debt restructuring under Chapter 11 allows large businesses to stop paying interest on debt while they reorganize, many very small businesses do not owe interest. Your biggest debt backlog may be to suppliers, who aren't charging interest on overdue bills but who are complaining loudly that they haven't been paid.

If you have problems paying bills, either personal or business, try to call creditors—*before* you reach the point of thinking about bankruptcy—and work out a repayment plan. Even the IRS will sometimes negotiate in connection with back taxes. Seek competent legal and accounting help, along with credit counseling, and you may be able to keep both your personal and business credit intact.

Chapter Highlights

• Most self-employed people must rely on their own financial resources—credit cards, personal loans, life insurance and margin loans, home equity lines of credit, family, friends.

• Loans from family and friends should be by written agreement, at stated rates of interest, with a specified schedule for repayment.

• A solid credit record, including credit cards, overdraft checking, and a home equity line of credit, should be in place before you leave a salaried position and become self-employed.

• A well-thought-out business plan is a must in securing financing from most sources.

- Bank loans are more often available to established businesses than to start-ups; bank financing includes short-term lines of credit and term loans.
- The SBA guarantees loans made by banks to small-business owners otherwise unable to secure a loan; counseling and loan application preparation is available through Small Business Development Centers, Small Business Institutes, and SCORE.
- Other sources of capital include state and local programs and, for the lucky few, venture capitalists.
- Bankruptcy, personal or business, is a last resort when you are unable to pay your bills.

Part II

Fringe Benefits

4 Keeping Fit: Health and Disability Insurance

- Jim A., a self-employed investment adviser, has comprehensive health insurance as a dependent of his wife, a salaried marketing manager at a midsize corporation.
- Debbi M., an attorney, participates in group health insurance offered by the state Bar Association.
- Steve W., an architect, dropped a similar group health policy he had carried through his professional association when it became too expensive, substituting an individual policy with a $2,000 deductible.
- David S., an insurance broker, has his coverage through the Council of Smaller Enterprises (COSE), a division of the Greater Cleveland Growth Association.

Four self-employed individuals. Four distinct approaches to acquiring health insurance. Four entrepreneurs concerned about what the future may bring.

Right now adequate health coverage is one of the biggest problems for the self-employed. It can be difficult to buy health insurance in the first place, and more difficult to keep it if you, a family member, or an employee develops an expensive illness. But difficult does not mean impossible. Health insurance can be very expensive, but it is generally available one way or another.

This chapter describes failed efforts at health insurance

reform on the federal level and successful experiments with reform on the state level, so that you, as a solo entrepreneur, can be prepared for the future. Practically speaking, it describes what you can expect to find in buying and paying for health insurance today. Finally, it covers the important topic of disability income insurance, the type of insurance that will replace lost income if you are unable to work for any length of time because of injury or illness.

Health Insurance Reform

When President Bill Clinton was elected in 1992 he promised health insurance coverage for all. By the time the fall of 1994 rolled around Congress had given up after a political battle over competing health reform proposals. The consensus of the American public, expressed in survey after survey, was clearly that something must be done to curtail escalating insurance costs and to help the growing number of Americans without any health insurance. Congress could not reach a consensus as to what that something should be and is unlikely to try again in the near future.

What might have been: With a phase-in period of several years, most (but not necessary all) Americans would have been covered under a basic benefits package, with optional extras available to those willing and able to pay more. Insurance companies would have had to cover everyone without regard to age or preexisting conditions. Individuals might have been required to buy insurance.

A major stumbling block: Who was to pay the tab. Under some proposals employers would have had to pay 80 percent of the cost for their employees. This would have had a major impact on your pocketbook if you expanded your business by hiring employees, although there might have been subsidies for smaller employers. But self-employed people covered under a spouse's plan might have had to foot the bill for their own coverage. Dependent coverage, except for children, could

THE VOCABULARY OF HEALTH REFORM

- *Managed competition.* A way of reducing health care costs through competition by creating groups of medical providers and groups designed to act as purchasing cooperatives of medical services for large numbers of individuals.

- *Purchasing cooperatives.* These organizations contract to provide medical services to groups. They could be formed by states (some have already done so), created by voluntary alliances of small businesses, or made up of the employees of large corporations.

- *Universal coverage.* Would entitle all citizens to a given set of health-care services.

- *Universal access.* Would allow all citizens to purchase a given set of benefits at roughly the same price.

- *Employer mandates.* Would require employers to provide health insurance for employees.

- *Individual mandates.* Would require individuals to purchase health insurance for themselves.

- *Single-payer system.* Provides tax-financed universal coverage by government, without an insurance intermediary. The Canadian system is a single-payer system.

- *Experience rating.* Premiums are adjusted to reflect claims experience; if someone in your family or business gets sick, premiums are raised.

- *Community rating.* In its pure form, premiums are based only on where policyholders live.

- *Modified or adjusted community rating.* Allows insurers to consider age and/or gender in setting health insurance premiums. Health experience is not considered under either community rating or modified community rating.

PRIMARY SOURCE: "Health Reform: Examining the Alternatives," Washington, D.C.: Employee Benefit Research Institute, March 1994.

have been a thing of the past. Details remained to be worked out.

On the plus side of health reform: Without an employer to pick up part of the cost, the self-employed would probably have been able to deduct 100 percent of health insurance premiums. Right now, just 30 percent is deductible. With a full 100 percent deduction, a $3,000 premium paid by someone in the 31 percent tax bracket actually costs $2,070 after taxes. With the current 30 percent deduction, the out-of-pocket cost of the same premium in the same tax bracket is $2,721.

Independent contractors, however, would have faced a complex situation. Right now, as described in chapter 6, the IRS is waging a battle against independent contractor status. If federal reform is ever enacted, that battle could become a full-fledged war.

The current classification issue revolves around the fact that income taxes are withheld from employees' pay but paid quarterly by the self-employed. Since it's much easier to collect taxes en masse than in scores of individual checks—and since it's much more likely that the taxes will actually be collected—the IRS prefers to classify workers as employees whenever possible. To ensure independent contractor status, it helps to incorporate your business and to have income from many clients. Making a mistake is expensive, often resulting in back taxes, interest, and penalties being assessed by the IRS.

The same thing is likely to happen with health insurance, but the cost of misclassification will increase with the addition of back health insurance premiums. Under most health insurance reform measures, employers may have to forward premiums for employees and pay the bulk of those premiums while independent contractors will be responsible for their own. This could create an enormous incentive for employers to shift employees to independent contractor status. Anticipating this possibility, the Clinton plan gave the Treasury Department extensive new power to write rules classifying workers as either employees or independent contractors. These rules would have affected you whether you had been an independent contractor or had hired others in that capacity.

State-by-state reform, meanwhile, isn't waiting for Congress. Hawaii has been a model for employer-provided health care for two decades. Minnesota, Oregon, and Vermont have also passed legislation intended to provide health coverage for all. Insurers in New Jersey must offer standardized health insurance plans to all residents without regard to health status, age, gender, occupation, or where they live within the state.

Florida and Washington State have instituted purchasing cooperatives to pool the resources of individuals to buy health services. California has a similar purchasing cooperative that is limited, initially, to employees of small businesses; the Health Insurance Plan of California (HIPC) enrolls only businesses with at least three employees. In its first year of operation, HIPC members saw premiums drop by more than 6 percent. Maryland now has cost controls on physicians' fees. New York requires insurers to use "community rating," charging uniform premiums so that people with preexisting conditions or those likely to get sick can't be charged more.

In the small-business marketplace insurance reforms have passed in at least thirty states. These reforms, according to the Health Insurance Association of America, typically include guaranteed access to coverage, renewability, and continuity of coverage. Price caps also may apply.

These reforms are significant. Until five years ago all small-business policies were "underwritten," meaning that an applicant's medical status was carefully considered before a policy was issued. With guaranteed issue, notes Sanford Herman, vice president of group medical insurance at the Guardian Life Insurance Company, "we are moving in the work force to insurance on demand." Continuity of coverage means that once someone is covered and has satisfied a plan's preexisting condition provisions, no restrictions can be imposed if the person changes jobs or the employer changes insurance companies. In other words, if you satisfied a preexisting condition clause when you were working for someone else, then went out on your own and took out a new policy, you would be treated as if there were no gaps in coverage.

COMMUNITY RATING

Community rating, under which all the residents of a particular area are charged identical health insurance premiums, is a controversial concept. Its advocates claim that it will guarantee access to health insurance because insurers won't be able to raise rates for people who are sick or likely to become sick. Its critics believe that it won't work unless it goes hand in hand with universal coverage, because young, healthy people will drop out as their premiums rise to cover the costs of insuring older, sicker people.

In New York State, which introduced pure community rating in 1993, that is exactly what has happened. Premiums dropped for older policyholders but rose sharply for young, healthy individuals. As a result, many of those young people dropped their health insurance, figuring, as one *Wall Street Journal* report put it, that "they either won't need coverage or they'll be able to get it at a reasonable price when they do." What happened next? The insured population rapidly became older and sicker; within one year, as just one example, Mutual of Omaha reported that the average age of its New York policyholders had increased by 3.5 years. And insurers had to raise premiums across the board to provide their insurance.

You won't benefit from these reform measures unless you live in a state that has enacted them. But it isn't that simple. You may also need to meet specified size requirements. In some states, sole entrepreneurs can be defined as a group if they can prove that they run a business. You don't have to be incorporated to do so, says Herman, but you do have to show that you really are a business. In other states small business is defined as at least two or three people; here you are thrust back into the individual marketplace where it can be truly tough to find affordable insurance.

If you live in a state that has reformed or is reforming its health care delivery and/or health insurance system, you may find health coverage more accessible and more affordable. If you live in a state where access to health insurance is not guaranteed, you may find that a preexisting condition makes it impossible or exceedingly expensive to secure coverage. Even here, however, there is hope. A dozen states require Blue Cross–Blue Shield plans to offer periodic open enrollment and to accept all applicants. If you live in one of these states—Alabama, Maine, Maryland, Massachusetts, Michigan, New Hampshire, New Jersey, New York, Pennsylvania, Rhode Island, Virginia, and Vermont—or in the District of Columbia, ask your state insurance department when the next open enrollment period will take place.

Buying Health Insurance

You need health insurance. You and your family need the peace of mind that comes with knowing that sizable medical bills will be paid.

TIP

Should you gloss over health problems when applying for health insurance? No. When it comes to what insurers call preexisting conditions, answer questions honestly. Failing to do so may mean a disallowed claim later on or even a canceled policy. In any case you shouldn't assume that a preexisting condition will make you ineligible for coverage. Different companies have different responses, depending on just what the condition is: Some worry about a history of heart attacks more than cancer while others do the reverse. Some will not cover you at all if you have a medical history of certain conditions, while others will not cover the particular condition for six months or a year. If you are forthright and disclose the condition in your application, it will still be treated as a preexisting condition. You may have to wait for it to be covered, but the policy cannot later be canceled.

Health insurance currently comes in two basic forms, fee-for-service policies and managed care, with the first rapidly giving way to the second.

Fee-for-Service Policies

Traditional health insurance policies are fee-for-service arrangements. You go to the doctor you choose, the doctor bills you, and you or your doctor submits a claim to your insurance company for reimbursement. Your out-of-pocket expenses are limited to the amount of any unmet annual deductible as well as by a co-payment, which is usually 20 percent. You may owe more if reimbursement is limited to what the insurance company considers "reasonable and customary" payment for the particular service in your location. As insurers attempt to keep costs down, such limitations are increasingly common. In addition, preventive services such as checkups are usually not covered at all.

Fee-for-service policies can be either basic or comprehensive.

Basic protection includes hospitalization, surgical, and medical benefits. But basic policies are limited and seldom worth the expense. Before you pay premiums for basic protection alone, think about whether you can pay out-of-pocket costs for routine medical care yourself. If so, apply premium dollars where they'll count most: to insurance that will cover the catastrophic costs associated with serious illness. After all, you can budget for Band-Aids; you can't easily budget for a triple bypass.

Major medical insurance is the most important health insurance you can carry. Whether you purchase it as a supplement to basic coverage or as part of a comprehensive policy, look for a lifetime benefit of at least $1 million; an unlimited lifetime benefit is better still. You also want a "stop-loss" provision, which will limit your share of coinsurance after a specified level of benefits has been reached.

You can keep costs down by choosing a policy with the largest deductible you can afford. Costs and savings vary with location, but an individual major medical policy offered by Guardian in

> **TIP**
>
> **Deductibles should apply to a calendar year, rather than to an illness. Ideally, too, there should be a carry-over period into the next calendar year so that you're not faced with meeting a new deductible in January for an illness that began in December.**

St. Louis, for example, costs $2,017 a year with a $2,500 deductible; the price includes $150,000 of life insurance.

Another cost-cutting technique is to pay a larger portion of your medical bills in the form of coinsurance. Some insurers offer coinsurance choices ranging from a 90 percent–10 percent split—the company pays 90 percent, the insured pays 10 percent—all the way to a half-and-half sharing of costs between insurer and insured. Be careful here, though. While you can cut premiums by as much as 40 percent to 50 percent if you take a fifty-fifty split with no cap on your out-of-pocket expenses in the form of a stop-loss provision, you could also wind up poor. Going fifty-fifty is OK if you can afford to do so, but only with a stop-loss provision to limit your exposure.

Managed Care

Managed care, in contrast to traditional fee-for-service coverage, is a system both of financing and of delivering health care services. It typically covers preventive services and treatment (most fee-for-service arrangements cover only treatment) through a network of medical providers. Sometimes the providers are located in a central facility; this is the case with many health maintenance organizations (HMOs). Sometimes they practice in private offices but participate in a preferred provider organization (PPO). Managed care is at the heart of health reform proposals, both federal and state. Elements of managed care have also inched their way into traditional fee-for-service plans, as insurers and employers alike adopt cost-containment measures such as preadmission certification (before hospitalization), second opinions (before elective surgery), and utilization review (to be sure patients are receiving appropriate services).

Because managed care often costs less than fee-for-service insurance, more and more employers offer economic incentives to attract employees to managed care options. For example, employees who choose to participate in a managed care plan typically have little or no out-of-pocket costs; there are no deductibles or co-payments in most HMOs, and often a nominal five- or ten-dollar payment per office visit. Employees who go "out of network" to a nonparticipating provider, by contrast, may pay 50 percent or more of the cost.

Some major medical policies cover more than others. In evaluating policies, check to see if these services are covered (hospital and medical care will be; dental care probably won't):

- Inpatient hospital services
- Outpatient surgery
- Physician visits (in the hospital)
- Office visits
- Skilled nursing care
- Laboratory tests and X rays
- Prescription drugs
- Psychiatric and mental health care
- Drug and alcohol abuse treatment
- Home health care visits
- Rehabilitation facility care
- Physical therapy
- Hospice care
- Maternity care
- Chiropractic
- Preventive care and checkups
- Well-baby care
- Dental care

SOURCE: *The Consumer's Guide to Health Insurance*, Washington, D.C.: Health Insurance Association of America, 1992.

As a result, enrollment in HMOs has more than doubled since 1985, with most members participating through employer-sponsored groups. This means that one way or another, the trend toward managed care will continue. As a self-employed individual, however, you may have difficulty finding a managed care plan that will accept you. You can enroll in a PPO through a commercial insurer, but only one in four HMOs accepts individual applicants. If you find one that will, you will have to pass a medical examination to be accepted. But once accepted, according to the Group Health Association of America, you'll find two pleasant features: First, it's very rare to find an HMO that imposes waiting periods before covering preexisting conditions. Second, most HMOs use community rating, which means that the adverse health experience of members—bypass surgery, for example—does not affect their premiums.

You may pay less for health insurance under managed care; you may also have fewer choices when it comes to health care. One of the hallmarks of managed care is the use of medical providers organized into groups or networks: HMOs and PPOs are the most common, but there is a whole alphabet soup of options that boils down to this fact: in order to receive full benefits you must use a medical provider from a preselected panel. (Several states, however, have passed legislation that gives HMO enrollees the option to visit an out-of-network provider.) One of the other key elements—although you'll often find this in fee-for-service plans as well—is that benefits may be paid only for services that are "medically necessary," a definition made and implemented by insurers.

As employers try to cut costs, managed care is becoming an increasingly important component of corporate health care coverage. Employees must often make a choice: full coverage through plan physicians or partial coverage through standard deductibles and co-payments if out-of-plan providers are used. As a solo entrepreneur, you face a similar choice. If you can find one that will accept you, you can probably keep costs down by enrolling in a managed care plan. But bear in mind that there are trade-offs to be made.

Managed care is designed to curb the explosive increase in medical costs while reducing out-of-pocket expenditures by patients, but it sometimes has the less-desirable effect of limiting both patient choice and physician independence. Responding to many complaints of medical complications and even deaths resulting from insurer interference in medical decisions—refusing timely referral to specialists or limiting hospital stays, for example, sometimes unwisely—New Jersey's health department set out in 1994 to rewrite the rule book for managed care in the state.

Managed care plans can offer low-cost comprehensive health care but may not meet your needs. For example, a managed care plan may not cover you in other locations. If you travel frequently, whether on business or pleasure, you may be better off with a traditional fee-for-service plan that is not linked to a group of medical providers in a specific area. If you do decide that managed care is for you, shop around and compare both benefits and costs before you enroll.

Before you sign up for a managed care plan, ask these questions:

- Exactly what is covered, and what is not?
- Are doctors board-certified? Board-eligible? Well regarded in the community?
- What specialists participate in the plan? When patients need to see other specialists to whom are they referred?
- How are doctors paid? (Some payment methods seem to offer doctors incentives to see patients less often and restrict referrals to specialists.)
- What is the turnover rate among doctors? (Will you get to see the same physician on a return visit?)
- What is the usual wait for an appointment? What about emergencies?
- Which hospitals does the plan use?
- What happens if you become sick or are injured away from home?

Other Health Policies

There are two types of health insurance most people should skip. Both are frequently sold by mail.

Hospital Indemnity Policies

Hospital indemnity policies provide daily cash benefits during hospitalization. They do not directly pay medical bills, although the money can be used for anything you like. Their limited benefits, especially in an era when hospital stays are increasingly restricted—multiple bypass surgery only warrants three or four days in some hospitals these days—make little sense unless you are unable to secure more comprehensive coverage.

"Dread Disease" Policies

"Dread disease" policies pay benefits only for a specific named condition. They are generally not worth buying, unless you have a very good reason (besides irrational fear) to think that you will come down with cancer rather than some other, equally expensive disease. In fact, you want health insurance that will reimburse or cover the costs associated with any illness or accident.

Two other specialty types of health insurance may be worth considering, especially as you grow older.

Medicare Supplement Insurance

Medicare supplement insurance, often called "Medigap" insurance, fills in the gaps in Medicare coverage.

Major changes are under way in Medicare as Congress grapples with ways to rein in soaring costs. Instead of expanding Medicare to cover those unable to secure other health insurance, as was once suggested in the fervor for health insurance reform, it looks as if Medicare beneficiaries will pay more for less. For now, Medicare comes in two parts: part A, hospital insurance, and part B, medical insurance. Both have deductibles and coinsurance. Both become available when you reach age sixty-five, although you must pay separately for medical benefits under part B.

If you keep working between ages sixty-five and seventy, and if you have a group health insurance policy for your business, that policy will provide primary coverage. But do enroll in Medicare at age sixty-five, even if you will keep working. If you delay, there will be a hefty surcharge when you do enroll.

Medicare currently covers only 35 to 45 percent of health care costs. In addition to its deductibles and co-payments, it limits reimbursement to "approved" amounts, and excludes many important—and expensive—items altogether: out-of-hospital prescriptions, eye examinations and eyeglasses, routine immunizations, custodial nursing home care costs, preventive screenings, and so on. That's where Medicare Supplement insurance comes in.

MedSup or Medigap policies are available through private insurance policies, Blue Cross–Blue Shield plans, and retirement associations. There are ten standard packages (not all are available in every state), each designed to plug at least some of the gaps in Medicare coverage. The basic policy, plan A, covers the co-payment under Medicare part A, the 20 percent co-payment of allowable physician charges under part B, and the first three pints of blood. The other policies offer this core package plus additional benefits ranging from skilled nursing home payments to outpatient prescription drugs. Although the policy packages are standardized, prices are not. Be sure to shop around and compare carefully before you buy.

If you will want one, be sure to buy a Medicare Supplement policy when you first become eligible for Medicare at age sixty-five. You cannot be denied a policy based on preexisting conditions for the first six months after this date. If you miss this open enrollment opportunity, you may not be able to get the coverage you want.

CONSUMER PROTECTION IS BUILT INTO MEDICARE SUPPLEMENT REGULATIONS

Because so many older people were sold overlapping and duplicative policies, agents and companies can now be penalized for selling duplicate coverage. In fact, some issuers have adhered a bit too carefully to the letter of the law and refused to issue a MedSup policy to someone holding a group policy with minimally overlapping benefits.

In addition, newly issued Medicare Supplement policies must be guaranteed renewable; they can't be canceled unless you fail to pay your premiums or you significantly falsify information on your application.

Long-Term Care Policies

Long-term care policies insure against the costs of long-term custodial care in a nursing home or at home. Medicare and MedSup policies cover only brief periods in a skilled nursing home, on a doctor's orders, following hospitalization. Long-term custodial care, which can be needed by young accident victims and middle-aged sufferers from debilitating illness as well as by infirm elderly who need help with activities of daily living, is not covered by any other type of insurance. And long-term care is expensive. One year in a nursing home, on average, costs about $40,000; in high-cost urban areas, figures of twice that amount are not unusual. Around-the-clock custodial care at home can run almost as much.

Long-term care policies, a relatively "new kid on the block" in the insurance world, have not yet been standardized the way MedSup policies have been, but they are vastly improved over earlier models. If you are interested in a long-term care policy, for you or for your parents, look for one that does not require a period of hospitalization before nursing home benefits are payable or a stay in a nursing home before home care benefits can be paid. Look for a policy that covers Alzheimer's disease and.

other organic cognitive disabilities, one that pays benefits not only if you are ill but if you are unable to perform specific activities of daily living, and one that includes an adjustment for inflation. These policies typically pay a specified amount per day; without a cost-of-living adjustment these dollar amounts can become woefully inadequate over time.

Health Insurance Choices for the Self-Employed

You're heard all of the horror stories. You know that securing affordable health insurance as a solo entrepreneur can be a challenge. Nonetheless, there are a number of ways to embark on the quest for health insurance.

Links to the Corporate World

You may be pleased as punch to be on your own, but you may not want to sever all your ties to the world of employment. There are two ways corporate ties can be helpful.

First, if you are still considering embarking on a career as your own boss, or have just recently cut the ties that bind, you may be eligible under the COBRA rules for continuation insurance from your prior employment. COBRA is an acronym for the Consolidated Omnibus Budget Reconciliation Act of 1986, the law providing that workers and their dependents can retain benefits under certain conditions.

Most companies with more than twenty employees must abide by these rules and provide continuation coverage for eighteen months to employees who leave, whether voluntarily or involuntarily; dependent coverage can continue for thirty-six months. The employer must notify you if you are eligible, you must reply within a specified time, and you must pay the entire premium plus a 2 percent administrative charge. You may find this expensive, especially while you're in the start-up stages of a new business, but it can be more expensive to do without health insurance altogether.

TIP

If your prior employer is self-insured, as more and more
large companies are, you may not be eligible for COBRA
coverage. You'll probably have to ask, since plan documents can confuse the issue by bearing an insurance company name when there is no underlying insurance; many
self-insured companies hire an insurance company to administer the plan. If you are not eligible for COBRA, find
out if your group policy contains a conversion provision
allowing you to convert the group policy to an individual
one. The cost will be high, and benefits may be curtailed,
but conversion may be worthwhile—especially if you have
any preexisting medical conditions that could make securing a new policy difficult.

How do most self-employed workers find health insurance?
Through another family member's employment. In fact, according to Paul and Sarah Edwards, authors of *Working from
Home* (Tarcher/Putnam, 1994), many spouses are employed
expressly for the purpose of obtaining or keeping health insurance.

Under our current yet-to-be-reformed health insurance system employed spouses can obtain dependent coverage for their
partners. It doesn't matter whether those partners are self-
employed, unemployed, or working for a company with less
desirable benefits. It's uncertain what will happen to dependent
coverage under reform—much depends on just which measure
is enacted—but Paul and Sarah Edwards believe that many employed spouses will leave their salaried jobs to work with their
self-employed husbands and wives. Meanwhile, if your spouse
has good health insurance on the job, take advantage of dependent coverage under that insurance.

Going with a Group

Just as the Clinton administration hoped to curb health care costs by forming purchasing cooperatives, you may be able to control your own health insurance expenditures by joining a group. You may have a number of choices:

State Purchasing Cooperatives

Your state, like California and Texas, may already have a purchasing cooperative for small businesses. Your state insurance department or commission, probably located in your state capital, can provide this information.

Associations

Trade and professional associations, fraternal and business groups, and civic organizations all pitch group health insurance. Some of these offerings are better than others. Some of these groups simply sell their mailing lists to marketers. Some are insured through offshore companies, which can pose a problem if payment of a claim is in dispute (see p. 112). Other associations actually contract with an insurance company and provide discounted rates to their members. Insured plans can be a good buy, but be sure to check on the stability of the insurance com-

---

TIP

You may be keeping your salaried job, while getting your own venture under way, but don't drop dependent coverage even if both you and your spouse work for companies with health benefits. If you drop your coverage while your spouse keeps hers, and then her company downsizes, you might have to prove that you are insurable in order to get back your coverage. And, even if you opt out of your company health plan, the other employer may still coordinate benefits with the coverage you could have had. This could mean sizable uncovered medical bills.

pany providing the benefits just as you would if you were buying
an individual policy. If you don't currently belong to a group
with worthwhile health benefits, and can't find one to join, you
might look into benefits offered by one of the several organizations set up for this purpose: three such organizations are Support Services Alliance, 800-322-3920; Small Business Service
Bureau, 800-222-5678; Co-op America, 202-872-5307.

Local Chamber of Commerce

Your local chamber of commerce may offer health insurance
to its members. To become a member—useful for making
contacts with other business people in your community as well
as for securing health insurance—you must be in business in
the chamber's local area and you must pay membership dues.
These dues vary both by the size of your business and by the
size and program offerings of the chamber itself, but the U.S.
Chamber of Commerce indicates that the smallest firms, with
one to three employees, might pay dues ranging from $125 to
$200 a year.

An outstanding example of a chamber of commerce with
health benefits is Cleveland's Council of Smaller Enterprises.
COSE, as it is known, is the Small Business Division of the
Greater Cleveland Growth Association. With more than thirteen
thousand members, COSE is the largest local small business
organization in the United States. As such, it now offers twelve
different group health insurance plans, both traditional fee-for-
service insurance and managed care through preferred provider plans, point-of-service plans, and health maintenance
organizations. Most important, COSE is for *small* business; the
average insured group has seven employees, but the solo entrepreneur is welcome as well.

Similar, although usually less extensive, programs are available
elsewhere. Contact your local chamber of commerce for information. This is a particularly good route to follow if you are interested
in a health maintenance organization; national organizations re-
cruiting by mail are less likely to offer HMOs while community-
based chambers of commerce can more readily do so.

Regional Business Coalitions

Regional business coalitions are also being formed under the umbrella of the National Business Coalition on Health (NBCH). Most of the eighty-four coalitions in existence in mid-1994 focus on the needs of large employers, helping them negotiate for better pricing and quality controls in health care delivery through health maintenance organizations and preferred provider organizations. But NBCH is extending its reach to small businesses, including the one-person business. At this writing, groups in Denver, Madison, Milwaukee, Memphis, and the Tampa area are developing a product for the small employer market, with more regional coalitions to follow. For information, write to the National Business Coalition on Health, 1015 18th Street NW, Suite 450, Washington, DC 20036.

Commercial Insurers

Many insurance companies have withdrawn from the individual health insurance market over the last few years in reaction to what they perceive as overregulation by the states. When New York State instituted community rating in 1993, for example, forbidding companies to base premiums on health-related risk factors, a number of companies simply stopped issuing insurance in that state. Group insurance, historically, has been less regu-

---

TIP

A good insurance agent, one experienced in meeting the needs of small businesses, can be invaluable in finding the right health insurance and in helping you cope with subsequent problems. Look for an agent who has been in business for a while, who belongs to a professional association such as the National Association of Health Underwriters or the Association of Health Insurance Agents, and who has had advanced training such as that denoted by the designation Chartered Financial Consultant (ChFC) or Chartered Life Underwriter (CLU).

---

lated and consequently easier to obtain—if you qualify as a group. In at least fourteen states a sole entrepreneur is a group; in others you must be a two- or three-person firm to qualify. Your insurance agent can tell you if you are eligible to buy group insurance.

A number of insurance companies write policies for small businesses. For example, Guardian has a one-person health plan but it's a package deal; in many states you must also purchase at least $150,000 of group term life insurance, which makes the policy more expensive.

Celtic Life, headquartered in Chicago and selling policies in more than half the states, covers groups of three or more through group insurance and covers sole proprietors through "key employee" health plans. Celtic also writes individual insurance, which you can buy as a sole proprietor. Which is better? If you are healthy, and therefore have a choice, Peter Harmon of Celtic suggests this approach: If you intend to remain a one-person operation, consider individual insurance. With an individual policy (it can cover your family as well), you may be able to tailor deductibles and coinsurance amounts to suit your budget. If you ever hire employees, however, you'd better hope that they are insurable; you won't be able to include them on your policy, and they will have to obtain their own insurance.

If you own your own company and expect to add employees, you might do better starting off with a one-person group plan; once the original plan is in place you can add employees without regard to the state of their health. In addition, according to Roy Wilkinson of Wilkinson Benefit Consultants, group plans may not have as many restrictions and limitations as individual policies. An individual policy might limit coverage for organ transplants to $100,000, for example, while a group policy would be unlikely to contain such a restriction. You may also find higher lifetime maximum benefits in a group policy, sometimes even unlimited benefits.

Note, though, that in order to be eligible for group insurance you must generally work a minimum number of hours per week. Celtic's Key Employee plan requires that you work at least thirty hours a week. If you decide to retire early, before you are eligible for Medicare and a Medicare Supplement policy, the policy will be discontinued and you could face a big hole in your financial safety net. Meanwhile, if you want a group policy and have no intention of retiring early, be sure you work enough hours and can prove that you do. If you're working only twenty-five hours a week (lucky you!) and want a policy that requires thirty hours, be sure to put in the extra five hours a week and document them in a diary.

Buying an individual policy is another option. In more than half the states insurance companies must issue a policy to anyone who applies, regardless of health. Elsewhere applicants for individual insurance must meet medical underwriting standards. If you are healthy and can meet the standards, you may

---

TIP

Having trouble finding time, while running your business, to research the health insurance marketplace? Here are two suggestions:

• You can narrow your search by consulting Quotesmith, which tracks about four hundred companies offering both individual and small-group coverage. Explain to the representative on the toll-free line, 800-556-9393, the type of coverage you want, and you'll receive a printout listing the policies that meet your needs. The service is free to consumers; if you buy a policy (there is no obligation to do so), the insurance company pays Quotesmith a fee.

• For more detailed advice, including plan recommendations, consult Wilkinson Benefit Consultants at 800-296-3030. For a fee of $270 (for individuals and for businesses of up to three people) Wilkinson will do a thorough evaluation and prepare a report on the three plans that best meet your needs. You also receive a price summary of another eight to ten insurance companies or HMOs, so that you can put prices into context. Follow-up consultation is included in the initial fee.

want to look at an individual policy because it may have better benefits at a lower cost than a small-group plan.

But there are trade-offs, so be sure to look beyond price and compare policy provisions carefully. Just to confuse the issue, small-group plans often have the advantage of carryover provisions on preexisting conditions. Most individual policies require a one-year wait before coverage for preexisting conditions, even if you've had other coverage. Small-group policies, on the other hand, are generally required to provide immediate coverage for preexisting conditions if you've met waiting periods under another policy.

Risk pools are a last-resort option if you are unable to secure any other health insurance because you are in poor health or work in a hazardous occupation. About half the states now have risk-sharing pools providing health insurance for the uninsurable; contact your state insurance department to see if your state is on the list. The major drawback is cost. Premiums typically run 125 percent to 150 percent of the average premiums charged in the state by private insurers, but they can be much more. Another drawback is that benefits are usually limited. For those without access to insurance, however (at least until reform measures are passed on the national level), risk pools can provide peace of mind.

TIP

Until recently you had to incorporate your business in order to deduct the cost of family medical insurance. Now, under a 1994 "tax advice memorandum" by the IRS (a memorandum is not quite as binding as a ruling, but tax analysts say you can act on it), you can put your spouse on the payroll and pay your family's medical expenses with pretax dollars. Your spouse must be a legitimate employee and be paid a reasonable salary. You will also have to remit payroll taxes on your spouse's behalf. Consult your tax adviser to make sure the arithmetic works out favorably.

Although the health insurance industry says that coverage is available for every type of business, and indeed it is in states with guaranteed-access laws, a 1992 survey indicated that you could have a tough time securing insurance in some fields of work. If your state hasn't joined the small-business reform movement, you could face a tedious search for health coverage if your business is considered hazardous (quarrying, logging, farming, pilot-training, pest-control), is low-paying or seasonal, with high employee turnover (service stations, convenience stores, car washes, ski resorts, beauty salons, dry cleaners, restaurants), or has a high rate of claims (physicians' offices, nursing homes, law firms). But don't give up. There are hundreds of insurance companies with different sets of requirements. A good agent or broker can help you negotiate your way through the maze and find affordable insurance, no matter what your line of work.

Selecting a Company

It can be so difficult to find health insurance that you may cheerfully go with any company that will issue you a policy. Don't be hasty. It can be even worse to have health insurance with a shaky or dishonest insurer than to have no health insurance at all.

Unfortunately, financial difficulties have shadowed a number of formerly stable companies in recent years. Even some Blue Cross–Blue Shield plans, along with some well-known commercial insurers, have foundered under the weight of junk bonds or depreciated real estate holdings. Insolvent insurers are often taken over by other insurers, and state guaranty funds may step in to protect you if your company fails and is not taken over, but your safest bet is to select a stable and solvent company in the first place. Before you buy, check ratings assigned by A. M. Best Company, Standard & Poor's, and Moody's. Ask your insurance agent for the rating report or look for it in your local library.

Be particularly careful with association group policies; some (not all) are insured through offshore companies that are not regulated in the United States at all. When companies are not regulated you have no recourse when problems arise. If you are considering an association group policy, find out who the insurer is and check the company's stability as described above.

HEALTH INSURANCE CHOICES FOR THE SELF-EMPLOYED

- Coverage as a dependent of an employed spouse
- Through carryover (COBRA) benefits from your own prior job
- Through an association policy
- Enrolling in a health maintenance organization or joining a PPO thru a commercial insurer
- Joining a health alliance; your state insurance commission can tell you if your state has an alliance
- Buying a small-business group policy; in some states a small business may have just one employee
- Buying an individual policy; in more than half the states insurance companies must issue a policy to anyone who applies, regardless of health.
- Participating in a "risk pool," if your state offers one, for people unable to secure health insurance elsewhere.

Disability Income Insurance

This crucial part of your protection package replaces the income you would lose if an illness or injury put you out of commission for a lengthy period of time. Health insurance pays medical and hospital bills; disability income insurance provides income so that you can carry on during an extended period when you can't work. This form of insurance does not appear immediately susceptible to change as part of health reform and should definitely be part of your insurance plans.

But disability income insurance can be both complicated and hard to find, especially if you work out of a home office. Insurers experienced heavy losses in the 1980s, both because medical advances made disabled survivors out of people who might have died in an earlier era and because there was a significant increase in claims for mental and nervous disorders and substance abuse. As a result, underwriting standards have been tightened and individual disability insurance is harder to buy. But hard does not mean impossible. While insurers used to favor professionals, in fact, some are now actively seeking small-business owners.

In shopping for disability coverage here's what you need to know:

Amounts of Disability Insurance

The amount of disability insurance you can buy, typically expressed as a monthly dollar amount, is pegged to how much you earn. As a self-employed person with a fluctuating income be prepared to document your income with tax returns. No matter how much or how little you earn, however, you generally can't buy insurance to replace more than 60 percent to 70 percent of your income; insurers don't want you to be tempted to receive benefits in lieu of working.

TIP

If you received employer-paid disability benefits from a salaried job, you would owe income tax on those benefits. When you buy your own policy and pay your own premiums, the benefits are tax-free. This means that a benefit equivalent to 60 percent of your predisability earnings is actually worth considerably more if no taxes need be paid. It may also mean, insurance adviser Peter Katt suggests in the *AAII Journal*, that you should resist the temptation (if you are incorporated) to deduct premiums paid by the corporation; if you do so, you will have to pay taxes on any benefits you receive at a time when paying additional taxes could be a real hardship.

Working from Home

If you work in a home office and spend almost all your time there, be prepared to look long and hard for an insurer willing to sell you a disability income policy. The problem, of course, is that it's hard for an insurance company to verify disability if you're your own boss and your home and workplace are the same. You'll find it easier if you spend a lot of time out of the office, with your clients or on the road; in fact, UNUM, one of the major issuers of disability income insurance, requires most home-based workers to spend at least half their time away from home. Anne Mitchell, a second vice president and actuary at UNUM, notes that it's also helpful, although not required, to have a separate entrance to your home office and customers or clients who visit you there.

Be careful. Meeting the requirement of spending at least half your time away from your home office, assuming that you can do so, could disqualify you from claiming a home office deduction (see chapter 6).

But even the true stay-at-home businessperson should be able to find a disability policy. Jeff Sadler, an insurance agent in Orlando, Florida, notes that attitudes are loosening a bit. "Before, someone who worked out of a home office wasn't even discussable," he says. "Now, with so many people laid off, going into business for themselves, companies are being more understanding. If you've been in the same field for a long time and have a good income, even though you're now working out of your house, there's a good chance of getting a policy." Just be prepared to shop around and to prove that you've had steady income over a period of time; many carriers now want to see tax returns. Some—Guardian is one example—want a description of occupational duties and may write disability policies for home-based businesspeople with longer elimination periods and shorter benefit periods.

Defining Disability

Disability can be defined as the inability to perform your own occupation or any occupation. If you are in a highly specialized field, such as speech therapy or architecture, you'll want a policy that defines disability as the inability to perform your own occupation. The classic example provided by insurance agents is the neurosurgeon who can no longer perform surgery but who might be able to teach; "own occupation" coverage would pay benefits that would help to make up the difference between what a surgeon earns and what a teacher is paid.

In other fields, suggests Jane Ann Schiltz, director of individual disability insurance marketing at Northwestern Mutual Life Insurance Company, you should ask yourself what else you might be able to do. "If you can't do your own occupation because you can't write or dial a phone or sit at a desk," Schiltz says, "perhaps you can't do much else either, and wouldn't need own occupation coverage." Note, too, that as a self-employed person you probably perform a wide range of tasks from white-collar to blue. Some policies pay benefits only for total disability that prevents a business owner from performing administrative duties; manual tasks such as stocking shelves or loading boxes are not covered.

Many individual disability policies require that you be totally disabled before benefits begin. Some will pay for partial disability, typically for six months or a year, but often only after a period of full disability. Two other wrinkles to consider:

Residual Benefits

"Residual" benefits, a popular feature in policies issued to executives and professionals, permit the policyholder to make up a portion of lost income until retirement age (assuming you buy a policy with benefits payable to age sixty-five) if you can do part of your job but not all of it. Benefits are pegged to loss of income; with a 30 percent loss of income, you would receive 30 percent of your monthly benefit. In a policy covering your own occupation you would receive this benefit regardless of any income you may be earning in another occupation. You need not be totally disabled first or meet the requirements of an elimination period (see p. 118) in order to collect residual benefits.

Recovery Benefits

"Recovery" benefits supplement a shortfall in earnings while you're getting back on your feet. Recovery benefits are designed for occupations with a client base; if clients go elsewhere while you're laid up with a disabling illness or injury, it could take a while to get back to prior income levels even after full recovery. Mitchell points out, though, that this is subjective; because it's hard to prove that income is down from lost clients rather than from a downturn in the economy, some companies are pulling back from offering recovery benefits.

Duration of Coverage

You can buy coverage for a few years, to age sixty-five, or for life. Your best bet: coverage to age sixty-five, with an extension if you are still working. While you can save money on premiums by electing a shorter benefit period, you will also be in a bad way if you suffer a chronic disability that makes it impossible for you to return to work.

TIP

You may be able to buy group disability coverage if you have at least one employee, although group discounts typically apply only to groups of three or more (five in Kentucky). But Jane Ann Schiltz of Northwestern Mutual points to one potential disadvantage. To buy and keep group coverage you must be and you must remain a group. If you have one employee and then you don't, you are no longer a group and you no longer have coverage. You're probably better off buying an individual policy unless you have a stable staff of three or four people.

A lifetime coverage rider (some insurers require separate riders for illnesses and accidents) can be purchased to extend your policy beyond age sixty-five, but it's generally not necessary to do so. Many policies provide that if you are still working at least thirty hours a week, you can renew your policy to age seventy-five and receive benefits for up to two years.

Elimination Periods

A better way to keep premiums down is to self-insure for a longer period before benefits begin. Disability income policies typically come with waiting or elimination periods ranging from sixty to ninety days; periods of six months or a year may also be elected. If you can support yourself for several months—if you have adequate savings and/or a working spouse—elect a longer waiting period and you'll save considerable sums. See table 4.1.

Note, though, that disability insurance premiums for women recently increased significantly as insurers moved away from unisex pricing and toward gender-distinct pricing. Since women (up until age fifty or so) submit more disability claims, premiums for their individual disability policies are proportionately higher. In the group market, which is subject to more state regulation, unisex pricing still prevails.

Table 4.1: Sample Annual Premiums for a Forty-Year-Old Professional or Executive Who Is Part of a Three-Person Group with an Employer/ Employee Relationship, with Benefits Paid to Age Sixty-Five, for a Monthly Disability Benefit of $3,000

WITH A NINETY-DAY ELIMINATION PERIOD: $1,054
WITH A SIX-MONTH ELIMINATION PERIOD: $972

SOURCE: UNUM Life Insurance Company of America.

Costs

Disability insurance premiums are generally level, based on your age when you take out the policy. Some companies offer annual renewable disability income insurance, similar to term life insurance, which can help you keep premiums manageable when your business is new and income is unpredictable. Under one policy issued by Northwestern Mutual Life Insurance Company, for example, a forty-year-old man could pay an initial premium of just $918 a year for a $3,000 monthly benefit payable to age sixty-five after a ninety-day waiting period; the premium for this policy would rise to $2,340 a year by the time he reached his mid-fifties. This is the cost of a policy purchased at that age. Similar coverage for a forty-year-old woman would start at $1,635 and end at $2,643 a year.

Policies can also be a mixture. If this forty-year-old man wants the same $3,000 benefit but doesn't want premiums that will rise to $2,340 a year, he could take a policy that is half level premium (at $753) and half annual renewable (at $421) for a total first-year premium of $1,174. This combination policy will top out at $1,886.

Optional provisions, or "riders," can add to your premium cost. Not all are worthwhile. Buyers have shown relatively little interest in a rider that provides extra benefits toward a child's college education should the insured parent be disabled. Other more common riders offer a cost-of-living adjustment that increases benefits (but only after they've begun) by an inflation index and the right to purchase more insurance (if your income increases) without regard to the state of your health. Katt suggests that both are expensive and unnecessary. Consider buying the best basic benefit you can afford, with residual benefits, and skip the extras.

Disability Coverage for Your Business

As the owner of a small business, however, you may want to consider two types of business disability insurance as well as individual disability income insurance.

Disability Overhead Expense Protection

Disability overhead expense protection will help to pay a variety of expenses—rent, utility bills, accounting fees, insurance premiums, employee salaries—during a period when your own income is curtailed because of illness or accident. Optional provisions under some contracts will pay partial benefits if you are able to work part time. Benefits may not be payable if the injury or illness is such that you are able to perform administrative and managerial duties but not manual chores.

With some insurance companies you may be able to elect a shorter waiting period for a business overhead policy than you have on disability income benefits. And some insurers offer an optional partial overhead expense benefit. UNUM's owner-manager overhead expense policies, as an example, will pay 50 percent of the overhead expense benefit for the first six months of a residual disability.

Business overhead expense policies typically have short benefit periods of a year or two. The idea is that a business owner not recovered by that time should give serious consideration to closing the business. With business overhead policies too, expense vouchers must generally be submitted to the insurance company before the policyholder is reimbursed. At UNUM a forty-year-old man would pay $16.96 per $100 of monthly benefit for a policy with a one-year benefit period after a thirty-day elimination period. This comes to $848 for a $5,000 benefit. A woman of the same age, buying the same policy, would pay $25.24 per $100 or $1,262.

Disability Buyout Policy

If you are in a partnership or corporation, you may also want to consider a disability buyout policy so that any one of you can afford to buy out another who is unable to work and unlikely to return. While many partnerships and corporations carry key person life insurance to enable a buyout if a partner or owner dies, disability buyout insurance can be just as important. Policy benefits can be paid in a lump sum or in installments. Some insurers require that a buy-sell agreement be in effect before the benefit is paid. UNUM's lump sum benefit under a buyout policy with its gender-neutral rates costs $5.66 a year per $1,000 of total benefit.

How to Buy Disability Income Insurance

A number of companies write individual and business disability income insurance, but four insurers—Paul Revere, UNUM, Provident Life & Accident, and Northwestern Mutual Life—dominate the market. Start your search with an agent representing one or more of these companies. If you can't find an individual disability income policy, either because you're just starting out and don't have a track record or because your occupation is a problem for most insurers, don't give up. You may be eligible for a group policy through a professional or trade association.

Chapter Highlights

• National health insurance reform may mean major changes for the self-employed.

• More than half the states require that insurers offer small businesses guaranteed access to health insurance, renewable policies, and continuity of coverage. In some states these measures apply to one-person businesses.

• In buying health insurance you must choose between fee-for-service plans and managed care.

• In fee-for-service arrangements you go to the doctor you choose, the doctor bills you, and you submit a claim to your insurer for reimbursement. You can keep costs down by buying a major medical policy with the largest deductible and co-insurance you can afford.

• Managed care, as a system of both financing and delivering health care services, controls costs by limiting access to medical providers. If you belong to a managed care plan and go outside the network of providers, you will pay more.

• Hospital indemnity policies and dread disease policies are generally not worth buying, but you may want to consider Medicare Supplement and long-term care insurance.

• If you have difficulty buying health insurance on your own, consider buying it through an association such as a local chamber of commerce.

• Disability income insurance replaces income lost if you are unable to work because of illness or injury. Business overhead expense protection pays ongoing expenses while you are unable to work. A disability buyout policy can provide the funds to buy out a disabled partner.

5 Property Insurance: Are You Covered?

In August 1992 Hurricane Andrew wiped out much of southern Florida. In the summer of 1993 floods damaged or destroyed large areas of the Midwest. In fall 1993 fires ravaged southern California, and in early 1994 earthquakes hit the same area. In each of these natural disasters small businesses were destroyed along with people's homes.

And then there are the individualized disasters: the electrical fire that wipes out a home office, the professional photographer whose camera equipment is stolen from a parked car, the client who trips in your office, breaks a leg, and sues.

Just as you need homeowners insurance to protect you against the hazards that can damage or destroy your home, so do you need insurance against the perils that can damage or destroy your business. If your office is in your home you need both—and the two should be integrated to eliminate gaps and duplication.

You may believe that your home office is sufficiently covered by your homeowners or tenants policy; chances are, however, that it is not. You may also believe that you face minimal risk of loss and that insurance is something you can place low on your totem pole of priorities; again, you could be wrong. This chapter describes personal property insurance for home owners and

> ## TIP
> Many self-employed people, asked to rank priorities, put property and liability insurance very low on the list. You too may be more interested in paying the rent, putting food on the table, and plowing any extra cash back into your business. Before you decide to skip insurance altogether, think about how much risk you face in your particular business. If a fire or a lawsuit could wipe you out it would be wise indeed to consider protective insurance now.

then tells you what additional coverage you need to protect your business, whether you work in a home office or in outside premises.

Homeowners Insurance

The standard homeowners policy (or tenants policy, if you rent) protects you against financial loss from theft, from physical damage (if, for example, your kitchen catches fire), and against liability claims (if a friend slips on a throw rug and is injured or your dog bites someone).

Under the *physical damage* portion of your policy, typically with a $250 deductible, your house is covered to the amount you designate. This should be at least 80 percent of its replacement value—not the market value, but what it would cost to rebuild your home from the foundation up if it were totally destroyed. If you follow the 80 percent rule you can recover in full from a partial loss, such as a fire limited to a single room. In fact, it may be wiser to buy 100 percent coverage on your entire house, including the foundation; the 1991 Oakland fire was so hot that many foundations were wiped out along with the houses they held. You can skip the value of the land the building sits on, however; this is unlikely to be destroyed.

Other structures on the same property are covered for up to 10 percent of the insured value of the home—except if a separate structure houses your office, in which case it is not covered under the homeowners policy at all. Your personal property, the contents of your house, is insured for up to 50 percent of the value of the house on standard policies, although you can (and probably should) elect more coverage. It's also vitally important to clearly understand whether the personal property coverage extends to the business-related property in your home office.

Protection against *liability* claims is limited to $100,000 in the standard homeowners policy; you probably should raise this limit. It can cost as little as $10 or $15 a year, depending on your insurance company, to raise liability limits from $100,000 to $300,000. In this litigious age that's not too much coverage.

You can also purchase an *excess liability* (umbrella) policy for additional protection, picking up where the liability limits on both your homeowners insurance and your automobile insurance leave off. Umbrella policies not only offer larger limits, they cover more potential problems, including libel, slander, and invasion of privacy. Be aware, though, that business-related liability is generally not covered at all in either the liability portion of your homeowners policy or an umbrella liability policy. If you are sued because a computer repair person is injured in your office or because your advertising is claimed to have damaged another company, you need commercial liability coverage.

What else is not covered under homeowners insurance? With some variation from policy to policy, company to company, you

---

TIP

Be sure you update your homeowners insurance limits regularly, even if you have inflation protection, because rebuilding costs may outdistance inflation. Be sure, too, that you at least consider an endorsement that will pay the added cost of conforming to new building codes; otherwise, if your town or county has changed the rules, it could cost you a lot more to rebuild to meet the new standards, and your insurance may not cover the cost.

may need separate endorsements or policies to cover these excluded or limited items:

• Personal computers and other electronic equipment worth more than $2,500, along with the data you store on your computer. A home-based business will typically have a computer, a printer, a copying machine, a fax machine, and a telephone-answering machine—for a total value of much more than $2,500. Some homeowners policies may provide coverage up to $10,000 for business equipment and furniture, according to Barbara Taylor Burkett, a consultant to the Insurance Information Institute, but only if the business is "incidental" rather than primary. This is an important distinction but one that can be difficult to pin down. You can add "incidental office occupancy" coverage to most homeowners policies for as little as thirty dollars or so a year. But don't sit back and relax with this addition until you've clarified what it means.

"Incidental," to some insurance companies, means a business grossing under $5,000 a year. To others it means a business producing less than half of your total income; USF&G Corporation is one company that uses this rule of thumb. To still others it means incidental to the building's purpose as a residence; a representative of State Farm, for example, told me that you can run a full-time business out of your home and it will be considered incidental for the purposes of your homeowners policy so long as you have no signs, no parking lots, and no parade of customers marching through your home. My own insurer, AMICA Mutual, applies full property damage and liability limits to business pursuits under a homeowners policy with an "incidental office" endorsement.

If you add incidental business coverage to your homeowners policy, find out exactly what it means to your insurer; you don't want any unpleasant surprises if and when you file a claim.

• Business liability is specifically excluded under most homeowners policies. If you have any outsiders coming to your home office—whether regular customers or the occasional package deliverer or repair person—you need a business liability policy.

Just think about this scenario, put forth by Burkett in *How to Get Your Money's Worth in Home and Auto Insurance* (written under the name Barbara Taylor; McGraw-Hill, 1991): "One of your clients slips on your highly waxed floor as he steps into your office and breaks a leg. As a result, he misses a flight to Chicago, losing an opportunity to bid on a $10 million construction job. He sues you." Without business liability insurance you could be up the proverbial creek without a paddle—or any hope of rescue.

• Flood damage is not covered at all under homeowners policies and cannot be added by endorsement. You need a separate policy. If hurricane-driven floodwaters damage your home, you may collect under your homeowners policy only if you can prove that wind damage occurred first and made it possible for the water to gain entry. If you live in an area susceptible to flooding, even if only in a so-called one-hundred-year flood, ask your insurance agent about the federal flood insurance program. If you build or purchase a home located in a designated floodplain, you may be required to purchase flood insurance. Otherwise it's optional but very possibly a good idea. Just ask all those folks in Iowa.

• Earthquakes are also specifically excluded under standard homeowners policies. But earthquake coverage may be readily obtained, wherever you live, as an endorsement to your homeowners policy. It costs more in earthquake-prone regions such as the West Coast than it does elsewhere, and deductibles everywhere are higher than on other property insurance—usually 10 percent of the value of your home—but having the insurance may make it possible for you to rebuild.

• Valuable personal property, such as cameras or jewelry, are covered only to very limited dollar amounts. For full coverage you need a separate personal articles floater or endorsement.

Business Insurance

If an endorsement to your homeowners insurance isn't offered by your insurer or won't be adequate for your business, or if you rent or own an office outside your home, you need a commercial policy protecting against financial loss from theft and physical damage, liability, and business interruption. You may purchase this protection separately or in a single-package policy. There are significant differences from policy to policy and from company to company, so you should start out by consulting an insurance agent specializing in small-business coverage, preferably one familiar with the kind of work you do. Business insurance may be tailored one way for a potter, quite another for a publisher.

Note, however, that it can be very difficult for a start-up home-based business to secure business insurance. Premiums are low, in the neighborhood of $300 to $500 a year, so there isn't much incentive for companies to issue the policies. And risks are greater when a business is new, so many insurers insist on at least a two-year track record. USF&G Corp. is one of the exceptions. According to vice president Ben Griffin, it will insure new home-based businesses—but it will first take a long hard look at your personal bill-paying history as well as the amount of debt you carry. "Our concern," says Griffin, "is that you not be tempted

---

A CHECKLIST OF PROPERTY INSURANCE

- Homeowners or tenants insurance
- Automobile insurance
- Flood insurance
- Personal articles floater
- Earthquake endorsement
- "Incidental office occupancy" endorsement for the home office
- Office equipment endorsement, to protect hardware
- Business data policy, to protect software and data
- Liability coverage
- Business interruption insurance
- Contingent business interruption insurance
- Malpractice or errors-and-omissions insurance
- Businessowners policy

---

to 'sell it to the insurance company' [by fraudulently claiming a loss] if you have trouble making mortgage payments."

You'll want information and quotes from two or three independent agents. But your first challenge will be finding agents willing to work with very small businesses. Griffin suggests asking other self-employed people whom they use, then calling each agent and saying, "I'm not going to generate big premiums; do you want an account my size?" You might also try a trade or professional association in your field; some offer package insurance policies to members. And you can call some of the well-respected companies that sell directly to consumers. (The two top-rated homeowners insurance companies in *Consumer Reports* studies in both 1989 and 1993 were AMICA Mutual and USAA; both sell directly rather than through agents, although they may not offer the business coverage you need). With each agent or company, ask for a written proposal including both recommended coverage and what it will cost.

Physical Damage

If your business is located in your home, your homeowners policy will cover damage to the premises from fire, wind, and so on, to the limits of the policy. Your business equipment, however, will be covered only up to a value of $2,500; if you have added a special endorsement to your homeowners policy, your coverage could be as much as $10,000 or, depending on the company, $15,000. Think about what you own: if someone were to break in and walk off with your computer, copier, fax machine,

---

TIP

In comparing policies, Wyckoff, New Jersey, insurance agent Steven P. Puntasecca suggests that the single most important question to ask is, What's *not* covered? Some policies are standardized, others are not, so the only way to determine exactly what protection you'll have is to ask this key question.

telephones, and answering machine, would $2,500 be enough? If not, pick up the telephone right now and call your insurance agent or company about an endorsement to your policy. You may also want to consider a separate electronic data-processing (EDP) policy (see page 131).

If you rent or own office space outside your home (even if that space is in a converted shed in your backyard), you need a separate property insurance policy. Property insurance is available to cover buildings, furnishings and equipment, data-processing equipment (often covered separately), records of accounts receivable (both tangible records in the form of software and intangible records consisting of the information itself), inventory, and so on. You choose exactly what you want to cover, what potential catastrophes you want to protect against ("perils," in insurance jargon), and what size deductible you can afford. The bigger the deductible, in any kind of insurance, the lower the premium.

Take as large a deductible as you can afford to pay out of your own pocket. But don't underinsure, making yourself vulnerable to catastrophe. And don't buy any insurance policy, file it, and forget it. Notify your insurer when you make improvements to your property; otherwise that new wall of storage cabinets or laser printer may be uninsured.

If you rent business space outside your home (even if that space is simply a room in a multiunit office incubator), be particularly aware of what your landlord's insurance policy covers and what you are required to cover on your own. For example, your insurance company should pay for damage to your inventory and equipment if a pipe breaks, while your landlord's policy should cover damage to the building. Similarly, your insurance company should cover liability claims if someone is injured on your premises, while the landlord's policy will cover liability for injuries incurred in lobbies, hallways, and elevators. If you include a "mutual waiver of subrogation" in your lease, as suggested by attorney Fred S. Steingold, author of *The Legal Guide to Starting and Running a Small Business* (Nolo Press, 1993), you won't get caught "in the cross-fire between two insurance companies."

TIP

You can't prevent a natural disaster, but you can take some steps to protect your business. For example: a periodic cleanup, tossing accumulated papers and stacks of magazines, will greatly reduce fire hazard in your office. Chances are you'll never read those old magazines anyway.

Electronic Data Processing Coverage

Your first line of defense against damage to valuable data is an off-site storage system. Back up your data disks regularly and store the disks in another location. If you have specially designed software rather than off-the-shelf programs that are easy to replace, you should keep copies of these in another location as well.

You may also want insurance that will reimburse you for the cost of reproducing and replacing important programs and data. While EDP equipment is generally insured under the contents section of a property policy, some hazards—such as fire damage caused by electrically generated power surges—are excluded. If you are heavily dependent on your EDP equipment, you'll want a separate EDP policy and possibly a business data policy as well, covering a wider range of perils. (And, of course, you want a surge protector for each piece of electronic equipment.)

Business Interruption Insurance

If you're temporarily out of business because of circumstances beyond your control, says Sean Mooney of the Insurance Information Institute, you face two kinds of losses: lost revenue from lost sales, which may never be made up, and ongoing expenses that you'll have to pay even while no income is coming in. Ongoing expenses are obvious if you're renting space and, perhaps, paying employees. But even if you're a one-person band in a home office, you could face ongoing lease payments for equipment, insurance premiums, and other financial commitments.

Let's say your apartment burns, along with your client records. You may have to suspend operations until you can put your living quarters and office back in shape and reconstruct your client lists. Business interruption insurance can make it possible to start over without a significant loss of income.

Or let's say you produce crafts and, thanks to the holidays, make more than half your year's income in the month of December. You could buy business interruption insurance with higher limits for the month of December, just to cover the possibility of being out of business in that critical month. Of course, if you must have your Christmas crafts on hand by October in order to sell them in December, you'll want this peak-season coverage in effect for the entire three-month period. Again, talk to your insurance agent or company to work out exactly what you and your business need.

Note, though, that business interruption insurance kicks in only if your business grinds to a halt because of damage to something you insure. An example would be a piece of equipment or the building itself. If you might possibly be out of business because of something that happens to someone else—a fire at your distributor, for example, halts the flow of merchandise you plan to sell for the holidays—you'll need *contingent business interruption insurance.*

Whether or not you need business interruption insurance, of course, depends on the kind of business you operate. If you could be back in business in a matter of hours simply by setting up a laptop computer in another space, you may not want to bother with business interruption insurance. However, if you will need to replace inventory or equipment or data before you can begin to think about getting up and running again, you should talk to your insurance agent or company about this coverage.

Whether you need any business insurance at all also depends on your own attitude toward risk. In general, for most self-employed people with moderate income, says Saint Louis financial planner Katharine McGee, "property and liability insurance are way down on the priority list. It's a question of shifting risk. If an occasional computer repair person is the only person who sets foot in your home office, are you willing to assume the risk that this person might be injured? Or do you want to shift the risk to an insurance company?"

Liability Insurance

If you do have regular foot traffic in your office—whether customers or clients, package deliverers, or repair people—you should give some thought, at the very least, to protection against liability claims. As defined by Sean Mooney, in *Insuring Your Business*, "liability insurance protects the assets of a business when it is sued for something the business did (or failed to do) that caused injury or property damage to someone else." If you are sued, you may be liable for damages. Even if you win, you may face costly attorney's fees that could have been paid through an insurance policy.

Again, you have to assess the degree of risk you face. If you run a catering business or you manufacture a product that could

---

TIP

"Be prepared" applies to good business planning as well as to Boy Scouts. One way to be prepared for a catastrophe that would interrupt your business is to know where you could set up temporary quarters if you were forced to do so in the aftermath of a fire or other disaster. If all you need is a space for your laptop computer, you may not need to worry, but if you're a potter who needs a kiln or a desktop publisher who needs specific hardware and software, you might give some advance thought to alternate facilities. Just knowing where they are located can produce peace of mind. So can knowing where all of your important clients, suppliers, and advisers can be reached; print out and periodically update a list of telephone numbers, then keep one copy in your office and another in an outside location.

conceivably malfunction and hurt someone, you are at far greater risk than if you run a one-person graphic arts studio designing book jackets for publishers. If clients come to your place of business, you are at greater risk than if you meet them in their own offices—although one school of thought suggests that you could do costly damage by breaking a valuable vase in a client's home.

If you *are* at risk of liability claims, you have several choices: a commercial general liability policy, a package business policy incorporating liability coverage, or, if you work at home, an endorsement to your homeowners policy. For most self-employed men and women either the package business policy or the homeowners endorsement will do the trick. (Restaurant owners are an exception; if you run a restaurant, you must have a commercial general liability policy.)

Understand, however, that none of these policies covers certain types of liability. You'll need separate malpractice or errors-and-omissions insurance, for example, if you run a law office or accounting firm, where your work itself could somehow harm your clients. Evaluate your own specific risk before you decide to buy. As attorney Steingold notes, if you're a publisher, but all you publish is self-help instruction booklets that never mention names, then you don't need insurance against claims of libel.

TIP

Auto insurance can be a tricky issue for the self-employed. If you use your car for business on a regular basis, you may find that your company will reject a claim. Beefing up your coverage so that business use is covered is generally inexpensive and should be considered. On the other hand, if you have switched from commuting by car to working at home, you may even be able to *save* money. Talk to your insurance agent to be sure you have the right coverage at the right price.

But you might need errors-and-omissions coverage, in case you leave some vital information out of one of your instruction booklets.

Package Policies

Rather than purchasing property damage, liability, and business interruption coverages separately, you can buy them in an all-in-one package. Here are some varieties to consider:

Businessowners Policy

The Businessowners Policy (BOP) is designed specifically to meet the needs of most small offices and stores. (If you run a restaurant, as noted earlier, forget about a BOP; you need coverage tailored to the specific liability risks you run.) Some elements of the BOP provide broader protection than individually purchased policies; others do not. Check with your insurance agent to see exactly what you need.

BOPs, like homeowners policies, include coverage for property damage and for liability. Property damage typically covers replacement value, or what it would cost to replace your building; it's also possible to select actual cash value coverage, which would reduce premium costs but also reduce the reimbursement you would receive if you suffered a loss. BOPs also cover other people's property on your premises; if you are doing alterations, for example, and a fire destroys suits left to be altered, you would be covered.

And, just as a homeowners policy typically provides some living expenses if you are forced out of your home in the aftermath of an insured disaster, the BOP will cover indirect costs of a disaster. This could include debris removal, fire department charges, and loss of income and expenses for up to twelve months during a period of reconstruction.

Liability coverage under a Businessowners Policy is similar to liability coverage under separate commercial general liability

> **TIP**
>
> Although the standard form of BOP includes business interruption coverage, some insurers do not include it automatically for home-based businesses on the grounds that it's too difficult to calculate the risk. If you want this coverage, be sure it is included in your policy.

policies. The big difference, according to Sean Mooney, is that the BOP has a "single limit" of coverage for all types of liability. "The single limit in the BOP makes decisions on how much liability to purchase less complicated," Mooney says, "but it also reduces flexibility." For example, if you have a bicycle store, where you assemble and repair bicycles, you might need more product liability coverage than you could obtain in a BOP.

Combination Policies

The BOP is available to the self-employed, at home or in outside space. But with more and more people working at home, some insurers are creating new insurance forms, or combinations of old forms, specifically to meet the need.

One of the first is HomeWork from Continental Insurance (now CNA), an endorsement to homeowners policies incorporating the important provisions of the BOP. HomeWork, specifically designed for the home office, offers some advantages. For one thing, at $175 a year (in 1994, over and above the premium for the basic homeowners policy) it costs less than the minimum of $300 or so for a BOP. It does cost more than the incidental office endorsement available for $20 to $30 on some homeowners policies, but, as noted, you have to be very careful about making sure that the incidental office endorsement gives you full protection. With some companies incidental office occupancy may not cover a full-time business; with others it may extend property protection but not liability coverage.

HomeWork also covers business interruption, including one year of income and extra expenses, just as a commercial policy would; business interruption is usually not available as an endorsement to a homeowners policy. Its liability coverage includes product liability and advertising liability. Liability limits are the full limits on the underlying homeowners policy, and, if you have an excess liability (umbrella) policy, HomeWork would extend to its full liability limits as well.

Note, though, that HomeWork is currently available as an endorsement only on the homeowners policies issued by CNA Insurance Companies; you can't have coverage with another company and add HomeWork. Other companies, however, are beginning to follow suit with similar products; Aetna Life and Casualty has already done so. Ask your agent or insurer if it plans to do so as well.

Meanwhile, you may find what you need (on top of whatever homeowners policy you now have) by purchasing an In-Home Business Policy from RLI Insurance Company. This specialty insurer, based in Peoria, Illinois, does not write homeowners insurance. But it does offer the In-Home Business Policy specifically designed for home offices (an office in a garage within one hundred feet of your home is also covered) with up to $50,000 in comprehensive coverage on business personal property, on- and off-premises. You might want extensive off-premises coverage if, for example, you often have crafts awaiting sale at a consignment shop or art gallery. The policy also features up to $1 million in business liability protection, one year's loss of income, and medical expense liability of $5,000 per person.

At this writing (in late 1995) the policy is available in every state except Maine. Premiums for the basic policy ($300,000 business liability, $5,000 on-premises business property, $1,000 off-premises coverage, one year loss of income, and $5,000 per-person medical expenses) run from $150 to $225 a year, depending on your location and the type of business you operate, except in Texas where premiums are twice this amount.

The RLI policy does not cover every small business. Some with exceptional potential for product or professional liability—caterers, chemists, and architects among them—are ineligible. But it is designed for a wide range of business categories, including financial planners, craftspeople, desktop publishers, graphic artists, bookkeepers, photographers, and manufacturers' representatives. Their needs are similar yet different. Where a financial planner might be concerned about a client slipping and falling in her office, a craftsperson displaying at fairs could fear liability from a display tent blowing over in a high wind and injuring someone. Both incidents would be covered under the RLI policy.

TIP

Insurance companies have long been considered secure financial institutions. But no institution can be accepted, these days, at face value. Before you pay your property and liability insurance premiums to a company you'll need to stand behind you in case of loss, be aware of two potential pitfalls: (1) a formerly solid U.S. company that has run into hard financial times and, even worse, (2) "offshore" insurers poised to take your money and run. Following the 1992 Los Angeles fires, many merchants were victimized by Caribbean-based companies. With fully paid insurance policies, many merchants have yet to collect—and the state can't go after the companies because they are located elsewhere and are not subject to state law.

Before you sign up with any insurer, check with your state insurance department to make sure the insurer is licensed in your state; better yet, do business with a company (no matter where you live) that is licensed and supervised under New York State's tough rules. Also check the insurer's ratings from A. M. Best, Standard & Poor's, and Moody's; two of the three should give the company their top rating before you sign on.

Filing a Claim

Insurance is one purchase you hope you never use. If you do suffer an insured loss, however, here's what to do:

• If the loss was due to burglary or theft, contact the police and file a report. Your insurance company will require a police report before paying the claim.

• Notify your agent or insurance company without delay. They will arrange for an adjuster to look over the damage and give you an estimate of the cost of repairs or replacement. They will also help you fill out claim forms and gather the documentation you need to prove your loss. (An inventory, prepared in advance, will be a big help. So will relevant receipts and serial numbers from missing equipment.)

• Take pictures of any damage, then make temporary repairs to protect your property. If you have to put up plywood to replace broken windows, for example, your insurance will probably cover the cost. But don't make permanent repairs until the insurance company has had an opportunity to inspect the damaged property.

• Get an estimate from your own contractor, to compare with the insurer's estimate of the cost of repairs. If the damage is sizable, you may also want to call in a public adjuster, a licensed professional who will act as your agent in negotiating a settle-

---

TIP

Use a video camera, along with a written inventory, to record what you own. Keep a current "evacuation kit," with irreplaceable documents and copies of the records you will need to restart your business: financial data, client and supplier lists, serial numbers and receipts for office equipment. Update both your inventory and evacuation list periodically.

ment with your insurance company. The fee for this service, agreed to in writing in advance, is generally about 15 percent of your insurance settlement. But don't accept the services of the first adjuster who appears on the scene; talk to more than one, and check their qualifications with your state insurance department.

Insurance Tips from the Small Business Administration

• Use your insurance dollars wisely. Insure against the biggest potential loss, with the largest deductible you can afford.

• Don't try to save money by not insuring against perils you consider unlikely; if the probability of loss is really small, the premium will also be small.

• Select an insurance agent or company carefully; then have that agent or company provide as much of your property and liability insurance as possible. Coordinating coverage will help to eliminate gaps and duplications in coverage.

• Keep your agent or company informed of upgrades and additions.

• Keep complete records of insurance policies, agent, and company, with a duplicate list outside your office.

Chapter Highlights

• Homeowners or tenants insurance will protect you against loss from theft, physical damage, and liability, but only on personal property. To protect your business you need additional coverage.

• An "incidental office occupancy" endorsement to your homeowners policy may provide the protection you need, but the definition of "incidental" varies significantly from insurer to insurer; be sure you understand exactly what is covered and what is not.

• Commercial physical damage and liability coverages may be bought separately or in a combined form called the Businessowners Policy, or BOP. The BOP also usually includes business interruption insurance.

• Separate policies are available to cover special needs; an example would be electronic data-processing policies.

• Some insurance companies are designing policies tailored to home-based businesses. As you comparison shop for coverage, ask whether such policies are available.

Part III

Tax Traps

6 Tax and Consequences

Sherry J. was audited the very first time she took a home office deduction. Timothy Y., in a cash flow crunch, skipped a quarterly estimated tax payment. Bob R. faced back taxes and penalties after the IRS decided that a computer consultant was really Bob's employee.

Taxes can be a big headache for the self-employed. When you hold a salaried job, your employer withholds income tax and sees to it that Social Security tax is paid. You owe extra, and must pay quarterly estimated taxes to make up the shortfall, only if you have other income, such as that from interest, dividends, and capital gains.

When you're self-employed, on the other hand, you are responsible for your own income tax and self-employment tax. If you hire employees, you must withhold and pay payroll taxes, including Social Security, unemployment insurance, and workers' compensation. With employees or without, you are also vulnerable to a host of special taxes and special considerations and must cope with what seems to be an IRS conviction that you are out to cheat or are, at the very least, susceptible to temptation. Some self-employed businesspeople may in fact be tempted not to report cash payments, just as others may be tempted to write off personal vacations as business trips. Far more common,

I suspect, are the self-employed who get into tax trouble because they don't understand the rules or are too busy to follow them to the letter.

It's hard to take time from starting or running a business to deal with taxes. However, not only is it essential, but you'll also find it easier in the long run to follow the rules and keep proper records. Because the rules are complicated, you should consult a tax adviser who is familiar with the way your particular business is run. It will help, of course, if you know what to discuss with your adviser. Here, then, are some of the things that you need to know about federal income tax rules for small business; the individual states, discussed later in this chapter, have rules of their own.

Business Income Tax Basics

As a business, even a one-person business, you should have a federal employer identification number, you must decide whether to use cash or accrual accounting, you must determine your fiscal year, and you must file quarterly estimated taxes. You must also keep good records. The following pages cover the rules.

Federal Employer Identification Number

A federal employer identification number (EIN) is required for any business with employees. As a sole proprietorship with no employees, you won't actually need an EIN unless you open a Keogh plan. For all other purposes you may use your Social Security number. But attorney and author Fred S. Steingold suggests that it's a good idea to get an EIN anyway. "It helps you separate your business affairs from your personal affairs," he notes, "something every small-business person needs to do."

It's easy to acquire an EIN; just file Form SS-4 with the IRS.

> **TIP**
> Are you starting small? Making a few hundred dollars from crafts, perhaps, while you continue a salaried job? You must include this income on your federal income tax return if you have net earnings of $400 or more from self-employment in a calendar year. Net income is total business income reduced by deductible business expenses.

Cash Versus Accrual Accounting

Under the far simpler and somewhat more flexible cash method of accounting, you report income when it is received and expenses when they are paid—just as you do on your individual income tax return. Most self-employed people use the cash method, which permits you to time deductions and income (typically accelerating the first and deferring the second from one year to another) if it makes tax sense to do so.

Under the accrual method, which must be used if you maintain an inventory in your business, income is reported when it is earned—when goods are sold or services are rendered—even if you receive payment at a later date. Similarly, expenses are deducted when obligations are incurred.

Which method you choose makes a difference: Sell a service in December and get paid for that service in January, and you report the income for tax purposes in December under the accrual method and in January under the cash method. Report it in January and you pay taxes on it, in the form of quarterly estimates, over the course of the succeeding year. Once you decide which method you're using for your business, you need permission from the IRS before you can make a change.

Fiscal Year

In the past, owners of partnerships, S corporations, and personal service corporations could defer taxes by putting the business entity on a fiscal year other than the calendar year used to figure personal income taxes. This neat arrangement let you structure income and deductions to your best advantage. This is no longer possible. You must now generally use the calendar year for both personal and business returns, unless you can demonstrate a compelling reason for using a different tax year for your business. There are some exceptions, but the rules are complicated; consult your tax adviser.

Estimated Taxes

If your estimated federal income tax and self-employment tax will be $500 or more for the year, you generally have to make estimated tax payments on a quarterly basis. In fact, you are supposed to make approximately equal quarterly payments—a tough thing to manage when income is as erratic as it often is for the self-employed. But it's OK to start the year making estimates based on the prior year's income (see next paragraph), then amend the estimates if income soars or falls short of expectations.

Changes in the 1993 tax legislation make those estimates a bit easier to calculate. You can avoid penalties, if you are married and filing jointly and had an adjusted gross income of $150,000 or less in the previous year, by paying quarterly estimates totaling your entire federal income tax for the previous year. If your income is higher, you can avoid penalties by paying 110 percent of the previous year's tax. In either case, if you can predict your income for the year with reasonable accuracy, you can avoid underpayment penalties by paying at least 90 percent of the current year's tax liability on a quarterly basis.

Keeping Good Records

Adequate documentation is crucial and serves two purposes: it helps you file your income tax return with minimum hassle, whether you prepare the return yourself or hire professional help, and it's essential to prove your case should you face an audit.

As a general rule, every piece of paper relating to a taxable or tax-deductible item should be kept for a minimum of three years after the due date of the return, including extensions; for a return filed in 1996 for the 1995 tax year, this means keeping records until 1999. However, because the IRS has six years to challenge a return if it believes you omitted more than 25 percent of your gross income, most tax advisers recommend keeping business-related tax records for at least six years. (Some states require that tax-related documents be kept longer; check with your tax adviser.)

Some records should be kept indefinitely, including income tax returns for prior years, annual financial statements and the ledgers substantiating those statements, and documents relating to improvements to real estate and other depreciating assets. If your business is incorporated, items that should be kept indefinitely include stockholder records, minutes of board of directors meetings, retirement and pension records, and so on.

Some additional record-keeping tips:

- Contemporaneous logs are a big help when it comes to documenting travel, meals, and entertainment deductions.
- On-the-spot notes about automobile usage should include before-and-after mileage, tolls, and the purpose of each trip.
- Notes related to business meals and entertainment (particularly useful these days, as the deduction becomes more suspect) should include whom you entertained and the specific business purpose.
- You may want to include some notes in your own tax file so that you'll remember, if you're questioned several years later, just how you arrived at the numbers you used on your return.

Business Structure

What kind of business do you have? Are you a sole proprietorship, a partnership, an S corporation, or a C corporation? Different tax rules apply to different business structures. But

---

TIP

While the IRS has always required canceled checks as
proof of payment, it now takes a somewhat gentler tack: if
you cannot provide a canceled check to prove payment of
an expense item, you may be able to prove payment with a
statement from a financial institution showing the check
number, amount, payee name, and the date the check
amount was posted to the account. But don't take chances.
Keep your canceled checks as well as supporting documentation for any tax deductions you claim.

---

corporations (both C and S) must keep separate records because they file separate returns. So must partnerships. Sole proprietors, because there is no separate filing requirement, have
the toughest time making a distinction between personal and
business finances. You must make a deliberate effort to separate
the two.

Sole Proprietorships

Chances are, as a self-employed person, that you operate as a
sole proprietor. This is the simplest form of business organization, since you *are* the business. As a plus this means that all you
have to do to go into business is say that you're doing so. As a
negative this means that there is no formal separation between
your business finances and your personal finances (although, if
you're wise, you'll keep a separate business checkbook, as described in chapter 2). When you figure your taxable income for
the year, from all sources, you must add in any business profit
and subtract any business loss.

But this doesn't mean melding your personal and business
finances and taking unauthorized deductions. Where many sole
proprietors get into trouble with the IRS, if they are audited, is in
blurring the lines: the kids play computer games on the "business" computer, or groceries are carried home in a car written

off as a business expense, or your home office doubles after hours as the family TV room. Many IRS-generated headaches can be avoided if you follow the record-keeping advice in chapter 2 and keep things separate.

Business income and deductible expenses for sole proprietorships are reported on federal income tax returns on Schedule C-EZ or Schedule C, but the total is then merged with all of your taxable income and deductible expenses for the purpose of determining how much you owe. Incidentally, if you file either a Schedule C or a Schedule C-EZ, you must file it along with a Form 1040; if you have self-employment income and business expenses, you cannot use either Form 1040A or Form 1040EZ.

Schedule C-EZ

If you have a new or small business, you may be able to use the simpler and shorter Schedule C-EZ. Introduced in 1992, this form may be used only if you

- have gross receipts of $25,000 or less;
- have business expenses of $2,000 or less;
- use the cash method of accounting;
- did not have a net loss from your business;
- have only one business as a sole proprietor;
- have no employees for the year;
- have no inventory at any time during the year;
- are not required to file Form 4562, Depreciation and Amortization;
- do not deduct expenses for business use of your home; and
- do not have prior-year unallowed passive activity losses from this business.

You must meet every one of these requirements in order to file a Schedule C-EZ. Many, if not most, smaller sole proprietorships are home-based, but home-based businesses wishing to claim a home office deduction must file the longer and more complicated Schedule C along with Form 8829, Expenses for Business Use of Your Home. (More information on taxes and the home office starts on page 159.)

Schedule C

Schedule C must be attached to your tax return for all other sole proprietorships. It includes spaces for details on a range of business expenses, from advertising to wages, along with space for other, nonlisted expenses. Be careful, however. While deductions are more valuable if you can take them on Schedule C, because they are fully deductible, instead of on Schedule A, where they may be subject to limitations (for example, miscellaneous itemized deductions can be deducted on Schedule A only to the extent that they exceed 2 percent of your adjusted gross income), the IRS is cracking down on any Schedule C deductions that don't really belong.

Most of the Schedule C expense categories are self-explanatory, but a few can use clarification.

Car and Truck Expenses. Business use of your car is deductible, but only business use. This includes trips to see clients but not travel between your own home and office. If you use your car for personal use as well as business use, be sure to keep mileage logs of your business trips. Then you may take either the IRS-

---

TIP

Tax preparation fees in general are subject to the 2 percent rule on miscellaneous itemized deductions—deductible only if, together with other miscellaneous deductions, they exceed 2 percent of adjusted gross income. But the IRS has finally ruled that small-business owners may fully deduct the portion of tax preparation fees related to the business portion of the tax return. Ask your tax preparer to separate his or her charges into those related to your Schedule C and those related to the rest of your return. The cost of preparing Schedule C may then be deducted as an expense, which will reduce your adjusted gross income.

designated per-mile deduction for business miles traveled (29 cents per mile in 1994) or actual expenses (gas, oil, tires, repairs, and so on) for the proportion of time the car is used for business. Either way, you may also deduct direct costs, such as tolls and parking fees. For more information, see IRS Publication 917, Business Use of a Car.

Depreciation. The 1993 tax law permits immediate write-offs for equipment expenditures up to $17,500 per taxpayer (up from $10,000 under prior law), assuming that your business shows a profit of at least as much as you spent on equipment. If your Schedule C shows a loss, you may either carry forward the expenditure and deduct it when you do have income or depreciate it over the period of time allowed by the IRS. The choice must be made for the year you place the equipment in service.

"Per taxpayer," incidentally, means per taxpaying unit; if you and your spouse have separate sole proprietorships but file a joint income tax return, you have $17,500 to spend between you. Other business equipment must be depreciated over time in accordance with schedules provided by the IRS; in general, most business property is depreciated over either five years (computers, typewriters, copiers, and the like) or seven years (office furniture).

Equipment that is used partially for business and partially for pleasure (examples might be a car phone or a VCR) must be depreciated over time, with the business deduction taken on a pro rata basis for the actual percentage of time the equipment is used in business.

Travel, Meals, and Entertainment. Take a client out to lunch to negotiate the terms of a deal and the expense is a legitimate deduction. But lawmakers have been whittling away at deductions for meals and entertainment, so that you may now deduct only 50 percent of the cost. Even so, be sure to keep scrupulous records of what you did, who you did it with, and the precise business purpose.

Telephone. Business use of your telephone is included on the Utilities line on Schedule C. Note, though, that special rules apply if you have an office at home: the basic telephone service charge for the first line into your home is not deductible, although itemized long-distance telephone calls on that line are deductible. If you want to deduct basic telephone charges, install a second line for your business. Having a business telephone, just like having a separate business checking account, also helps to prove that you're serious about running a business.

Wages. Wages are what you pay others; you cannot include anything you pay yourself or withdraw from the business for personal use.

Home Office Deductions. Formerly listed as an expense along with all of the other expenses on Schedule C, expenses for business use of your home (whether that home is a house, a condo, a rental apartment, a mobile home, or a boat) now appear in a separate category on Schedule C and must be supported by a separate form, 8829. This separate form includes a calculation for the percentage of your home used exclusively for business as well as information about allowable deductions and depreciation of the home itself. See page 159 for a full discussion of home office deductions.

Husband-and-wife enterprises deserve a special note here. Whatever the business has as a net profit is taxable on your joint income tax return, whether or not you have a formal partnership agreement. And if you work together, according to Lawrence E. Kraus, a CPA in New York City, you are each liable for your own self-employment tax. Alternatively, one of you could work for the other. In this instance, where your spouse is your employee, you

---

TIP

An accounting code system, offered free by most long-distance telephone carriers, makes record keeping easy for toll calls; just assign your own number to business calls in general or to each client, put it in after you dial the number (you'll get a tone as a prompt), and you'll have documentation both for the IRS and to submit to clients if expenses can be reimbursed.

TIP

The deductibility of home offices has been greatly restricted in recent years—so much so that some people consider the deduction a red flag to the IRS, almost inevitably leading to an audit, and question whether it's worth taking. If you meet the rules and legitimately qualify for a home office deduction, by all means take the deduction. Just be prepared to provide full documentation in case you are questioned.

---

will deduct the wages you pay as a business expense and pay income tax on those wages on your joint return. You must also, in this instance, pay Social Security and Medicare taxes, file payroll tax returns, and issue a W-2 at the end of the year.

It may seem like an expensive nuisance, but formalizing your business arrangement may make abundant good sense. It will give each of you business standing, Social Security credits, and a formal stake in the business should the marriage falter.

LIMITED LIABILITY COMPANIES

The limited liability company, attorney Thomas H. Campbell writes in the *Journal of Financial Planning,* "is the only business entity available that allows every member, including managers, to enjoy limited liability while the entity is treated as a partnership for federal income-tax purposes." Whether or not a particular LLC can file a tax return as a partnership, however, depends on whether it has some of the particular characteristics of a corporation as interpreted by the state. In general, to be taxed as a partnership, an LLC should not have more than one of these characteristics: centralization of management, free transferability of interests, continuity of life. If it does, in most jurisdictions, it will be taxed as a corporation. Upon request, the IRS will issue a ruling as to whether a particular LLC meets the requirements and can be taxed as a partnership.

Partnerships

Partnerships are not taxable entities. A partnership must figure its profit or loss and file a return (Form 1065), but this is for information purposes only. The partners report their individual shares of the profit or loss on Schedule E, Supplemental Income and Loss, filed along with Form 1040. "In other words," according to Steingold, "a partner's income is treated like a sole proprietor's income on Form 1040; it's listed in a separate schedule and then blended with other income listed on the first page of the 1040."

S Corporations

If your business is structured as an S corporation, it works very much like a partnership for income tax purposes. Form 1120S is filed as an information return and then you, as a shareholder, report your portion of the profit or loss on Schedule E and meld the number with your 1040 income.

Although S corporations generally need not pay federal income tax, they may be subject to other taxes, such as those on capital gains and certain types of passive income (for example, dividends, interest, and rental income). In states and localities that do not recognize S corp status, they may also be subject to state and local taxes.

Regular C Corporations

These formal business organizations do pay income tax, using Form 1120 or Form 1120-A, while shareholders pay taxes on dividends distributed by the corporation. Because corporations may not deduct the dividends they pay (salaries, by contrast, are deductible), this is a form of double taxation; the same money is taxed twice, first to the corporation and then to the individual. For most small companies, Kraus points out, the point is academic; most money is taken out in the form of salaries.

But the spread between the corporate rate and the individual rate has widened in recent years; corporations pay a maximum tax rate of 34 percent on earnings of up to $10 million (except that personal service corporations are taxed at 35 percent), while individuals top out at almost 40 percent on the federal level. This disparity creates an incentive to leave money in the corporation. In fact, you may have good reason to do so if, as one example, you're looking to future expansion.

Good reason or not, there are a couple of pitfalls here for the unwary small-business person doing business as a corporation. The IRS can impose penalties if you take what it calls too much compensation. Suppose you take a small stipend in the early years, while you build the business; when you finally feel comfortable and take a larger sum, the IRS may decide that this is "unreasonable compensation" and tax some of the income as dividends. One way around this is to establish a compensation formula at the outset, then keep good records of corporate meetings. (Corporations are required to have regular meetings and to keep minutes, but some small corporations fail to honor these rules.)

The IRS can also impose penalties if you take too little compensation, leaving accumulated earnings in the corporation. In the latter instance, the IRS may impose penalties based on what the dividends would have been if you had paid them out. You *are* allowed to retain certain reserves, but there are no hard-and-fast rules governing the amount. If you are in the enviable position of having surplus cash, consult your tax adviser.

TAX FORMS FOR BUSINESS

Sole proprietorship	Schedule C (Form 1040) or C-EZ
Farming	Schedule F (Form 1040)
Partnership	Form 1065
Corporation	Form 1120 or 1120-A
S corporation	Form 1120S

Which form you use depends on how your business is organized.

Changing Business Structure

Is your business an S corp? If it is, and you are earning enough to be taxed at the highest federal rates (currently 39.6 percent on taxable income exceeding $250,000, against a high of 34 percent for most corporations), you may want to consider a change in your business structure. But don't act hastily. There are still good reasons for being an S corporation, among them:

- C corps must withhold and pay payroll taxes. An S corp must withhold and pay payroll taxes on salaries but may also make tax-free distributions to shareholders. (Note, however, that President Clinton's health reform proposal would require shareholders in a personal service S corp to pay self-employment tax on distributions.)
- The capital gains tax rate is 28 percent for individuals (and for S corp shareholders); the rate goes up to 35 percent for C corps.
- An S corp permits you to save on taxes by income splitting—giving shares to your children, once they are at least age fourteen and will be taxed at their own, lower income tax rates.
- If you plan to sell your business in the near future, stick with being an S corp. Because appreciated assets are subject to double taxation, taxes on the sale will be higher if you are a C corp.

On the other side of the coin:

- Fringe benefits for owner-employees are deductible by C corps and are not taxable to recipients. Many fringe benefits for S corps are deductible to the corporation but they are taxable to the recipient.
- In a C corp you may borrow against your tax-qualified retirement plan. In an S corp you may not.

Consider your own situation and talk to your tax adviser. It doesn't cost much to switch corporate status. Once you move from S corp status to C corp, however, you may not move back again for at least five years.

Special Situations

Start-up Expenses

The Internal Revenue Code draws fine distinctions in many areas. Expenses involved in starting a business venture face one set of tax rules, for example, while expenses in an ongoing business face another.

If you are just getting started, many of the costs that would be deductible for an operating business—including legal fees, marketing surveys, and advertising—are not immediately deductible. Instead you may treat such costs as capital expenses so that they become part of your "basis" in the business, recoverable when you sell or go out of business, or you may amortize them over five or more years. You must make this decision when you file your tax return in the year you start your business with respect to costs such as these:

- Traveling to look over business possibilities or to find customers or suppliers.
- Conducting market surveys or starting to advertise.
- Retaining professional advisers, including lawyers and accountants, and the actual cost of incorporation or drafting a partnership agreement.
- Beginning to hire and train employees.
- Analyzing available facilities, labor, and supplies.

Home Offices

A very special word is owed to the legions of self-employed who toil in offices, workshops, and laboratories at home. Because the IRS apparently has it in for those who do, you must be meticulous when it comes to meeting home office rules and claiming home office deductions.

The rules keep getting tougher. A home office has long had to be your principal place of business, but that definition has recently been narrowed by the Supreme Court to mean that you must spend most of your time there. If you are a salesperson who is on the road a great deal, a computer consultant who spends most of your time in clients' offices, or a contractor or interior decorator whose days are spent on location, you probably won't qualify for a home office deduction under current rules, even if you have no other office of your own and no place to do the marketing and paperwork that goes with running a business. The overriding factors now are both the amount of time spent at each business location and the relative importance of the activities performed at each location. There is just one exception: if you regularly meet clients, customers, or patients in your home office, you may qualify for the deduction even if you spend large amounts of time elsewhere.

A "home" containing an office, by the way, may be a house, apartment, condominium, mobile home, or boat. One husband-and-wife team I know, an independent film producer and a writer, set up shop on a houseboat moored at Manhattan's Seventy-ninth Street Boat Basin.

If you do spend most of your working hours in your home office, or you meet customers there, you must still meet the other key rule before taking a deduction: the office must be exclusively an office. The only exceptions are that you may use a personal living area as part of a day-care center or use personal space for storing inventory. Otherwise, home office deductions are limited to spaces that are 100 percent office. So don't watch television in your home office or put up overnight guests on a convertible couch. You can, however, use part of a room for your office if that is all you have; just be sure to erect a partition or some sort of barrier—one consultant marked off a portion of her bedroom floor with masking tape—so that the office is clearly an office.

If you qualify for the home office deduction, you must use Form 8829 to document your deductions. A key element of this form compares the area used exclusively for business with the total area of your home. Don't guess. Do the measurements, so that you can come up with the precise percentage that will determine all of your deductions. Then follow these rules:

• Direct expenditures, such as painting your office or building shelves for your office, are deductible in full.

• Indirect expenditures, such as utilities, are then deducted in the proportion applicable to the office. Note, though, that no portion of landscaping or lawn care is ever deductible as an office expense, and that the IRS can get sticky when it comes to apportioning things like electricity. If your work space occupies 20 percent of your home, you might be able to deduct more or (more likely) less than 20 percent of your electrical bills—more if you operate an electricity-intensive business, such as a beauty parlor with hair dryers, less if you run a real estate business. Don't forget that your normal household utility use includes generating hot water for showers and washing machines as well as running appliances that have nothing to do with your business.

• Deductions for the business use of your home may not create a business loss for tax purposes. You may never deduct more for the expense of running a home office than you earn. If home office expenses do exceed your income, the excess may be carried over into the next tax year. Note, though, that you must show a profit for three or more years of any consecutive five-year period; if you don't, the IRS may classify your business as a hobby and disallow all of your business deductions.

If you are going to claim a deduction for your home office, whether you own your own home or rent an apartment, you must list your deductions in this specific order:

1. Expenses that are deductible because you own a home, whether or not you take a home office deduction, including real estate taxes and mortgage interest. If you use 20 percent of your home as an office, then 20 percent of your real estate taxes and mortgage interest may be claimed as a deduction on your Schedule C; the balance of both is claimed on Schedule A.

2. Expenses that are directly business-related but not necessarily home office–related, such as office supplies, telephone, and salaries.

3. Household expenses related to the business use of your home, including the applicable percentage of utilities (see above), cleaning services, and homeowners or tenants insurance, plus the full amount of expenses related solely to the home office, such as painting the walls.

4. Depreciation of the portion of your home used for business.

What this means, in short, is that regular business expenses, along with mortgage interest and real estate taxes, are deductible, whether or not your business earns a profit. But expenses

---

AN EXAMPLE OF HOME OFFICE DEDUCTIONS

In an example provided by the accounting firm of Ernst and Young, a self-employed bookkeeper earned $7,500 in her first year in business. She used 20 percent of her home regularly and exclusively for her office. Her tax calculations looked like this:

Gross income from business use of home:	$7,500
Minus business percentage (20 percent) of mortgage interest and real estate taxes:	−2,000
Minus other business expenses (supplies, transportation, et cetera):	−5,000
Modified net income:	500
Business use of home expenses	
Maintenance, insurance, utilities (20 percent):	800
Depreciation (20 percent):	+ 700
Total:	1,500
Deduction (limited to modified net income):	− 500
Expenses carried over to the next tax year (subject to earnings in the next year):	$1,000

SOURCE: Peter W. Bernstein, ed., *The Ernst & Young Tax Guide*, New York: John Wiley & Sons, 1994, p. 460.

related to having your office at home—such as the portion of your utility bill that goes toward lighting, heating, or cooling your office—may be deducted only if your business makes money. If you can't claim all of your deductions because you haven't made enough money, you may carry unused deductions into succeeding tax years. Sooner or later, though, unless you make a profit, you will lose the deductions.

When You Sell Your Home

When a home is purely a residence, tax on any profit earned when you sell may be deferred so long as you buy a new residence of at least equal value within two years. Similarly, when a home is purely a residence and you are at least age fifty-five when you sell, $125,000 of profit may be permanently excluded from tax. If you have taken a deduction for a home office, however, you have converted part of your home to business property and you will owe tax on that portion of the gain. But special rules apply; here is what you need to know:

• If you do not claim the home office deduction in the year of the sale, you may still be able to defer tax on the entire profit in your home by moving to another residence within the two-year period.

But be sure to actually move your office to another location for that year or to disqualify your home office space for the deduction by using it for another purpose. Julian Block, a tax attorney in Larchmont, New York, and author of *The Homeowner's Tax Guide* (Runzheimer International, 1991), suggests moving the cat's litter box into your home office and taking pictures to document the fact. A better tactic—one perhaps more likely to be accepted by the IRS in the event of an audit—is to actually move your office to an outside location.

• When you sell your home after claiming a home office deduction for any period of time—even if it was years ago—you must adjust the "cost basis" (the purchase price of your home for tax purposes) downward to reflect the depreciation deductions that you took or could have taken while the office was in use. The result of a lower purchase price, of course, is a higher profit and hence more tax due to Uncle Sam.

• If you are over age fifty-five and eligible for the $125,000 tax exclusion when you sell your home, you can lose as much as the full exclusion if you take a home office deduction in two of the five years preceding the sale. The exclusion will apply only to the gain on the portion of your home actually used as your residence.

• In a real estate market where home values have been falling, the above may actually be good news. That's because you can never claim a loss on the sale of a home—except on the portion of a home used as business property. If your home is currently worth less than you paid for it, and you plan to sell, keep your home office deduction in force.

Substantiating Your Home Office Deduction

When it comes to proving that you are entitled to home office deductions, you want as much evidence as possible. As you prepare your income tax return each year, put all of the relevant documents in the file with your return. It's a lot easier to do so at the time than to reconstruct your files if your return is examined two or three years later.

Tax publisher Commerce Clearing House suggests that you keep a diagram showing your home office as a portion of your home, photographs of the home office, and the following documents:

• Form 1098, showing the interest paid on your mortgage;
• Property tax bills, along with canceled checks;
• Utility bills, along with canceled checks;
• Receipts and canceled checks substantiating capital improvements, maintenance, and repairs; and
• A copy of your lease and canceled rent checks if you use a portion of a rental unit as your office.

When You Expand Your Business

Finding help with a growing business is discussed at much greater length in chapter 10. But hiring salaried help inevitably leads to tax complications. And, notes CPA Bernard Kamoroff, it will "just about double" your paperwork burden.

When you become an employer you take on a number of responsibilities. You must keep payroll records, withhold taxes, remit withheld taxes to the federal and, in some cases, state taxing authorities, and give each employee a year-end record of taxes withheld. You must prepare quarterly and year-end payroll tax returns, pay your half of each employee's Social Security and Medicare taxes, and pay unemployment insurance, workers' compensation, and, in some states, disability insurance for each employee.

There are several ways around this dilemma, from using unpaid interns to relying on consultants. But the IRS is waging all-out war on employers who call workers "consultants" or

---

TIP

Hiring your teenage kids (once they reach age fourteen) can save some money on family taxes. First, the money you pay your youngsters will be taxed at their (usually) lower income tax rate. Second, the standard deduction (in 1995, $3,900 on an individual return) offsets income; if you pay your child no more than this, no tax will be due. Third, while income tax must be withheld from wages, a child employed by parents (either sole proprietors or in a partnership consisting only of parents) need not pay Social Security or Medicare taxes until the child reaches age eighteen. Federal unemployment tax need not be paid until the child reaches age twenty-one. The youngster must perform actual work, the wages you pay must be reasonable, and you should keep records documenting the hours worked and the wages paid.

"independent contractors" when they are in fact employees. Misclassify an employee, deliberately or not, and you can wind up owing back taxes and penalties.

How could this happen? Look at this scenario: You've found a computer guru, a genius at dealing with both hardware and software. She insists that she is a consultant, so you don't go through all of the employer-employee rigmarole described above; instead you simply file a 1099 form at the end of the year, summing up the fees you've paid. You learn what a mistake you've made when your computers and programs are running smoothly, you don't need your self-employed "consultant" any longer, and she files a claim for unemployment insurance. Your books are audited and you're slapped with back taxes and penalties. If your fees to the consultant were $30,000 a year for three years, according to the California Society of Enrolled Agents, you could owe the government as much as $80,000 in back taxes and penalties.

Don't fall into this trap. The IRS offers guidelines that can help you determine who is an independent contractor and who is an employee. The guidelines, unfortunately, are somewhat vague. But you can generally treat helpers as independent contractors, responsible for paying their own taxes and providing their own fringe benefits, according to James Urquhart III, a California attorney and author of *The IRS, Independent Contractors and You!* (Fidelity Publishing Company, 1993) if you use people who are clearly in their own established independent businesses. Two key indicators are (1) the business is incorporated (although, of course, many small businesses are not), and (2) the worker has multiple sources of income from the independent business.

In addition, you'll strengthen your case if you:

- Do not control where the work is done (it's better if it is not performed on your premises, although with such specialists as computer consultants this may be impossible);
- Do not set the hours that the person must work;

- Do not have any say about whether the contractor chooses to hire assistants;
- Have a signed contract, including a termination date;
- Cannot unilaterally fire the individual; and
- Pay the person by the job rather than by the hour, week, or month.

On the other side of the coin, you may yourself act as a consultant or an independent contractor in performing services for others. That's exactly what a whole host of people do in occupations including (but not limited to) freelance writers, truck drivers, graphic artists, computer programmers, and real estate agents. If the shoe is on this foot, Urquhart suggests that you can protect your independent status against a challenge by the IRS by:

- Working for several clients;
- Printing business cards;
- Advertising in the Yellow Pages or in a professional or trade journal;
- Billing by the assignment on your own printed invoices; and
- Working under a written agreement that can be terminated early only for cause.

State Taxes and Fees

Federal taxes, one might think, are enough to deal with. But states have taxes too. And cash-poor states are adding more and more taxes, fees, and licenses that cost small businesses big bucks.

Most states have some form of personal income tax; almost as many also tax unincorporated businesses. A few states tax gross receipts, while others have special taxes on specific types of business ventures. Counties and large cities sometimes have taxes of their own, frequently taxing such business assets as machinery, equipment, furniture, and fixtures. Some jurisdictions tax inventories; others tax vehicles. And corporations, of course, are subject to their own tax rules.

Where you live and do business has a lot to do with the weight of your tax burden. A major study published in 1993 by the NFIB Foundation, the research arm of the National Federation of Independent Business, found significant variation. For example, a restaurant paying taxes of $19,000 in Austin, Texas, would pay over $42,000 in Seattle. A plumbing firm with an annual tax bill of $43,000 in Memphis would owe more than $56,000 in Portland, Oregon. In general, the NFIB study found the highest small-business taxes in Portland, Oregon; Detroit; Washington, D.C.; Seattle; and New York City. The five cities with the lowest taxes were Manchester, New Hampshire; Montgomery, Alabama; Austin, Texas; Houston, Texas; and Raleigh, North Carolina.

If you're still thinking about setting up shop or might consider a move, be sure to factor in state and local taxes. If you live in tax-hungry New York City, for example, it might be worth forgoing a home office deduction in order to locate your business just north of the city in New York State or Connecticut. Similarly, a Washington, D.C., resident might headquarter her business in one of the surrounding suburbs. But don't make an off-the-cuff decision either to move or to stay put. Crunch the actual numbers before you decide. And remember that state and local taxes are deductible on your federal income tax return, so that the net taxes you pay are not the sum of the parts.

Facing an Audit

If you're self-employed, you're likely to face an IRS audit. That's the simple truth. As a spokesman for the IRS told me recently, anything that makes your return more complicated raises the likelihood that your return will be examined. And self-employment income, along with a Schedule C, certainly does make an income tax return more complex. Claiming a home office deduction only adds to the complexity.

What the IRS doesn't often admit to, however, is its belief that self-employed people have more opportunity to conceal income and exaggerate deductions than do salaried people. In order to keep the self-employed from succumbing to temptation and giving in to these opportunities, the IRS increases the audit odds.

With Schedule C filers, the odds of being audited increase with income—not net income, after expenses, but the gross income you report. For the 1993 tax year (the latest figures available at this writing), gross income between $25,000 and $100,000 had a higher chance of being audited than reported gross income under $25,000; Schedule C filers with incomes over $100,000, however, had twice as much chance of being audited.

With or without a Schedule C, every return is examined by computer and given a numerical score. The higher the score, the greater the likelihood that the return will be examined. What triggers a high score? With variation among geographic regions (even the IRS knows that property taxes are much higher in some parts of the country than in others), audit "triggers" include:

- Income reported by you that doesn't match income reported to the IRS by clients, banks, brokerage houses, and so on. The matching program is so thorough that you should be very careful to see that numbers match up. If a client includes reimbursed business expenses on your 1099 form, for example, be sure that you note the discrepancy.
- Deductions out of line with your income. If you earn $30,000 and claim $5,000 in charitable contributions, you can expect your return to be flagged for a closer look.
- Casualty losses. With all of the natural disasters in recent years, from floods to hurricanes to earthquakes, more home owners and business owners will be claiming casualty loss deductions. But these losses are hard to document. You need to prove three numbers: the cost basis of your property (essentially what you paid for it), its fair market value immediately before the loss, and its fair market value immediately after the loss. Even then,

casualty losses are deductible only to the extent that they exceed $100 (per loss) plus 10 percent (in aggregate) of your adjusted gross income.

The latest wrinkle in stepped-up IRS efforts to monitor small business and the self-employed is something called the Market Segment Specialization Program. The idea here is to focus on particular types of small business, training revenue agents to understand the ins and outs of the business so that they can more accurately focus on problem areas and turn up telltale discrepancies.

Detailed guidelines have been issued, so far, for seven types of businesses: air charters, attorneys, bed-and-breakfast operations, gas retailers, mortuaries, taxicabs, and trucking. Guidelines are under way in many more areas, including auto retailing, entertainment, garment manufacturing, grocery retailing, insurance brokerage, coin-operated laundries, construction, and door-to-door selling. If you are in any one of these areas and your return is examined, you can expect to encounter a revenue agent with a detailed knowledge of how your business works and the kind of revenues you should be

Table 6.1: Average Itemized Deductions on Federal Income Tax Returns for 1992

ADJUSTED GROSS INCOME	MEDICAL EXPENSES	TAXES	INTEREST	GIFTS
$ 15,000–$ 20,000	$ 5,442	$ 1,747	$ 5,333	$1,417
$ 20,000–$ 25,000	3,734	2,125	5,191	1,138
$ 25,000–$ 30,000	4,247	2,216	5,422	1,273
$ 35,000–$ 40,000	2,991	2,627	5,435	1,401
$ 40,000–$ 50,000	3,641	3,263	5,811	1,450
$ 50,000–$ 75,000	4,588	4,379	6,856	1,734
$ 75,000–$100,000	5,239	6,214	8,867	2,368
$100,000–$200,000	6,088	9,854	12,174	3,776
$200,000 or more	15,600	37,679	22,114	9,906

SOURCE: Internal Revenue Service, Commerce Clearing House.

taking in. By 1999, in fact, the information is expected to be incorporated into the computer scoring system that selects returns for examination.

What is the IRS looking for? Try these on for size: Attorneys who write family ski vacations off as business trips. Bed-and-breakfast owners who eat food bought for guests who didn't show up, then claim the food as a business deduction. The guidelines have been published in manuals, which are available to the public. Call your local IRS office or write to IRS FOI Reading Room, P.O. Box 388, Ben Franklin Station, Washington, DC 20044.

If your return is selected for examination (the IRS prefers this word to the scarier *audit*), the examination method will vary with what the IRS expects to find.

- A *correspondence audit* may be used if one or two relatively simple items are questioned and the necessary backup evidence may be submitted by mail. If you do send documentation by mail, however, always send copies and keep the originals.
- *Audits in an IRS office* are more frequent. Here you will be asked to bring all of your records pertaining to specific items. Bring those records, but don't bring anything else; the last thing you want to do is open up the audit to other questions. In fact, it's a good idea to let your tax preparer attend this meeting in your place; he or she knows the ropes and is more likely to keep the questions within bounds.
- A *field audit*, conducted in your home or office, is the most serious situation because it means that the IRS wants to see your office and may want to delve into more records. If you're scheduled for a field audit, ask to have it relocated to your tax preparer's office and let the tax preparer represent you.

If you are called for an audit, don't panic. It may be a simple matter of resolving discrepancies between two numbers. It may even wind up with your getting a refund. Keep these key points in mind:

• The better prepared you are, the better the outcome is likely to be. Keep complete records and bring with you to the audit those you need to substantiate particular deductions.

• Better yet, send your tax preparer to the audit in your stead. He or she is more likely to keep the examination on track, less likely to volunteer information that may open up other areas for examination.

• The IRS is not responsible for advice it gives, whether over the telephone or in one of its publications.

• A professional tax preparer can be a big help (see chapter 10 on how to select accountants and other advisers), but in the end, you and you alone are responsible for what is on your return.

• The IRS exchanges information with state tax authorities; if you owe the federal government more money after an audit, chances are that you will owe your state more money too. Consult your tax adviser about what procedure to follow.

• An audit isn't the last word. You do have the right of appeal, first within the IRS and then in court. There is even a special Small Tax Case Division within the Tax Court; disputes about less than $10,000 may be resolved there with minimum formality and at minimum cost.

Chapter Highlights

• Business tax basics include obtaining a federal employer identification number, or EIN, deciding whether you will use cash or accrual accounting, determining your fiscal year, and paying quarterly estimated taxes.

• Your business structure determines the tax forms you use. Sole proprietors report business activity on Schedule C (or Schedule C-EZ), which is attached to your Form 1040. Home office deductions must be supported by a separate Form 8829.

• Home office deductions are tougher to substantiate now that the home office must be not only your principal place of business but also the place where you spend most of your time.

• Partnerships file Form 1065 to report partnership income, but the partners report their individual shares of the profit or loss on Schedule E, with Form 1040.

• S corporations are very much like partnerships. Form 1120S is filed as an information return, but shareholders report their own profit or loss on Schedule E.

• Regular C corporations do pay income tax, using Form 1120 or 1120-A.

• With the current spread between individual and corporate tax rates, some S corporations are considering a change to C corporation status. Get expert advice before you decide that a switch is right for you.

• State taxes can have a big impact on the cost of doing business. Investigate the state tax situation before you establish or move your business.

• The IRS is targeting small businesses in tax audits. Keep complete records so that you can substantiate deductions if your return is examined.

Part IV

Planning Ahead

7 Planning for Retirement

One of the nice things about being self-employed is that no one (except, perhaps, your ever-loving spouse or your worried children) can tell you that it's time to slow down, time to retire. Nonetheless, the time will probably come when you want to consider working fewer hours or, perhaps, not at all. Long before that time comes you should be building a retirement nest egg—because one of the not-so-nice things about being self-employed is the lack of a company pension. Right now, every penny you have is probably invested in your business, violating the cardinal rule of investing: diversify, diversify, diversify.

Right now, too, you're probably so busy building your business and providing for current needs that retirement seems very far away. But the years have a way of passing and the day will come sooner than you may think. When it does, having that nest egg firmly in place will give you flexibility, let you decide what you want to do on the basis of how you feel rather than because you must keep on earning in order to survive.

For most wage earners, the basic building blocks of a comfortable retirement are Social Security, a pension, and personal investments. But you are self-employed and Social Security may be the only one of the three that you can count on—unless you start planning now.

If you've come from a salaried job, of course, you may have brought a pension with you. If you've always been self-employed, you must structure your own pension if you are to have one at all. You should also, ideally, have investments outside of your own business. Social Security and pensions, both the kind you bring with you from the corporate world and the kind you create for yourself, are discussed in this chapter; investment strategies and investment vehicles are described in chapter 8.

Depending on the type of business you operate, you may also be able to beef up your retirement income by selling the business when you want to retire (passing on your business is discussed in chapter 9); a buyout can be structured to provide income in installments. Supplemental income may also be forthcoming, after you retire, through a postretirement job or by tapping the equity in your home.

Before evaluating your personal sources of future retirement income, however, it's a good idea to figure out just how much you'll need. This gets easier as you get closer to retirement, but it's a useful exercise at any age. As you do a budget for current expenses and postretirement expenses (refer back to the budget worksheets in chapter 2), remember two things:

1. You can expect to live a long time in retirement. The average sixty-five-year-old now lives about eighteen years after retirement, with women outdistancing men by almost four years. But averages are just that: averages. You may live twenty-five or thirty years after retirement, and you don't want to run out of money before you run out of time. Just to be on the safe side, do your retirement planning as if you will live to age ninety-five.

2. The dollar will continue to lose purchasing power to inflation. Even at a relatively modest inflation rate of 4 percent, you will lose half of your spending power in eighteen years (see table 2.1, page 40). The only way around this is to build a nest egg that will continue to grow in retirement. That means investing for growth and not just for income, even into your sixties and beyond.

Social Security

As a self-employed individual, you pay and pay and pay into Social Security. The self-employment tax, as it's called, consists of both the employee and the employer share of Social Security—or, including the Medicare tax, 15.3 percent of your taxable income from self-employment. What's more, as of January 1994 there is no ceiling on taxable income subject to the Medicare tax. You'll pay 12.4 percent of income up to the ever-increasing Social Security "wage base" ($62,700 in 1996) but another 2.9 percent of *all* of your income toward Medicare.

In return, what do you get?

While it's still the bedrock of retirement planning, Social Security was never designed to provide all of an individual's retirement income. A sixty-five-year-old retiring in January 1996 could receive a maximum monthly benefit of $1,248. But the average retired worker in 1996 actually received $720 a month. How much *you* will receive depends on the number of years you've worked and how much you've earned over those years.

How much of your preretirement income Social Security will replace depends on where you fall on the wage scale. If you earn the maximum currently subject to Social Security tax, you can expect to receive about 28 percent of your preretirement income (up to the wage base) from Social Security retirement benefits. If you earn an "average" income your ratio will be 42 percent. And if you're at the bottom of the wage ladder you'll probably get about 56 percent of what you earn.

What's more, if you have a livable income (from all sources) after retirement, you may wind up paying income taxes on most of your Social Security benefits. Since January 1, 1994, as much as 85 percent of Social Security benefits is taxable if you are single and have an annual income of $34,000 or more or if you are a married couple filing jointly with income of $44,000 or more. "Income" for this purpose means adjusted gross income plus tax-exempt interest from municipal bonds plus half of Social Security itself. If you earn less than this but more than $25,000 as a single or $32,000 as a married couple, up to 50 percent of Social Security is subject to tax. At lower income levels, all of Social Security is still tax-free. Relatively few Social Security recipients are affected by the tax—but, since the income levels are not indexed to inflation and will not rise, more and more people will be affected each year.

Another potential problem for many two-income couples is that Social Security is still firmly rooted in the demographic reality of the 1930s: lifelong marriages in which women stayed home, dependent on the financial support of their husbands. This is emphatically not the reality of the 1990s, but working women must still make a choice: They may take full Social Security based on their own earnings or half of their husbands' retirement benefits. They may not have both. For many women, half is greater than the whole, and their own earnings do not count.

An example: when Jim retired at age sixty-five in 1994, after earning $40,000 in 1993, his last year of work, he received $1,076 in monthly retirement benefits. His wife, who had been a homemaker for most of their marriage, received the spouse's 50 percent, adding $538 to the couple's monthly income for a combined family total of $1,614. Jim's neighbors retired at the same time. But Ted and Caroline each earned $20,000 for a total of $40,000. Each received a monthly Social Security check of $752, for a total of $1,504. The same yearly family income, the same monthly contributions over the years, and $110 less each month from Social Security.

This isn't the whole story, of course, because Caroline had other benefits stemming from her earnings: She could have received Social Security disability benefits, based on her own earnings record, if she had become unable to work because of illness or injury. Her children would have received Social Security survivors' benefits, again based on her earnings record, if she had died when they were young. And she had a choice about when to retire. While Jim's wife could not collect Social Security benefits until Jim retired, Caroline could have retired at age sixty-two and started to collect reduced retirement benefits based on her own earnings record.

Social Security, although drastically in need of updating, does offer several benefits. Its retirement benefits may also provide benefits for a spouse (including a divorced spouse after at least ten years of marriage) and dependent children. Its survivors' benefits are a form of life insurance, providing payments to your spouse and dependent children after your death. Its disability insurance provides monthly income if you are unable to work at all because of an illness or injury. And Medicare provides both hospital insurance and voluntary medical insurance for men and women over age sixty-five, along with benefits for some disabled younger people.

When it comes to receiving retirement benefits, you have three options under Social Security:

• Retire at the so-called normal age of sixty-five and receive full benefits (unless you were born after 1937, in which case the normal retirement age begins to get later and later until, for those born in 1960 and thereafter, it will be sixty-seven)

• Retire early, at any time after age sixty-two, and receive a reduced benefit (reduced by 20 percent at age sixty-two, 13⅓ percent at age sixty-three, and 6⅔ percent at age sixty-four)

• Retire later and get a bonus (of 3.5 percent to 8 percent, depending on when you were born) for each additional year of work up to age seventy. In addition, if you keep on working, you'll probably add a year or more of high earnings to your Social Security earnings record; this in itself will increase your benefits.

Just when you will retire, of course, depends on a number of factors: how well your business is doing, your continuing enthusiasm for the business, the state of your health, your need for income. You don't have to decide now; when you do decide, however, be sure to apply for Social Security (and for Medicare) several months in advance. Benefits are not automatic.

You can (and should) find out exactly how much you can expect from Social Security by calling Social Security toll-free (800-772-1213) and asking for Form SSA 7004, Request for Personal Earnings and Benefit Estimate Statement. Mail in the

---

TIP

If business is still going well and holding your interest after you turn sixty-five, think about putting off Social Security retirement benefits until you reach age seventy. If you start to receive Social Security while you keep working, before age seventy, you'll face several penalties:

• "Earnings limitations" will take one dollar out of your Social Security check for every three dollars you earn over specified limits (in 1996 the penalty-free zone stopped at $11,520).

• You will still be paying into the Social Security system via the self-employment tax; this will increase your long-term benefits but cut your current take-home pay.

• If you earn enough, you may wind up paying income tax on as much as 85 percent of your Social Security check. The combination of all three can result, for some middle-income Social Security recipients, in an effective tax bite of well over 50 percent.

---

completed form and you'll get a statement within a few weeks, showing your year-by-year earnings (on which Social Security has been credited) and a personalized estimate of the benefits you'll receive.

Do this every three years, and use this statement to make sure Social Security has an accurate record of your earnings. If they've made a mistake, the quicker you call it to their attention, the quicker it can be corrected. Use this statement, too, to figure out what else you'll need in the way of retirement income.

Pension Plans

Have you left a corporate position, willingly or unwillingly, to become self-employed? If so, if your company offered a traditional defined benefit pension plan, you may have a pension waiting in the wings. If it had a defined contribution plan, such as a 401(k) plan, you may have had a lump sum distribution available. Here's what you need to know about each:

• The traditional defined benefit pension plan guarantees a dollars-and-cents payout at retirement, with the company obligated to provide enough money to make that payout. How much you will receive is usually based on a formula, typically some combination of how much you've earned and how long you've been with the company. The more you've earned and the longer you've been there, the higher your pension will be. Many plans, in fact, give greater weight to the last few years of employment, when wages tend to be much higher.

When you leave a company with a defined benefit plan long before retirement, you give up all of the pension growth you could expect as your salary grew and your years with the company lengthened. If you worked with the company long enough to be vested, typically at least five years, you will still be entitled to the pension you earned. But it is likely to be a pitifully small amount, especially since it will be frozen in place for all the years until your retirement and will not keep pace with inflation.

Nonetheless, it's worth remembering that you do have a pension coming to you. Keep your pension statements, keep track of your former employer, let that employer know when you change your address, and request your pension when the time comes. Defined benefit plans are guaranteed by the Pension Benefit Guarantee Corporation (PBGC), so even if your former employer falls on hard times, you should still have some money coming to you.

• With a defined contribution plan, such as a 401(k) plan or a profit-sharing plan, by contrast, your contribution is known while the amount you will receive at retirement depends on how wisely that contribution is invested over the years. Since most employees are too conservative, opting for guaranteed income instead of growth, retirement income is likely to be small. However, there may be matching contributions from your employer, which can increase your return. And there is typically a choice of investments, so if you are continuing your salaried job while starting your own business on the side, you can shift at least part of your portfolio toward greater potential for growth.

When you leave a company with a defined contribution plan, you may be entitled to a lump sum distribution. Many corporate dropouts want to use this distribution as start-up money for their new business ventures. Unless you have reached age fifty-nine and a half, however, using the money may entail a 10 percent tax penalty on top of ordinary income taxes. If you can afford to do so, try to put as much of the distribution as possible into an IRA rollover account. Doing so will preserve the tax breaks; it will also keep some money working toward your eventual retirement.

TIP

If you're starting your business as a moonlighter while keeping your salaried job, you may be tempted to borrow against your 401(k) plan for start-up cash. Many companies let you borrow up to half of the value of your account, to a maximum of $50,000. (You may borrow as much as $10,000, even if this amount is more than half of your account.) You'll pay interest, but that interest goes into your own retirement account.

Be careful, though, because loans against 401(k) plans (except those for home purchases) must be repaid within five years or when you leave your job, whichever comes first. Typically, while you're on the job, repayment is made through regular payroll deduction. If you expect to be able to quit within a year or two and pursue self-employment full time, think twice before you borrow from your 401(k) plan. If you don't have the money to repay the loan when you leave, the outstanding balance will be deducted from your 401(k) account. If you haven't reached age fifty-nine and a half (with some exceptions), you will owe a tax penalty of 10 percent on top of ordinary income tax; the combination could cut your retirement funds in half.

If you do need the money to start your business, note that there is an exception to the age-fifty-nine-and-a-half rule. According to Rolf Auster, professor of taxation at Florida International University in Miami, the 10 percent penalty doesn't apply if you leave your employer after age fifty-five. But the law is complex. In *What You Ought to Know About New Pension Withholding Rules* (Commerce Clearing House, 1992), Auster gives this advice: while you would normally want to roll a distribution into another tax-qualified account to avoid penalties, the situation is different if you need all or part of the money. Let's say you have $100,000 in your 401(k) plan and want to use $50,000 of it for your business. You could do one of two things: You could ask the plan administrator to roll over exactly $37,500 to your rollover IRA, with no withholding tax or penalties. The remaining $62,500 would be subject to the 20 percent withholding, which would leave exactly $50,000 for you. You would have to pay income tax on the $50,000, but because you have reached age fifty-five, there is no tax penalty.

Or, perhaps because you don't need the money right away, you could instruct the plan administrator to roll the full $100,000 into your rollover IRA. This way you have no income and therefore no withholding or penalties. But, and it's a big but, if you then turn around and withdraw $50,000 for your business (or for anything else) at a later date but before you reach age fifty-nine and a half, you must pay ordinary income tax on the full $50,000 and, because it is a "premature distribution," a penalty of 10 percent, or $5,000. You could have avoided the penalty, says Auster, by having the plan distribute the $50,000 directly to you in the first place. These rules are so complicated that you should consult a knowledgeable tax adviser before you make a move.

It's probably not a good idea to leave the money with your former employer, although you are often allowed to do so. Consider the investment options you have within the employer plan as well as whether or not you will have access to your money. Also, remember that defined contribution plans are not guaranteed

---

TIP

Although you are allowed to use money from a 401(k) distribution without tax penalty, so long as the money is put back into a tax-sheltered plan within sixty days, the IRS has come up with a new way to trip up unwary taxpayers. If money eligible for a rollover passes through your hands at all, the employer making the distribution must withhold 20 percent of the money. Although you can get back the tax on the amount you roll into another qualified plan, if you make the rollover within sixty days you won't get it back until after you file your federal income tax return for the year. That could be as much as fifteen months later; meanwhile, you're out the 20 percent. Worse yet, you'll be hit with a penalty tax if you don't roll over the entire amount; you'll have to come up with the missing 20 percent out of your own pocket, when you make the rollover, to avoid the penalty.

---

by the PBGC. Assets in the plans must be segregated from company assets, but if a company goes out of business you could well be caught in the middle.

Pension Plans for the Self-Employed

With no company pension plan, you're on your own when it comes to saving for retirement. Fortunately, Uncle Sam offers some tax-saving ways to put money aside. Try to take advantage of at least one tax-sheltered savings plan even while you are devoting every minute (and every spare dime) to building your business.

It's tough to put money aside in the early years of a business, but the earlier you start to save toward retirement (or any other goal), the better you'll do in the long run. Let's say you manage to save just $1,000 a year for each of the ten years between your

Table 7.1: Saving Early Makes a Difference

EARNINGS RATE: 7%

YEAR	INVESTMENT BEGINNING OF YEAR	CUMULATIVE INVESTMENT END OF YEAR	INVESTMENT BEGINNING OF YEAR	CUMULATIVE INVESTMENT END OF YEAR
1	$1,000	$ 1,070	$ —	$ —
2	1,000	2,215	—	—
3	1,000	3,440	—	—
4	1,000	4,751	—	—
5	1,000	6,153	—	—
6	1,000	7,654	—	—
7	1,000	9,260	—	—
8	1,000	10,978	—	—
9	1,000	12,816	—	—
10	1,000	14,784	—	—
11	—	15,818	1,000	1,070
12	—	16,926	1,000	2,215
13	—	18,111	1,000	3,440
14	—	19,378	1,000	4,751
15	—	20,735	1,000	6,153
16	—	22,186	1,000	7,654
17	—	23,739	1,000	9,260
18	—	25,401	1,000	10,978
19	—	27,179	1,000	12,816
20	—	29,082	1,000	14,784
21	—	31,117	1,000	16,888
22	—	33,295	1,000	19,141
23	—	35,626	1,000	21,550
24	—	38,120	1,000	24,129
25	—	40,788	1,000	26,888
26	—	43,644	1,000	29,840
27	—	46,699	1,000	32,999
28	—	49,968	1,000	36,379
29	—	53,465	1,000	39,995
30	—	57,208	1,000	43,865

SOURCE: Harold Evensky, CFP, Evensky, Brown & Katz, Coral Gables, Florida.

thirty-first birthday and your fortieth birthday; then you stop and don't save another dime. With compounding at 7 percent, your original $10,000 will become $57,208 by the time you turn sixty. By contrast, if you don't start putting money away until your thirtieth birthday, then invest $1,000 a year each year until you turn sixty, you will have put in $30,000, and at the end you will have $43,865 (see table 7.1). Surely, even now, you can manage to put $1,000 a year into a tax-qualified plan for retirement.

Here are your choices:

Keogh Plans

Specifically designed for the self-employed, Keogh plans (named after Eugene Keogh, the congressman who came up with the idea) let you put away a good bit of money toward retirement. The contribution itself is deductible and earnings grow tax-deferred; no tax is due on interest or dividends until the money is withdrawn. The idea was that you would then be retired and in a lower tax bracket. This may no longer be the case, with tax rates rising once again, but the tax-deferred compounding can still make a lot of sense.

Defined contribution Keogh plans are the most popular and make the most sense for most people. Here, as with the defined contribution pension plan described above, you put in a specified percentage of your income. The amount of money you'll have at the end depends on how much you've put in and how your investments have performed. Defined contribution Keoghs come in three flavors:

- *Money purchase* plans are the most restrictive. You decide at the outset what percentage of your income you will put away, up to the stated limit of 25 percent (actually a bit less because of the way the formula is calculated) and a maximum of $30,000, and then must put that percentage of income away every single year, in good years and bad. Many self-employed people find this a scary prospect.

• *Profit-sharing* plans let you put away up to 15 percent, up to a total deductible contribution of $22,500. (The $30,000 cap no longer applies here, as a practical matter, because new rules in the 1993 tax act limit the total annual compensation on which deductible retirement contributions can be based to $150,000; 15 percent of $150,000 is $22,500.) More important, you can reduce or skip payments if business isn't good.

• *Paired* or combination plans offer the best of both worlds. You designate a fixed amount for the money purchase portion and then can add more to the profit-sharing portion in years when profits are rolling in, to a combined total of 25 percent. You might choose to put away a basic 10 percent of income every year (remember, it's deductible, so the actual cost is less), then add up to 15 percent more in years when business is booming.

Note: for reasons best known to the IRS, spouses working together either as co-owners or as employer and employee are treated as a single individual for the purpose of determining deductible pension plan contributions. This won't matter if your combined income is $150,000 or less. If it is more, says Howard J. Golden, a partner of Kwasha Lipton, an employee benefits firm in Fort Lee, New Jersey, you must allocate pension contributions proportionately. Stay alert, though; there is a possibility that this rule will be modified or repealed in a tax simplification bill being considered by Congress.

Defined benefit Keogh plans are another, far less common, option. With these arrangements you designate a desired level of retirement income, then put away whatever it will take to reach that income. As Daniel Kehrer, editor of *IB* magazine and author of *12 Steps to a Worry-Free Retirement* (Kiplinger's Books, 1993), puts it: "As in the TV game show *Jeopardy*, you begin with the answer—an annual retirement income target of your choosing—then provide the question: How much must I contribute annually to reach that goal?"

Note, though, that your choices as to the retirement income you'd like to target are increasingly restricted. Not only does the law not permit annual retirement income of more than a specified amount (about $120,000 in 1996), but you can no longer make contributions based on annual compensation of more than $150,000.

Even so, a defined benefit Keogh plan has one major advantage: assuming that you are getting close to retirement age, you get to stash away a much bigger retirement nest egg, often much more than the 20 percent of compensation permitted under defined contribution Keogh plans. The disadvantages (yes, they're plural): You need an actuary to calculate the amount you can put away each year, and actuaries cost money—typically $1,000 or more per year (although the fees are deductible as a business expense). You're also committed to making this large payment, which may be tough in years when income doesn't quite meet expectations. Defined benefit Keoghs are most appropriate for self-employed women and men over age fifty with sizable self-employment income who want to fund a comfortable retirement and have relatively few years left in which to do so.

Note, though, that the IRS has cracked down on defined benefit Keoghs on the theory that the tax shelter was being abused by high-income professionals. The crackdown took the form of extensive audits of previously filed defined benefit Keogh returns, challenging both projected retirement dates earlier than age sixty-five and actuarial assumptions about interest earned in the plan. This retroactive punishment, with fines and penalties levied for interest rates that were previously acceptable, enraged actuaries and other pension professionals. Some companies took the IRS to court over the issue. Today's low-interest-rate environment makes challenges about interest rate assumptions less likely. However, although the IRS has lost every court case thus far, it has not given up.

So it pays to be careful in setting the actuarial assumptions on which a defined benefit Keogh is established. Be sure to get expert advice in this tricky area—and bear in mind that because you are funding to provide a specified benefit, rates of return well in excess of assumptions could cost you the ability to make contributions. In other words, in the words of David Wasserstrum, a New York City CPA who specializes in employee benefit consulting and administration, "to the extent that earnings exceed assumptions, your contributions go down; you can't create a larger benefit, because the benefit is fixed in advance."

With any Keogh:

• You may use a prototype plan from a bank, brokerage house, mutual fund, or insurance company. Or, at considerably greater expense, you can pay a pension consultant to design your own plan and file it with the IRS for approval. The expense is generally unnecessary, however, since prototype plans meet most needs.

• You must start your plan before year-end, initially, then can make annual contributions up until the date you file your income tax return. This is usually April 15, of course, but could be August or even October if you've secured tax filing extensions.

• Contributions must be made from earned income, not stock dividends and the like, and you can continue to make contributions as long as you have earned income.

• You must file an annual report with the IRS, on Form 5500. An exception from this paperwork chore: if your plan covers only you and your spouse and contains under $100,000, you need not file.

• You may not withdraw money before age fifty-nine and a half without a tax penalty, unless you are disabled or you annuitize withdrawals over at least a five-year period. You must start withdrawals by the April 1 after you reach age seventy and a half, although if you are still earning self-employment income, you may continue to contribute even as you withdraw.

• If you return to a salaried job and have no self-employment income, you can no longer contribute to your Keogh. But you may leave your prior contributions in place to continue growing tax-deferred.

• If you have any employees, you must include in your Keogh plan those who are at least age twenty-one, work for you full-time, and have been with you for at least one year (or two years, if you offer immediate vesting).

> **TIP**
>
> The annual fee you pay to maintain your Keogh account, which may start at thirty dollars at some discount brokers and work up to considerably more, is tax deductible—but only if you pay for it with a separate check (on your business account, of course) rather than letting it be deducted from your Keogh funds.

Simplified Employee Pensions

Keogh plans have been the vehicle of choice for the self-employed for a couple of decades now, but an upstart is moving in on the Keogh turf. The Simplified Employee Pension (SEP), sometimes called the SEP-IRA, is similar to a Keogh (the profit-sharing variety) but simpler to set up and administer—more, in fact, like an IRA. With a Keogh you must file annual returns with the IRS; with a SEP you can skip this task. With a Keogh, as noted, you must open the account by December 31, although you can fund it until your tax-filing deadline; with a SEP you have until that tax-filing deadline to both open and fund the account.

Pensions for the self-employed are so complex that there aren't many simple answers; about the only piece of generalized advice I found comes from David Wasserstrum, who says, "If you are self-employed, if you *know* that you will never have employees, and if you are satisfied with a plan that will limit contributions to $22,500 or 15 percent of earned income, then the SEP is almost always the best answer."

The SEP has the advantage of being completely flexible. You may vary the amount you contribute each year, up to a maximum of 15 percent of earned income (remember, that's really about 13 percent) and a cap of $22,500 a year; you may even skip a year entirely if you like. With a Keogh you can put away more toward retirement—but, as financial planner Katharine McGee notes, most self-employed people count themselves lucky if they can manage to put away 10 percent to 12 percent of their income.

But the SEP does have drawbacks if you have employees, because you must make contributions for every eligible employee—and "eligible" is defined as anyone over age twenty-one who has worked for you in three of the five preceding years. "Worked for you" means performing any service, with no time constraints (unlike Keogh plan rules, where employees must work one thousand hours a year in order to be eligible). As Wasserstrum points out, this could include a college kid putting in twenty hours a week for two or three months as a summer helper. You can't get off the hook just because an employee doesn't want to be bothered. You must open the account anyway. And because vesting is immediate, you might find yourself opening the account even as your employee waits on line behind you, then withdraws all of the money. So, again, if you have or expect to have employees, consider a Keogh, a 401(k) plan, or a salary reduction SEP (see page 199) instead of a SEP.

Individual Retirement Accounts

You remember the IRA . . . the $2,000 a year you could put away, tax-free, while the account grew, tax-deferred, until retirement. That $2,000 a year, of course, is now fully deductible only if you (and your spouse, if you have one) are not otherwise covered by a pension or if you earn below $25,000 as a single person or $40,000 as a married couple filing jointly. Contributions are partially deductible at earnings of up to $35,000 for a single and $50,000 for a married couple.

If your business is earning below these levels, as it well may be at the outset, an IRA may be the simplest way to stash some money away toward retirement. At higher levels of income (or if you also have a Keogh or your spouse is covered by a pension), you have to decide whether a nondeductible IRA is worthwhile. With these accounts (which should be kept separate from any deductible IRAs you may have), you can't deduct the contribution, but the growth continues to be deferred from taxes until you withdraw the money.

Some advisers think this tax deferral is worthwhile, even when

> ### TIP
> If you've left a salaried job where you were covered by a pension plan, you may under some circumstances be able to make a deductible IRA contribution. According to Howard Golden of Kwasha Lipton, this would be true if you were covered under a profit-sharing plan and no additional money (either contributions or other allocations) is being put into your account. You could *not* make deductible IRA contributions, however, if your prior coverage was under a defined benefit pension plan, where you are still entitled to receive benefits at a later date.

the contribution is not deductible. I'm not so sure, because the paperwork headaches can overshadow any financial advantage. If you make a nondeductible IRA contribution, you must file Form 8606 with your yearly federal income tax return, then hold on to that form virtually forever; you'll need it when you reach retirement age and start making withdrawals from the IRA so that you can calculate the tax due on the withdrawals. The process is complicated because the IRS insists that you cannot withdraw first from one IRA and then from another; instead deductible and nondeductible IRAs must be treated as an aggregate, with taxes figured on proportionate amounts.

You may be better off opening a SEP or a Keogh plan, even if you can't fund either to the full extent. With a SEP or a profit-sharing Keogh you can put in as much (up to the allowable ceiling) or as little as suits you.

Otherwise the rules for IRAs are similar to those for other tax-qualified retirement plans: You may take withdrawals, without penalty, after age fifty-nine and a half; you must start withdrawals after age seventy and a half. Annual administrative fees are tax-deductible if you pay them by separate check (assuming, of course, that you itemize deductions). And you have a choice of investment vehicles, although you should keep these guidelines in mind:

• Stay out of tax-free investments. There's no sense in erecting a tax-shelter umbrella over investments that are already tax-sheltered; you can't defer taxes twice on the same investment income. Moreover, since your Keogh, SEP, and IRA withdrawals will be taxed as ordinary income, you'll lose the benefit of the tax shelter in the end. Even municipal bonds, in a tax-qualified retirement account, become taxable eventually. You might just as well take the higher yield of a taxable investment and increase the yield by putting it within the tax shelter of your retirement plan.

• If you have many years until retirement, consider investing for growth within your retirement portfolio—although, again, be aware of the tax consequences. Since proceeds will be taxed as ordinary income, you lose the differential between capital gains tax rates and ordinary income tax rates. In 1994 the maximum capital gains tax was 28 percent, while the maximum federal tax on ordinary income was almost 40 percent. If you have sufficient funds to maintain investment portfolios both within a tax-qualified plan and outside, you might invest for income inside the plan and for growth outside.

• Specialized investments, such as zero-coupon corporate bonds, can be particularly well suited for tax-qualified retirement plans. That's because zeros, as they are called, do not pay interest but are taxed as if they do. Within a Keogh, SEP, or IRA there is no tax to pay.

That said, these are your basic Keogh, SEP, and IRA investment choices:

• *Certificates of deposit* at a bank, thrift, or credit union. When interest rates are high, you can lock in your return by using a CD of five or more years. When interest rates are low, consider "laddering" maturities, buying a new CD of a fixed length with each year's retirement contribution so that you can take advantage of changing interest rates.

Retirement plans at financial institutions are easy to establish and usually have few if any associated costs. CDs also have the advantage of federal deposit insurance—but be careful: under new rules, any and all retirement plans at a single institution are insured to a total of $100,000. If you left an IRA to accumulate that has now reached $30,000, and you've added a Keogh plan at the same institution that is now at a total of $80,000, you have $10,000 that is uninsured. Keep track of your accounts and move money from one institution to another if you will exceed insurable amounts. Retirement money can be transferred as often as you like, with no tax penalty, so long as the transfer is made directly from one institution to another.

• *Mutual funds* offer more flexibility, since, once you open a prototype Keogh, SEP, or IRA plan with a mutual fund family, you can invest in just about anything—stocks, bonds, treasury issues, and so on. When you have many years to retirement, a growth fund can help your retirement money keep pace with rising costs. As you get closer to retirement, you can shift a portion of your plan money to income funds to preserve principal. Yearly fees are usually low, in the neighborhood of twenty or thirty dollars; some fund families charge no fees at all. And if you choose a "no-load" fund, one without an up-front commission to a salesperson, all of your money goes right to work for you—although, if you want advice, it may be worth buying through a

---

TIP

Check both rates and rules at competing financial institutions before taking a CD anywhere. Interest rates vary considerably. And when it comes to rules, some institutions are more flexible about allowing withdrawals than others. For example: While the IRS permits you to withdraw money from a retirement plan without tax penalty, once you reach age fifty-nine and a half, some banks continue to charge their own penalties on early withdrawal from a CD. Worse, some institutions don't allow you to make early withdrawals even if you're willing to pay the penalty. Read the fine print before you buy.

broker and paying a load. Mutual funds, of course, are not insured; depending on the fund you choose, you do run the risk of losing principal. (More detail on investment vehicles, including mutual funds, is in chapter 8.)

• *Self-directed accounts* (if you can take the time from your business to manage an investment portfolio) let you buy and sell individual investments within your retirement plan wrapper. You can invest in stocks or bonds, in real estate, or in oil wells. But you will pay start-up fees and annual maintenance fees for a self-directed account at a brokerage firm, plus brokerage commissions on every transaction. If you do choose to go this route, compare both cost and service carefully before you select a firm; discount brokerage firms charge less than do full-service firms, as a rule, but they do not give advice. And bear in mind that capital gains within a retirement plan are taxed as ordinary income when the money is withdrawn, while capital losses cannot be deducted against other gains.

• *Annuities* are sometimes recommended as funding vehicles for Keogh, SEP, and IRA plans. But annuities are tax-deferred on their own and, as noted earlier, there's little point in wrapping a tax-deferred retirement account around a tax-deferred investment. Annuities can provide supplemental retirement income but should be separate from your tax-qualified plans.

Annuities come in two varieties: fixed and variable. Single-premium deferred annuities, bought with a lump sum that will provide installment income at a later date, are the most popular fixed annuities. Before you buy, find out the current interest rate

---

TIP

For more flexibility at low cost, open an account with a firm such as Charles Schwab or Fidelity. Both offer a wide variety of mutual funds, their own and others, with two distinct advantages: consolidated account statements, and the ease of switching from fund to fund with a single telephone call as your needs or objectives change.

as well as the minimum interest rate guaranteed in the contract; look for an annuity contract that permits you to bail out without penalty if the interest drops below a specified rate. Other questions to ask before you buy: What penalties are there for early surrender? How much will I pay in commissions (either up front or on redemption) and fees? How much of the cash value can I take as a loan, and how much will I pay for the privilege?

Although they are not tax-qualified—contributions are not deductible—annuities are subject to many of the same rules as qualified plans: withdrawals before age fifty-nine and a half, for example, are generally fully taxable as ordinary income and subject to tax penalties as well.

(You'll find information on variable annuities as investment vehicles in chapter 8.)

When You Have Employees

As your business grows and you add employees, you have additional options and responsibilities. First, if you have a pension plan for yourself, you must include eligible employees. With a Keogh, that's all employees over age twenty-one who have worked for you full time (at least one thousand hours a year) for at least one year. You don't have to *include* every employee (as you do in a SEP plan), so long as the plan is made *available* to every eligible employee; you do have some leeway in terms of the percentage of employees that must be covered. But all covered employees must be treated equally, which means that you can't contribute far more toward your own pension plan (as a percentage of salary) than you contribute for your employees. The single exception to these nondiscrimination rules—age-weighted plans, which permit you to consider age as well as income and therefore contribute a higher percentage for older employees—appears to be the target of a Washington crackdown.

The rules for covering employees under a SEP plan, as noted

earlier, are somewhat different. Eligibility rules include far more people—even the occasional part-time employee. Every employee must be included, willingly or not. And employees are immediately vested. SEP plans, as a result, are better suited to the self-employed person who does not have and does not intend to have employees.

Other options include:

• *401(k) plans.* These salary reduction plans can suit the needs of businesses with as few as ten employees—some benefits consultants write 401(k) plans for as few as four people—although administrative costs and paperwork burdens may reduce the appeal. Still, if you hook up with an insurance company (such as the Principal Financial Group in Des Moines) or a mutual fund group (such as T. Rowe Price in Baltimore) that specializes in these plans for the smaller business, you may find that the 401(k) works for you.

• *Salary reduction SEPs,* or *SARSEP plans.* These may be ideal for some small-business owners. Designed for businesses with under twenty-five employees, SARSEP plans let eligible employees make their own contributions in the form of salary deferral (up to 15 percent of salary, to a specified limit—$9,500 in 1996; it's going up each year), while you deduct those contributions as a business expense. To set up a SARSEP, at least half of all eligible employees must agree to participate. Both start-up and administrative costs are minimal.

Nonetheless, SARSEPs aren't for everyone. David Wasserstrum prefers 401(k) plans, even for the smallest businesses, even though they are more expensive to establish and administer. His reasoning:

1. A SARSEP is basically an IRA, so you can't borrow against it; the loan feature is a popular element of 401(k) plans.
2. You can't make matching contributions to a SARSEP, because of rules stating that contributions to a SARSEP must "bear a uniform relationship to compensation." If one employee chooses not to participate, matching con-

tributions for another employee would destroy this uniform relationship.

3. If your business should grow beyond twenty-five employees, you could not have a SARSEP and would have to start over.

Nonqualified Plans

Qualified retirement plans are the plans that, with the blessing of the IRS, let your investments grow, free of taxes, until you withdraw the money. Qualified plans, including Keoghs, SEPs, IRAs, 401(k) plans, and SARSEPs, must meet strict IRS requirements about how much may be contributed, when money can and must be withdrawn, how employees must be treated, and so on. *Nonqualified* plans include a range of employee benefits that may also be subject to IRS requirements but that tend to be more flexible.

Most nonqualified plans are more suitable for high-paid executives in a corporate setting. Some may work well for succession planning (see chapter 9), and some may suit your retirement-planning needs, especially if you have established a regular C corporation and if you have key employees whom you want to keep by offering such inducements. Here is a very brief overview of some nonqualified options, provided by Stuart G. Tugman, vice president of Jefferson-Pilot Life Insurance Company:

• *Deferred compensation agreements.* These provide benefits for death, retirement, and disability to employees and their beneficiaries. The funding is provided through life insurance, with the employer as the beneficiary. Premiums are not taxable to the employee or deductible to the employer; benefits are taxable to the employee and deductible for the employer.

• *Split-dollar life insurance.* The employer and the employee divide the cost and benefits of a life insurance policy on the employee's life.

• By providing the funds to hire and train a replacement, *key person insurance* indemnifies a business for the death of a key person and the resulting loss of his or her skill and experience.

All of these plans are complex and require careful planning and implementation; don't even think about them unless (1) your business is structured as a regular C corporation and (2) you get expert advice.

Investing on Your Own

Even while you're struggling to come up with the money to pay your self-employment tax each year, try to put some money aside for the future. Do so, first, through a tax-qualified plan, because these plans have at least two advantages: Your money grows faster when you don't pay income tax on interest and dividends as they accumulate. And, just as important, you're not likely to tap this money for other purposes because of the tax penalties you'll face.

As your business grows and income becomes more predictable, you should also plan to invest outside your qualified retirement plans and outside your business itself. (Investment strategies and vehicles are discussed in chapter 8.)

Chapter Highlights

• As a self-employed individual, you must provide most of your own retirement income.

• No matter how much you pay into Social Security in the form of self-employment tax, it will not provide sufficient retirement income; the maximum annual income for a sixty-five-year-old retiring in 1996 was $14,976.

• If you remained in a company pension plan as you moved into self-employment, try to leave it untouched so that it will continue to grow, tax-deferred, and be there after retirement, when you need it most.

- Pension choices, now that you are self-employed, include defined contribution Keogh plans: money purchase, profit sharing, or combination.

- Businesspeople who earn sizable amounts and are close to retirement can put more money away through a defined benefit Keogh plan.

- Simplified Employee Pension (SEP) plans are easier to set up and administer than Keogh plans, although, if you can afford to do so, more money can be contributed to a Keogh.

- Individual retirement accounts, especially if you qualify to deduct contributions, are another choice.

- When your business grows and you have employees, you may want to consider a 401(k) plan or a SARSEP.

- Nonqualified retirement plans are best suited to corporations.

- Investing on your own, outside a formal retirement plan, will provide additional income in retirement.

8 Investment Strategy

"How can I even think about investing when I just about make enough to support myself and my family?" says the owner of an Indianapolis market research firm. "Every extra penny goes right into the business."

You may feel exactly the same way, yet there are two very good reasons for investing outside your business. First, we've seen the need for retirement planning, so that you can leave your business behind when you're ready to do so; it generally takes both tax-qualified retirement plans and ordinary investments to make this possible.

Second, and at least as important, diversification is the golden rule of investing. This may be tough to go along with for someone with the entrepreneurial zeal to start a business, but putting all of your money into your business is the exact same thing as putting all of your eggs into one basket. If the basket drops, you'll have nothing but scrambled eggs. Put another way, in the words of financial planner Diahann Lassus, "Your business is the high-risk portion of your portfolio. You need to tone down the risk level in other investments in order to create a balance."

Here, then, is an overview of some investment strategies and vehicles you might use to reach your personal objectives, all tailored to the special needs of the self-employed.

Investment Guidelines

Before you invest, determine your investment objectives, your investment time line, and your tolerance for risk.

Determine Your Investment Objectives

Although they can and should be fine-tuned to suit your specific needs, there are three basic investment objectives: liquidity, income, and growth. Ideally your portfolio will be designed to achieve all three.

Liquidity entails keeping some portion of your investable assets in cash and cash equivalents (such as money market mutual funds, short-term CDs, and treasury notes and bills) so that you'll have money readily available if needed. This "cash cushion" serves several purposes. It can pay for an emergency roof repair on your home or cover your office rent during a slow period. It can also come in very handy if an irresistible opportunity comes along—as a Washington State potter found when a kiln became available at just the right price.

If your business is a sole proprietorship or a partnership, you can use your personal cash fund for your business; just keep records to document the transaction. If your business is a corporation, however, you must be extra careful; pay for roof repairs from a personal account and pay your office rent from a corporate account. If your home roof also shelters your office, you might pay for the job with two checks, one from each account, or pay the roofer with a personal check and reimburse yourself for the appropriate amount from your corporate account.

Income investments are those throwing off a steady stream of reliable income in the form of monthly interest (from bond funds), semiannual interest (from bonds), or quarterly dividends (from stocks; utility issues are often considered income investments).

Bonds are the investments most often associated with income. But bonds are not all alike. Some are issued by corporations and

---

TIP

An adequate cash cushion for people with salaried jobs usually consists of three to six months' living expenses. For the self-employed man or woman with erratic and unpredictable income, however, a two-year emergency fund makes a lot more sense. If your business is new or subject to cyclical swings, and if you don't have a spouse with a steady salaried income, you need to keep money on hand in cash and cash equivalents to cover lengthy periods when business income may be sparse.

---

some by municipalities and government agencies; some are short term and some have maturities stretching thirty years into the future. Some provide guaranteed income until a predetermined maturity date, while others can be "called" early so that the income comes to a premature end. (Bonds are discussed in more detail on pages 225–27.)

While investment income is often considered most important for the older investor who is retired and no longer earning current income, it can also help the self-employed individual level the peaks and valleys of erratic business income. If you come into a large sum of money, whether from a retirement distribution or an inheritance or a lottery, you may be tempted to plow the money right into your business. Before you use all of it this way, consider investing at least some of the money to produce income that will supplement your business earnings. Remember, your business is probably the riskiest investment you have; channel some investment dollars into other, less risky investment vehicles.

Note, though, that investing solely for income is not as safe as it may seem. Fixed returns tend to lose ground to inflation, and you need to keep some proportion of your investable dollars in growth investments (at every age) if you are to get ahead.

Growth investments, such as common stock, offer a trade-off. Although many stocks do pay dividends, you don't buy most stocks for current income. Instead you hope for appreciation over time. There is no guarantee, of course, and money invested for growth may also be lost. In fact, as a general rule, the amount of potential profit is directly related to the amount of risk. Blue chip stocks may produce steady growth with minimum risk, although there's no guarantee, but "aggressive growth" stocks or mutual funds offer the tantalizing promise of great rewards coupled with enormous risk.

Don't invest for growth with money you can't afford to lose. And don't invest for growth unless you have enough time to ride out market cycles and thereby reduce some of the risk.

Determine Your Investment Time Line

Before you invest at all, try to work out just when you'll need your money. The measuring rod should include both business and personal needs. On the business side, for example, you may plan to move from a home office to rented space; if so, you'll probably need additional funds when the time comes. On the personal side, you may want to buy a house or put children through college.

If any of these money-hungry events will occur within two to three years, you should keep your money in a form where it will be accessible when needed (but not necessarily in a low-return savings account or CD; some alternatives are suggested on pages 222–23). Common stock could be a mistake because the market might be down just when you must sell.

If you won't need the money for eight to ten years, however, you can invest in common stock in the hope that your investment will appreciate and be worth considerably more when you sell. To be on the safe side, though, because it is virtually impossible to "time" the market and either buy at the absolute low or sell at the absolute high, you should buy gradually through dollar cost averaging (see page 212) and then sell gradually over a two- to three-year period before you will need the money. (This is easy to determine if the money will be needed for a fixed purpose, such as a tuition bill. If you're not precisely sure when your need for money will arise, but you know that it will—perhaps because you plan to buy a house but are not sure exactly when—put less in stocks for the time being and more into cash equivalents and income-producing investments with staggered maturities.)

Determine Your Tolerance for Risk

You may think of investment risk solely as the risk of losing principal when market value goes down. In fact, investment risk comes in several varieties. Yes, you can lose principal if you must sell when prices are lower than when you bought. But you can also lose money if inflation outdistances income; your cash might be "safe" under your mattress or in a bank vault, but it would definitely lose value. Similarly, it may be safe in an interest-earning CD or Treasury bill, but unless your after-tax return beats the rate of inflation, which is unlikely in these conservative investments, you will actually lose money.

Then there is interest rate risk, the kind associated with investments (such as bonds) that lose value in inverse proportion to interest rates; when interest rates rise, in other words, bond prices generally fall. And, of course, there's the risk associated with broad economic conditions; this is the risk that companies in a problem-ridden industry will take years to recover or that an economy mired in recession will depress investment values across the board.

It's impossible to avoid any and all risk in investing. But it is essential to decide just which risk, and how much risk, you are willing to assume. You may spend enough sleepless nights worrying about your business; you needn't spend more worrying about your investments. The following investment strategies can help to minimize investment risk, leaving you free to concentrate on growing your business.

CHECK YOUR RISK TOLERANCE

Use this quiz to assess your own tolerance for risk:

1. I believe investing in today's volatile stock market is similar to spinning a roulette wheel in Las Vegas, because the odds are against me.
- [ ] a. agree strongly
- [ ] b. agree
- [ ] c. neither agree nor disagree
- [ ] d. disagree
- [ ] e. disagree strongly

2. My salary and overall earnings from my job are likely to increase significantly in the coming years.
- [ ] a. disagree strongly
- [ ] b. disagree
- [ ] c. neither agree nor disagree
- [ ] d. agree
- [ ] e. agree strongly

3. If I were deciding how to invest my retirement plan, I would choose investments that offered guaranteed returns and stability.
- [ ] a. agree strongly
- [ ] b. agree
- [ ] c. neither agree nor disagree
- [ ] d. disagree
- [ ] e. disagree strongly

4. If I were picking a stock to invest in, I would look for companies that were developing breakthrough products of the future, such as the next penicillin.
- [ ] a. disagree strongly
- [ ] b. disagree
- [ ] c. neither agree nor disagree
- [ ] d. agree
- [ ] e. agree strongly

5. If I were selecting an investment for my newborn child's college education fund, I would choose:
- [ ] a. federally insured certificates of deposit
- [ ] b. government-backed securities
- [ ] c. high-quality corporate bonds
- [ ] d. stock mutual funds
- [ ] e. corporate junk bonds

6. The following number of dependents rely on me for financial support:
- [ ] a. four or more
- [ ] b. three
- [ ] c. two
- [ ] d. one
- [ ] e. only myself

7. The number of years remaining until I expect to retire is approximately:
- [ ] a. currently retired
- [ ] b. less than 5 years
- [ ] c. 5–14 years
- [ ] d. 15–24 years
- [ ] e. 25 years or more

8. My total net worth (the value of my assets less debts) is:
- [ ] a. under $15,000
- [ ] b. $15,001–50,000
- [ ] c. $50,001–150,000
- [ ] d. $150,001–350,000
- [ ] e. over $350,000

9. **The amount I have saved to handle emergencies, such as a job loss or unexpected medical expenses, equals:**
☐ a. one month's salary or less
☐ b. two to six months's salary
☐ c. seven months' to one year's salary
☐ d. one to two years' salary
☐ e. more than two years' salary

10. **I would rather invest in a stock mutual fund than choose individual stocks on my own because a mutual fund provides professional management and diversification.**
☐ a. agree strongly
☐ b. agree
☐ 'c. neither agree nor disagree
☐ d. disagree
☐ e. disagree strongly

11. **I want and need to reduce the overall level of debt in my personal finances.**
☐ a. agree strongly
☐ b. agree
☐ c. neither agree nor disagree
☐ d. disagree
☐ e. disagree strongly

12. **When making investments, I prefer to have a guaranteed yield at a specified date rather than the possibility of a higher or lower return sometime in the future.**
☐ a. agree strongly
☐ b. agree
☐ c. neither agree nor disagree
☐ d. disagree
☐ e. disagree strongly

Give yourself one point for every *a*, two points for every *b*, three points for every *c*, four points for every *d*, and five points for every *e*. The higher your score, the more comfortable you are with risk. In the middle, with a score of 35 to 40, you have an average tolerance for risk and don't really like to gamble. Even if you're off the chart, however, with a score of 46 or more, be sure to diversify at least some of your portfolio into safer investment vehicles.

SOURCE: *Fidelity Focus*, Boston: Fidelity Investments (spring 1992).

Investment Strategies

Identifying Money to Invest

As a self-employed individual, you probably find it difficult to draw a hard-and-fast line between your business and personal finances. Unless your business is incorporated, in fact, you may not be required to do so. But you should track business income and outgo, so that you can identify business profits and know whether you are investing money earned from your business or money from another source, such as a spouse's salary or other, appreciated, assets.

Chapter 2 outlines ways to control spending and gain control of your finances, ways that can be put to good use in finding money to invest. In addition you might:

• Take a hypothetical pay cut. True, you may be barely supporting yourself in the early stages of a new business. But couldn't you get along with $1,000 less per year in take-home pay? Investing just $1,000 a year, consistently, can produce remarkable results over time, especially if you start early. Table 7.1 (page 187) demonstrates the surprising results.

• Take a loan against a whole-life insurance policy, using the money to invest at a higher rate of return than you are earning inside the policy. Do this carefully, since money building up inside the policy is not subject to current income tax. And bear in mind that even though you do not have to repay a policy loan, death benefits will be decreased by the amount of any outstanding loan. A loan may be more appropriate if you have an older policy, with large cash values, and a family that no longer needs the full face value of the policy to survive.

• Redeploy assets. If monthly payments on a car loan are finished or college tuition payments have (at last) reached an end, don't just let the money you've been allocating to these purposes disappear, unnoticed, in the family budget. Instead, since you've been getting along without this money, you should be able to use it for an investment program.

• Consider a garage sale. If you're like many people, with a basement or garage full of accumulated no-longer-used possessions, a well-run tag or garage sale can raise several hundred dollars or more. Don't spend the money. Invest it.

Investing with Small Sums

Don't fall for the notion that you can't invest unless you first save a sizable sum. It is not only possible to invest with relatively small amounts, it may be preferable to do so. That's because spreading investments over time, investing small sums on a regular basis, also helps to spread the risk. Here are some ways to do so:

Dividend reinvestment offers a low-cost, painless way to add to stocks you already own. Instead of taking dividends in cash each quarter and, probably, simply spending the money, you can often elect to have dividends automatically reinvested to purchase additional shares. The dividends are taxable whether you take them in cash or reinvest them, but reinvestment builds your investment portfolio and averages the purchase price over time.

Dividend reinvestment is a good way to put small sums to work and to do so at little cost. Seven out of ten companies with dividend reinvestment plans charge no commissions at all; others charge commissions but at rates that are lower than purchases outside the plan. And some companies even offer a discount on stock purchased through the plan.

TIP

Keep good records if you enroll in a dividend reinvestment plan. Each purchase will be made at a different price—and you'll need to know all of those purchase prices to calculate taxes due when you sell. Some companies will provide a computer printout of all of your transactions, but don't count on this. Set up a filing system and keep all of your statements.

Investment clubs are groups that get together and pool their money to invest. Each member might put in $20, $25, or $50 a month, then the group does research and decides where to invest. You can start your own club and play by your own rules, or you can secure advice and guidance by joining the National Association of Investors Corporation (NAIC), an umbrella organization of investment clubs around the nation. NAIC provides an enormous amount of useful information and investment research, all for an annual membership fee of thirty-five dollars. Information is available by writing to NAIC, 1515 East Eleven Mile Road, Royal Oak, MI 48067.

NAIC's Low-Cost Investment Plan may be more appealing to you, as a busy businessperson, than a club that requires attendance at meetings. With NAIC membership plus a five-dollar initial service charge on each initial stock purchase, you can get started in the dividend reinvestment plans of more than 110 participating corporations. With most you can get started by purchasing a single share. Once enrolled you can buy more shares directly through the company's dividend reinvestment plan, investing amounts of your choice at intervals of your choice. Information is available from NAIC.

Dollar cost averaging is the formal name for the disciplined investment tactic that involves investing on a regular basis. You can dollar cost average through dividend reinvestment, although the invested amounts will not be consistent, or you can do so by authorizing automatic transfers from your checking account to a mutual fund—many funds make it easy by reducing initial investment requirements if you sign up for automatic purchases.

Either way, the key is investing on a regular basis over a significant period of time. Putting in just $100 a month, for example, can get you started. And putting in that $100 (or more) a month (or quarter) means that you buy more shares when prices are down and fewer when prices are up, thereby producing a lower average purchase price over time. To dollar cost average effectively, continue the process over a period of at least two years; five years is better. Dollar cost averaging is no guarantee of investment success, but it is an excellent way to reduce investment risk.

Diversification

If there is one golden rule of investing, it is this: diversify, diversify, diversify. For you, as a self-employed individual, it means investing outside your business. It also means spreading your investment dollars among investment vehicles with different objectives and varying time frames. In fact, according to studies by CDA/Wiesenberger, selecting the asset categories for your investments is far more important than selecting the investments themselves.

Asset allocation is a more formal approach to diversification. Here you look at all of your investable assets (including your retirement plans and your business) as a single entity, then decide how to allocate the entire portfolio. The allocation can be done on several levels, according to your age, your investment temperament, and your objectives.

A very simple allocation model might designate one-third of your portfolio to cash, one-third to income investments, and one-third to growth. Here, if your business is your growth investment, the bulk of other investable dollars belong in the other two categories.

A more complex approach might allocate one-fifth each to cash, domestic stocks, international stocks, domestic bonds, and international bonds. Or you might choose to refine your allocation model still further and consider the common stock of small companies and the common stock of large companies as two different groupings; "small-cap" and "large-cap" stocks are known to perform differently. (Again, your own business might fill the riskier small-cap category, so that other stock investments should be in blue chips.) It's also important, if you buy individual stocks, to buy stock in companies in different industries. Similarly, within the bond grouping you can include short-term and long-term bonds, taxables and tax-frees. To keep risk down stick to "investment-grade" bonds, those rated Baa or above by rating agencies, or look for insurance-backing bond issues.

Real estate might be another category. Here you would ignore your personal residence (it is shelter, first and foremost, rather than an investment) but consider investing about 10 percent of your total investable assets either directly in real estate (which might, eventually, include a building used for your business) or indirectly through, for example, a real estate investment trust (REIT).

You can diversify on your own or achieve diversification through mutual funds (more on this on page 227).

You can also define your asset allocation model in terms of risk. A risk-based allocation model for a young single, prepared by the Minneapolis-based brokerage firm of Piper Jaffray Companies, might put half of the portfolio into the highest-quality investments, 30 percent into those with calculated risk, and 20 percent into speculative ventures. If this young single is self-employed, however, the business itself is likely to be his or her speculative venture, so the rest of the portfolio should stick to high-quality investments and (perhaps) some with calculated risk.

But asset allocation (like financial planning itself) isn't a one-time affair. The most carefully balanced portfolio will wind up out of balance as some investments do better than others. So you need to evaluate your investment portfolio periodically and re-balance as necessary. You may think this means selling good performers and keeping losers, since the winners are likely to make your portfolio top-heavy, but look at it as selling high and buying low—just what investors should do but rarely do.

You also need to evaluate your investment portfolio so that it keeps pace with your changing needs; as you age, for example, you may want to shift a larger proportion of your investments away from growth and into income.

Laddering maturities is a way to minimize risk with fixed-income investments. It works like this: Divide the amount you want to invest into five to ten equal amounts; then buy CDs, Treasury

TIP

If you haven't time to manage your investments on a day-to-day basis and are willing to go along with broad stock market performance, you might consider investing in an index fund. These mutual funds are designed to do no better and no worse than the market in general, although they do track different indexes. An often-used measure is Standard & Poor's 500 Index.

But index funds do have some drawbacks.

- Because they closely follow the market, they can be very volatile in the short term; buy an index fund only if you plan to hold for a while.
- By definition their performance will be average; you will have to forget about going for investment home runs.
- And because that average performance is reduced by expenses, it's wise to choose an index fund with no load (commission) and with low operating expenses (this number, called the expense ratio, is in the prospectus).

Note: asset allocation funds are not the same thing as index funds. Unlike index funds, which passively mirror the market, many asset allocation funds are actively managed to time the market. According to John Markese, president of the American Association of Individual Investors (AAII), such funds are very aggressive. Asset allocation funds that buy and hold are less aggressive, and hence less volatile, but the mix they choose may not be best for you. What's more, performance has often been disappointing.

obligations, or bonds with staggered maturity dates, one coming due each year for at least five years. As each maturity date rolls around, reinvest the money in a vehicle that will take you out one year further than the longest maturity you then have. Doing this lets you reinvest at varying interest rates and is a particularly good strategy when interest rates are low.

When rates are high and likely to decline, on the other hand, you would be better off locking in high rates for a longer period. But do so only if you expect to hold till maturity; bond prices fall when interest rates rise and you could lose money if you have to sell. Also, watch out for bonds that can be called; if the issuer redeems bonds early, your ladder will wind up with broken rungs.

Some analysts suggest that laddering works best if you have at least $50,000 to invest at one time; with smaller amounts, trans-action costs can consume too much of your return. If you stick to low-cost transactions, however, such as CDs or direct-purchase Treasuries (more on this later), you can construct a fixed-income ladder with as little as $10,000.

Finding Help

Help with asset allocation and specific investments is available from a number of sources, some more costly than others and some more objective than others.

Stockbrokers

Stockbrokers execute buy and sell orders for investors. They may call themselves "investment advisers" or "financial consul-tants," but brokers at full-service firms (the brokerage firms providing research and recommendations) are first and fore-most salespeople (unlike brokers at discount brokerage firms, who execute orders but do not give advice).

At full-service firms, how much brokers earn is determined not by how well clients do but by how much the brokers sell. This is clearly a form of compensation with a built-in conflict of interest; in fact, regulatory agencies are considering (but, so far, only considering) changing the rules. Meanwhile, since brokers receive a percentage of the dollar amount of every buy-and-sell transaction but nothing at all when your account is inactive, they are highly motivated to get you to trade. Moreover, since many full-service brokerage firms offer additional commissions to sell specific investment products, brokers are tempted to push those particular products—whether or not they are appropriate for the individual investor.

The temptation is too much for some brokers, who "churn" accounts with frequent trading to make more money for themselves. Most brokers are honest; they don't churn accounts and they don't recommend inappropriate investments. But even honest brokers are subject to temptation and, given the choice between two roughly equivalent investments, may recommend the product that earns them more. Try to do your own homework. And before you rely on a broker for investment advice, choose that broker carefully. Ask friends and other professional advisers for referrals, then interview several possible choices before making your decision. Talk to the broker to determine your comfort level, but also be sure to find out:

- How long the broker has been in business; ideally you want to work with someone who has been through a full market cycle of ups and downs.
- Whether the broker's definitions of "conservative" and "aggressive" investing match your own.
- Whether the broker's other customers are at all like you; if most are wealthier or trade more frequently than you expect to, you probably won't get the attention you deserve.

If you are willing to do your own research and make your own decisions, use a discount broker. The difference in cost can be substantial, although there are significant variations, depending on the size of the transaction and on the pricing technique of the particular broker. Some discount brokers base commissions on the dollar value of the transaction; they tend to be less expensive when you buy low-priced stocks. Others base commissions on the number of shares in the transaction and may be less expensive when you trade higher-priced stocks.

There is also a difference between the "big three" of discount brokers—Fidelity, Schwab, and Quick and Reilly—and the smaller firms known as "deep discounters." Table 8.1 shows the difference.

Financial Planners

Financial planners also recommend and may sell investment products, but they are more likely to do so within the context of your entire financial picture. They will draw up plans, for example, to help you pay for college or fund your retirement or build your business. Some planners specialize, in fact, in working with the self-employed.

Financial planners work for a fee, on commission, or for some combination of fee and commission. Fee-based advice is generally considered to be more objective, but it can be expensive, with a full plan running upwards of $3,000; targeted plans— looking solely at college funding, for example—may be less. Commission-based planners can give good advice as well but may face the same conflict-of-interest situation as stockbrokers.

Do your homework carefully before selecting any planner,

Table 8.1: Varying Commissions in 1993

AVERAGE COMMISSIONS

Deep discounters:	$ 53
Big three:	101
Full-service brokers:	239

COMMISSIONS ON 100 SHARES AT $100 A SHARE

Deep discounters:	$ 25
Big three:	49
Full-service brokers:	106

COMMISSIONS ON 500 SHARES AT $30 A SHARE

Deep discounters:	$ 25
Big three:	97
Full-service brokers:	314

SOURCE: Discount Brokerage Survey, New York: Mercer Inc., 1993.

bearing in mind that financial planners are unregulated and that anyone can hang out a shingle—although planners who sell investments or receive compensation for investment advice must be registered with the Securities and Exchange Commission. In addition to finding out how a planner is compensated, ask these questions:

- Will you tell me, at the outset, how much I will pay for the plan and follow-up monitoring?
- Do you receive any compensation beyond what I will pay, such as referral fees, when you recommend advisers or products?
- Will you provide regular written reports, summarizing fees?
- Will you give me names and telephone numbers of several clients?

Money Managers and Investment Advisers

Money managers and investment advisers can be helpful if you have a portfolio of at least $250,000 (some managers require $500,000). Instead of commissions (which tend to reward frequent sales), these professionals usually work for a percentage of the assets under management (which rewards performance; as assets grow, so do the earnings of the manager).

FINDING A PLANNER

Information about credentials and referrals to qualified planners in your area are available from:

International Association for Financial Planning, 800-945-IAFP
Institute of Certified Financial Planners, 800-282-7526
National Association of Personal Financial Advisors (fee-only planners), 800-366-2732
American Institute of CPAs, 800-862-4272

Money managers and investment advisers, however, often work only with discretionary accounts. This means that after discussing your investment objectives, they decide what to buy and what to sell to best meet those objectives. Check references very carefully before giving anyone discretion to trade on your behalf. It can be tempting to have someone manage your personal investment portfolio when you are busy running your own business, but it can be devastating if you choose a manager who mismanages your account. (In general, keep this in mind when selecting any financial adviser: no one cares as much about your money as you do. Even with advisers you trust, you must pay attention.)

It can also be difficult to measure the performance of money managers and investment advisers; you won't find comparative performance data published in newspapers or magazines as you will with mutual funds. When you ask an adviser about performance, Maria Crawford Scott, editor of the *AAII Journal*, suggests that you find out:

- Is reported performance a composite of all accounts or does it represent a particular model account? If the latter, does it reflect accounts similar to your own in size and strategy?
- Is reported performance net of fees and brokerage commissions?
- Does it cover a standard time period?

Investment Vehicles

Although the way you choose to allocate your assets is the key to investment success, the specific investments you choose within asset categories also play a role. Again, as a self-employed individual it's important to diversify in two ways: by investing outside of your business and by choosing a variety of investment vehicles.

The following is an overview of some investment possibilities.

TIP

Many brokerage firms are pushing *wrap-fee accounts*, combining investment advisory and brokerage services, as a way of making money managers available to investors with smaller portfolios ($100,000 or, at some firms, $50,000). Fees vary but tend to run around 3 percent of the assets under management. But it can be hard to know exactly what you're getting for the fees you pay. The SEC has proposed rules requiring wrap-account sponsors to disclose costs—including what percentage of the annual fee is paid to the manager—along with services provided and any conflict of interest. The SEC has stopped short, however, of requiring reports on performance.

Before you sign up for a wrap-fee account, the International Association for Financial Planning recommends that you ask the following:

- What fees, both direct and indirect, will I pay?
- What are the total costs associated with the program, and who is getting paid for what services?
- Are there any other expenses that will come out of my account? If so, how much?
- What would these services cost if I purchased them separately?
- Will I be paying for services I don't need?
- Will I have access to the money manager if I have questions?
- Will I receive regular performance reports? (This is important, because wrap-account performance, unlike stock or mutual fund performance, is not reported in the business press.)

When you have all of the information about the wrap account, compare its fees with the management fees of a mutual fund with similar investment objectives. Then

(*continued on next page*)

> **TIP** (*continued*)
> compare performance. It's worth paying fees for performance. But this means investment in equities. Cash, cash equivalents, and fixed-income investments do not yield the kind of return or require the kind of management that justifies wrap-account fees.

Cash and Cash Equivalents

Money in your checking and savings accounts and in money market mutual funds is money in cash. But you may want to consider cash equivalents that are liquid and accessible if needed yet return somewhat higher yields in the interim. These could include:

- Certificates of deposit. Short-term CDs don't earn much more than savings accounts. Go out at least a year, if you won't need your cash till then, and you can do better. And shop around; thrifts often pay higher interest rates than commercial banks, while credit unions may top them both. Before you commit to a fixed-time deposit, however, always find out what penalties you face if you need your money early. There are no longer any federal rules regarding penalties for early withdrawal; financial institutions can and do differ considerably in the penalties they impose.
- U.S. savings bonds, Uncle Sam's familiar EE bonds, are not often thought of in this context but actually can be a reasonable short-term cash equivalent. EE bonds pay a variable market rate of return. For the first five years, the rate is 85 percent of the average of six-month Treasury bills. Thereafter, the rate is 85 percent of the average of five-year Treasuries. Rates are changed twice a year. You may do better in EE bonds than in a CD. And EE bonds are easy to buy. Just fill out a form in your bank, write a check for the amount you're buying, and the Federal Reserve will send your bonds directly to you.

> ## TIP
> EE bonds pay interest from the first day of the month in which they are purchased. Buy bonds on the last day of the month and you can earn double interest for the month, first in the bank and then from Uncle Sam.

• U.S. Treasury bills are issued in three-month, six-month, and twelve-month maturities, in minimum amounts of $10,000 and multiples of $5,000 above this minimum. T-bills are sold at a discount, with the interest deducted in advance from the purchase price, which results in an actual yield higher than the stated yield. (U.S. Treasury notes and bonds are longer-term investments rather than cash equivalents. They are discussed on page 226.)

• Short-term bond funds, mutual funds investing in corporate or municipal bonds that mature within one to three years, are a way to achieve higher yields with less volatility than you'll find in intermediate or long-term bonds. They can also be a good alternative to savings accounts, CDs, and money market mutual funds, all paying painfully little in recent years.

One word of caution, however: although bond funds often come with check-writing privileges, try to withstand the temptation to use a bond fund as a checking account. Unlike money market mutual funds, which have a fixed net asset value, bond mutual funds have fluctuating share prices. Every time you write a check on a bond fund, you are selling shares at a different price. Each sale is a separate taxable transaction on which you must report capital gains and losses. Using a bond fund as a checking account will give you a real headache at tax time.

Common Stock

When you buy the common stock of a public corporation, you are becoming an owner of that corporation. You won't have much to say about the running of the corporation, of course, although

---

TIP

Because the interest on T-bills is subject to federal income tax in the year the bills mature, you can use these super-safe guaranteed-by-Uncle-Sam investments to bounce taxes into the next calendar year. Buy a six-month T-bill in July of 1996, for example, and it will mature in January 1997. Income tax on the interest won't be due until you file your return for 1997 in the spring of 1998.

---

you will be asked to vote, in person or by proxy, at the annual meeting. But you will share in the fortunes of the company to the extent that your investment will prosper when the company prospers and decline when the company's fortunes decline.

There are several ways to diversify individual purchases of common stock (purchases through mutual funds are discussed on page 227):

1. Buy shares in ten to fifteen companies, in different industries (for example: utilities, pharmaceuticals, food, financial services).
2. Buy the stock of large, well-capitalized corporations (among them, "blue chip" companies, such as Mobil Oil and AT&T) along with the stock of smaller companies (such as newer, high-tech ventures).
3. Buy for "value" in companies whose price looks cheap relative to earnings, assets, or dividends, and buy for "growth" in companies with rapid and expanding growth.
4. Include overseas investments along with domestic. While it's best to stick to mutual funds for the international portion of your portfolio, you can also gain international exposure through American companies doing business overseas.

Bonds

When you buy a bond, you are lending money to the issuer. Because bonds are debt obligations, bondholders typically get their money back before stockholders if an issuer runs into trouble. But bonds are also fixed-income investments, returning a predetermined yield if they are held to maturity. They do not hold the potential for capital appreciation inherent in common stock.

Since bond prices fall when interest rates rise, you can lose principal if you must sell early. Many bonds can also be "called," or redeemed early by their issuers; this often happens if interest rates fall and the issuer can save money by calling old bonds and issuing new ones at the lower rate, leaving you to reinvest your money at a lower rate of return.

Bonds, like stocks, come in several varieties:

• *Corporate bonds* are issued by corporations; their income is fully taxable and their value is only as good as the value of the issuing company—although bondholders do get their money before stockholders if a company goes under.

• *Municipal bonds* are issued by state and local government agencies and are backed, in most cases, by the taxing power of the government. Interest is generally tax-exempt for investors living in the issuing state, although in some instances interest on municipal issues may be subject to the alternative minimum tax. In any case, although tax-free income is always nice to have, don't let taxes be the tail that wags the dog; determine your investment objectives as a whole before you decide that tax-exempt investments are right for you. See table 8.2 for a comparison of taxable and tax-free yields.

• *Zero-coupon bonds*, unlike regular bonds, pay no interest during the life of the bond but return the entire yield at maturity. But there's a catch: while the bonds pay no interest, the IRS assumes "imputed interest," which is taxable each year even though you never actually see the cash. Taxable zero-coupon

Table 8.2: Comparing Tax-free and Taxable Yields

TAX-FREE YIELD	EQUIVALENT TAXABLE YIELD AT FEDERAL TAX RATE				
	15%	28%	31%	36%	39.6%
2.50%	2.94%	3.47%	3.62%	3.91%	4.14%
2.75	3.24	3.82	3.99	4.30	4.55
3.00	3.53	4.17	4.35	4.69	4.97
3.25	3.82	4.51	4.71	5.08	5.38
3.50	4.12	4.86	5.07	5.47	5.79
3.75	4.41	5.21	5.43	5.86	6.21
4.00	4.71	5.56	5.80	6.25	6.62
4.25	5.00	5.90	6.16	6.64	7.04
4.50	5.29	6.25	6.52	7.03	7.45
4.75	5.59	6.60	6.88	7.42	7.86
5.00	5.88	6.94	7.25	7.81	8.28
5.25	6.18	7.29	7.61	8.20	8.69
5.50	6.47	7.64	7.97	8.59	9.11
5.75	6.76	7.99	8.33	8.98	9.52
6.00	7.06	8.33	8.70	9.38	9.93
6.25	7.35	8.68	9.06	9.77	10.35
6.50	7.65	9.03	9.42	10.16	10.76

bonds are less of a headache, therefore, if you buy them solely for tax-deferred retirement plans, such as IRAs or Keoghs.

Treasury zeros are available and, like other Treasuries, are taxable on the federal level but exempt from state and local income tax. Fully tax-exempt zeros are sometimes available from state and local agencies. But zeros of any kind are extremely volatile investments; don't put your money in zero-coupon bonds unless you know you can leave it there until the bonds mature.

• *Treasury notes* are issued with maturities of two to ten years, at minimum denominations of $5,000 (for notes under four years) and $1,000 (for notes with longer maturities). *Treasury bonds* are issued with maturities longer than ten years, at a minimum purchase price of $1,000. Both pay interest twice a year. Both are available at a fee through stockbrokers and banks or at no cost through any branch of the Federal Reserve Bank. Note, though, that Treasuries cannot be sold directly through the Federal Reserve; if you do not hold them to maturity, you must sell through a stockbroker.

With any fixed-income investment—corporate, municipal, or Treasury—volatility increases with the length of the holding period. Investors are often willing to assume increased volatility (and risk) for the sake of increased yields. In recent years, however, the traditional yield curve has fluctuated. Instead of always earning much more by being willing to accept later maturities and the risk that goes along with tying up money for a considerable period, long-term issues have sometimes yielded little more than short-term issues—certainly not enough more to justify the risk involved. When this is the case, or when interest rates are expected to rise, stick with short- and intermediate-term bonds, going out no further than eight or ten years.

Mutual Funds

Virtually all of the investments discussed so far—cash equivalents, stocks, bonds, and Treasuries—can be purchased through mutual funds. These professionally managed investment pools, in fact, have a lot to offer.

• *Built-in diversification.* Since a mutual fund invests the pooled money of shareholders in a large number of individual stocks, bonds, or government issues, you are automatically diversified, without having to choose (and monitor) a wide number of individual issues.

• *Minimal initial investment.* Although most mutual funds require $1,000 as an initial investment, you can get started in some mutual funds with as little as $250. Subsequent investments may be smaller still. While you can certainly buy individual shares of common stock with $1,000, you won't be able to diversify, and commission costs may be steep. And you can't adequately diversify a bond portfolio with less than $50,000 or, some believe, $100,000; with bonds, for most investors, mutual funds are the only way to go.

• *Automatic transfers from your bank account.* Most mutual funds will arrange electronic fund transfers, so that you can easily and painlessly invest on a regular basis. This dollar cost averaging, as noted earlier (see page 212), is a disciplined way to build an investment portfolio at lower average cost.

• *Automatic reinvestment.* If you don't need current income, this is another good way to build your fund holdings. Instead of taking dividends in cash, authorize their reinvestment in the fund. Note, though, that (as with dividend reinvestment plans in common stock) dividends are taxable income whether they are reinvested or taken in cash.

• *Automatic withdrawal.* You can make arrangements to receive regular distributions from your fund holdings, an arrangement that can supplement self-employment income (if you've built up fund holdings before starting your business) or retirement income.

• *Fund "families."* If you select a fund within a "family' of funds, you can easily transfer money from one fund to another with a simple telephone call as your investment objectives, the economic climate, or fund performance indicate. (Bear in mind, though, that transfers from one mutual fund to another are actually sales and purchases, and taxes may be due.)

• *Retirement plans.* You can fund your IRA or Keogh plan through mutual funds, often at very low annual fees.

Although every mutual fund is, by definition, diversified, it's still a good idea to own from two to four mutual funds with different objectives and management styles. With over forty-five hundred mutual funds now in existence, picking a mutual fund is just about as tough as picking an individual stock. But you can narrow the field by matching your own objectives with twenty-one categories of funds listed by the Investment Company Institute. Here they are, with explanations as necessary:

1. Aggressive growth funds (seek maximum capital gain through aggressive investing techniques);
2. Balanced funds (seek income and long-term growth with a mix of bonds, preferred stocks, and common stock);
3. Corporate bond funds;
4. Flexible portfolio funds (the managers have enormous flexibility and can invest in whatever seems appropriate to them);
5. Global bond funds (invest in bonds worldwide, including the United States);
6. Global equity funds (invest in shares of companies worldwide, including the United States);
7. GNMA or Ginnie Mae funds (invest in mortgage-backed securities backed by the Government National Mortgage Association);
8. Growth funds (invest in the growth stock of well-established companies);
9. Growth and income funds (seek to combine long-term capital growth with steady income);
10. High-yield bond funds, sometimes called "junk" bonds;
11. Income–bond funds (a mix of corporate and government bonds to generate current income);
12. Income–equity funds (invest in common stock with good dividend-paying records);
13. Income–mixed funds (you guessed it: stocks and bonds);
14. International funds (invest in equities only outside the United States);
15. Long-term municipal bond funds;
16. Money market mutual funds (short-term cash equivalents, including treasury bills, CDs, and commercial paper);
17. Precious metals and gold funds;
18. State municipal bond funds—long term;
19. State tax-exempt money market funds (investing in

tax-exempt cash equivalents of a single state, appropriate for residents of that state);
20. Tax-exempt money market—national; and
21. U.S. government income funds.

These are the broad categories used by the Investment Company Institute, a trade association representing mutual funds.
There are other categories as well, including sector funds (such
as those concentrating in the health care industry), regional
funds (such as those investing only in Asia and the Pacific Basin), single-country funds (Japan or Germany), socially responsible funds (screening companies for social or ethical criteria as
well as financial performance), and index funds (seeking to
mirror a specific market index).

You can also diversify by buying equity funds with different
management styles. Some managers focus on "value" stocks,
whose prices are low when measured against per-share value
of the company's earnings or assets. Others concentrate on
"growth" stocks, those expected to exhibit steady appreciation.
Then there are "large-cap" funds, those holding the stock of
large corporations, such as those making up the Dow Jones
Industrial Index. And there are "small-cap" funds, generally
more aggressive and hence riskier, holding the stock of small,
emerging companies.

With more and more of the world's financial markets outside
of the United States, you also want to diversify by putting at least
a portion of your equity dollars overseas. The safest way to do

---

TIP

Don't buy mutual fund shares late in the calendar year.
Funds are required to make year-end distributions of capital gains. If you purchase shares right before the distribution, you will owe taxes on gains you never received. A call
to the fund you're considering will tell you the distribution
date.

this is through mutual funds, since it's very difficult for the individual investor to make judgments about overseas companies and to assume the currency risk that goes along with trading in other countries. More and more mutual funds focus on the burgeoning overseas market every year, some (international funds) investing only overseas and others (global funds) in a combination of domestic and foreign companies.

Loads and Fees

When you buy individual stocks and bonds, you pay a commission—usually evident but sometimes, especially in the case of bonds, hidden in the purchase price. Mutual funds are a bit different when it comes to pricing. Every mutual fund has administrative costs; a table at the front of each prospectus must tell you just what those costs are. Many funds also come with "loads" of one kind and another.

Loads are commissions. These days they may be "front-end," paid when you buy, or "back-end," paid when you sell. They may range from 2 percent to as much as 8.5 percent (rare, these days) of the amount invested. Or, if you buy a true no-load fund directly from the fund and not through a stockbroker, you may actually pay no commission at all. Some so-called no-load funds, however, have other costs. An example is "12b1 fees," named after the section of the regulations that permit them. These fees can cost more in the long run than any load because the same fee is levied year after year for as long as you hold shares in the fund.

Sometimes it's worth paying a load, but only if the advice you get is worth the price *and* only on a fund where performance can outweigh the fact that less of your money is working for you. This is most likely to be true of equity funds, where a top-notch portfolio manager can reap significant returns. But no-load funds also rank among the top performers; if you have the time and are willing to do your homework, you can pick a no-load fund that will work well for you. Busy self-employed people rarely

LEARNING ABOUT MUTUAL FUNDS

Information about mutual funds of all kinds is available in the annual directory published by the Investment Company Institute (available for $8.50 by writing to Directory, Investment Company Institute, P.O. Box 27850, Washington, DC 20038-7850). In addition to general information about investing in mutual funds, the directory lists more than forty-five hundred mutual funds by investment category, with toll-free telephone numbers so that you can call and request a prospectus.

Other information is available from:

- Mutual Fund Education Alliance, 1900 Erie, Suite 120, Kansas City, MO 64116. MFEA publishes a directory of no-load and low-load funds (for $10) along with educational information about investing in mutual funds.
- 100% No-Load Mutual Fund Council, 1501 Broadway, Suite 1809, New York, NY 10036, which publishes a directory of fully no-load mutual funds; cost: $4.
- *The Handbook for No-Load Fund Investors*, published annually by the No-Load Fund Investor, P.O. Box 318, Irvington-on-Hudson, NY 10533; (800-252-2042). This handbook includes strategies for mutual fund investing, statistical information, and a directory of funds; cost: $45.
- *The Individual Investor's Guide to No-Load Mutual Funds*, in bookstores or from the American Association of Individual Investors, 625 North Michigan Avenue, Chicago, IL 60611; cost: $24.95.

have much time, however, so you may choose to go with a stockbroker or financial planner whose advice you have found to be worth taking.

An increasing number of mutual funds are also sold in banks these day, most often in the low-load (2 percent to 3 percent) category. This can be convenient, if you like one-stop shopping.

If you choose to buy investment products from your bank, however, be aware that:

• Just because something is sold in a bank does not mean it comes with federal deposit insurance. Investment products are not bank products. They are not insured, they are not guaranteed, and you can lose money.

• Many banks offer the same mutual funds that you can buy elsewhere; this is good, because performance data can be found in newspapers and magazines. Some larger banks sell only their own proprietary or "private-label" funds; some of these funds have performed very well, but it can be difficult to monitor them or track performance.

Variable Annuities

Fixed annuities, discussed in chapter 7, are an insurance product designed to provide retirement income. Variable annuities serve the same purpose but work in a different way. Variable annuities are an investment vehicle combining an insurance "wrapper" with mutual funds. Both types of annuities offer tax deferral, but variable annuities offer the potential for more growth, along with greater risk.

The sellers of variable annuities stress their tax advantages. Note, though, that the tax-deferred buildup of earnings within an annuity has two limitations. First, as with an IRA, earnings are taxed as ordinary income when they are taken out; growth in an ordinary mutual fund, by contrast, is taxed at capital gains rates, which are lower. Second, the earnings become part of your taxable estate upon death.

Variable annuities also have sizable fees, which you should evaluate carefully before you invest. Those fees include a contract fee (typically a percentage of the assets under management), management fees (from under 1 percent to about 2 percent), plus insurance-related charges, such as mortality and expense risk charges. In addition, some states charge premium

taxes. With all of these associated costs, the mutual fund component of a variable annuity must do very well indeed before you
can come out ahead.

So stick to equities if you buy a variable annuity. It makes
little sense to pay annuity fees for fixed-income investments
and no sense at all to pay them for cash equivalents such as a
money market mutual fund. Even though equities carry the
most risk of loss, they also hold the greatest potential for gain—
and gain is what you need to outweigh annuity fees. (The
guaranteed death benefit feature of a variable annuity guarantees return of your entire principal, but only if you die;
if you live to take the money out, you may have less than you
expect.) You also need time; don't buy a variable annuity unless
you plan to leave the money in place for at least ten years.

Annuities are sold by insurance agents, financial planners,
stockbrokers, and some mutual fund companies (as direct
sellers, they typically have lower costs). They are also sold in
many banks.

Investments to Ignore

As a self-employed individual concentrating on building a
business, you should stick to bread-and-butter investments that
are easy to understand and do not require excessive time to
monitor. This means staying away, in general, from things
like options, hedges, straddles, and derivatives of all kinds,
no matter what some hot-shot salesperson says. If you don't
understand it, don't buy it. You have enough on your mind
running a business and planning for your family's financial
well-being.

Chapter Highlights

- Investing outside your own business provides essential
  diversification, especially since your own business is
  probably the riskiest part of your investment portfolio.

- Before you invest, determine your investment objectives, your investment time line, and your tolerance for risk.
- Investment strategies include identifying money that can be invested, investing with small sums when large sums aren't available, and diversifying your portfolio through asset allocation.
- Investment advice can be obtained from stockbrokers, financial planners, and money managers.
- Investment vehicles include cash equivalents, stocks, bonds, mutual funds, and variable annuities.

9 Time to Go: Estate Planning and Succession Strategies

If you are successful at what you do, your business is likely to become your single largest financial asset. Because it's also an emotional investment, however, it can be hard to view with the detachment necessary to plan for the day when it's time for you to relinquish the reins. Yet, inevitably, you will do so. Either you will be ready to retire and eager to pass the business on to your children or sell it to someone else, or you will die in harness and your business will become part of your estate. If you don't look ahead and make plans for these eventualities, both your business and your family may suffer.

First, you have to think about the future and plan both succession and exit strategies. Second, you have to take action so that your strategies can be readily implemented when the time comes. This chapter provides a framework for both planning and action. But tax laws change; so do personal circumstances. Before you take specific steps, be sure to consult experienced legal and tax advisers.

Estate Planning

Seven out of ten Americans, by some accounts, die without a valid will—"intestate," in the eyes of the law. Among family-business owners, according to a recent survey by the accounting firm Coopers & Lybrand (see box), many involve their children in the business, but only one-third mention in their wills the issue of continued family participation in the business. Too often, without advance planning, a business must be sold to meet financial obligations that arise after death. If most of your money is tied up in the business, for example, there may not be enough cash on hand to pay final expenses or estate taxes. Furthermore, as attorney Alex J. Soled points out in *Estate Planning* (Consumer Reports Books, 1994), "The laws of most states prohibit an estate from owning or running a business. . . . In some states, there is a requirement that a business be incorporated in order for the estate to run it. This will entail additional expense."

GOOD INTENTIONS

Family-owned businesses may *intend* to have the children carry on, but most do little to prepare for a smooth transition. These are the answers to the question in a 1993 survey of family-business owners: "If you plan to keep the business in your family, what steps have been taken to ensure the family's continued participation?"

My children already participate in the business:	77%
I have life insurance to cover estate taxes:	40%
It's addressed in my will:	35%
I have a buy-sell agreement for family succession:	29%
I have a management succession plan:	27%
A non–family member will manage the business until the children are old enough:	10%

SOURCE: *Growing Your Wealth Newsletter,* New York: Coopers & Lybrand, 1993.

In planning your estate and making provision for your family and for your business, take these steps:

• Determine your own objectives, and work out family issues that may conflict with those objectives. Is only one of your children, for example, interested in the business? How, then, can you be fair to all of your children?

• Write a will. While there are ways to pass assets along without a will, you also need this legal document to make sure your wishes are followed for all of your property.

• Minimize estate taxes. This can be achieved through a variety of techniques, each of which has both advantages and disadvantages.

• Consider life insurance, if appropriate, to provide liquidity and to ensure the continuation of your business.

• Consider specific succession strategies appropriate for your business, whether you operate as a sole proprietorship, as a partnership, or as a corporation.

Determine Your Objectives

Because you are self-employed, your business is probably a significant portion of your assets. In fact, despite your best efforts to separate business and personal finances, your property may be intermingled in a way that will make succession planning very difficult. This is likely to be true whether or not your spouse or children are involved in the business, but planning headaches can be multiplied many-fold when family emotions complicate strategic plans. If you want your family to benefit from your hard work, you have to plan your estate. If you want your business to continue when you are no longer actively involved—if it is the kind of business that *can* continue without you—you have to develop succession strategies. The two should go hand in hand.

Start the process by asking yourself the following questions. Be honest and specific in your answers.

1. What are your personal and business goals for the next five years? Ten years?
2. When do you plan to retire?
3. What would you like to happen to your business when you retire? When you die?
4. If you leave it to all of your children, is the business strong enough to sustain several owners?

Before you can write a will or implement other specific estate-planning strategies, you must know what you're trying to achieve. This is true for personal assets and it is true for business assets. If you are a sole proprietor the two may be intermingled. In fact, if you are a sole proprietor, especially if you are a one-person operation providing personal service, there may not be anything to pass along or to sell. In this case, your business equipment and furnishings simply become part of your estate. But if you have the kind of business that could continue— perhaps you have an established accounting practice with a valuable client list, or a pottery studio with an inventory of pots to be sold—you can implement many of the same strategies that a partnership or corporation can use to ensure succession.

First, however, think about whether there is a logical in-house successor to your business—a spouse, a child, or a key employee. This question of who should carry on after you may be a simple question if you are in a long-standing marriage and all of your adult children are either in or out of the business. It may be an extremely complex issue if you have remarried or might do so, if you have children from more than one marriage, if (and this may be the most ticklish question) some of your children work in and contribute to the business while others do not.

Start at the beginning: Does your spouse work with you? Can he or she carry on without you after your death? Will he or she want to continue after you retire? "One partner often wants to stop and smell the roses, while the other wants to keep working," notes New York accountant Stuart Kessler. "Often it's the husband who wants to slow down, while the wife feels she has a tiger by the tail and wants to keep going." A partnership agreement, even (or perhaps especially) between husband and wife, should spell out the rights each has to do as they wish and what happens if the partnership (marital or business) breaks up.

Divorce, unpleasant under the best of circumstances, often becomes a nightmare when husband and wife have worked together in a business. Both the family and the business can disintegrate under the pressure. Either the distraction of personal problems leads to the business deteriorating as less attention is paid to ongoing marketing and fulfilling customer needs, or, (a worst-case scenario) bitterness leads to actual sabotage, forcing business revenues downward to minimize the assets that must be distributed or the alimony that must be paid. Savvy divorce judges look at revenues over several years to take this into account.

There's little that can ease the emotional pain of a divorce between business partners—after all, business and personal lives have been interwoven in twenty-four-hour-a-day togetherness—but a prenuptial (or postnuptial) agreement, along with a partnership agreement, can help keep the business on an even keel. With these agreements, drawn up with the help of his-and-hers attorneys (*never* use the same attorney), you can spell out which assets each partner will get in the event of separation and how the business will be affected.

Do your children work in the business? All of them? If so, which one should most logically succeed you? It shouldn't neces-

---

TIP

A prenuptial agreement is also a good idea when the husband or wife is *not* involved in the spouse's business. Without one the business may have to be sold in order to divide marital assets at divorce. A premarital agreement could specify that whatever property each partner owns at the time of marriage remains his or her own, and that a business started by either partner during the marriage would be owned separately. Other property acquired during the marriage would then be split fifty-fifty.

sarily be the oldest child, even if that child has worked with you longest, if another has more leadership ability or business acumen. If you make this decision, however, know that one of your offspring may well resent the other. That resentment may harm both your business and your family. One solution, should family feuds break out after you are gone: mandatory arbitration. Just don't expect arbitration to bring your family closer together.

And what if you have three children and only one works in the business? Does that child take over the business when you retire? Does he or she inherit it when you die? If so, are you being fair to the other children? If not, and you split the business three ways, are you being fair to the one who has worked to make the business grow?

One solution to this conundrum: leave the entire business to the child who is actively involved, and leave equal amounts of other assets to the other children. A food broker in upstate New York did this when he left the business to the son who worked with him, leaving the house and other investments to the other son. One problem with this approach, if it kicks in at your retirement rather than at your death, is that the first child reaps the rewards of the business immediately, while the other must wait until you die. By that time, in fact, the assets may not be of equivalent value. The business may have prospered or faltered, while other assets may have appreciated or declined in value.

Another solution is to leave the business in thirds to the three children, so that the involved child has to buy out the interest of the other two. Life insurance (see page 259) can provide the necessary funds. Still another option, if your business is incorporated as a regular C corporation: leave controlling common stock to the active child, dividend-paying preferred stock to the others. In an S corporation, where preferred stock is not permitted, you would use nonvoting stock to accomplish the same purpose. Additional succession strategies are discussed, later in this chapter (page 264).

If you have a business that can survive you, whether you are currently thinking about retirement or planning your estate, you should train a successor. A spouse or adult child may work with you yet never learn enough to manage the business as a whole, unless you make a point of sharing the necessary information. Too many self-employed entrepreneurs are used to doing it all, and are reluctant to relinquish any decision-making authority. Yet an adult child strong enough to run your business may, quite understandably, not want to continually defer to your judgment. Jerome Manning, a trusts and estates attorney with Stroock & Stroock & Lavan in New York, says that such a successor "may want to come in only if he has a strong say and is not deferring to Pop or shining his shoes every day."

If authority is not shared, the end result is often rapid business failure. A study sponsored by National Life of Vermont examined more than seven hundred family businesses that failed within a few years of being transferred to the second generation. The study found, according to a report in *Forbes* (December 16, 1993), that 97 percent of the second generation blamed their parents for inadequately preparing either transition plans or estate plans. Don't let that happen to you.

If a family member could succeed you, start now to provide the necessary training. If you will have to rely on an outside person, start now to develop that successor. If you know that you rely on a key employee, think about strategies to ensure that employee's loyalty. And if you will have to sell your business to ensure its survival, start now to ascertain its value (see page 265) and to develop the necessary documents.

Write a Will

Many people shy away from writing a will. They may be unable to face their own inevitable mortality. They may believe that all of their assets will pass directly to a joint owner. (But they may not realize that additional assets, such as an accident settlement, may unexpectedly create an unplanned-for estate.) Or they may think they don't own enough to make a will worthwhile. (They may also be overlooking the hidden value in a house, in a pension plan, in life insurance, in the business they own; many of us are worth far more dead than alive.)

WORKSHEET: PERSONAL AND BUSINESS INVENTORIES

As you sit down to plan the future of your family and your business, prepare a personal inventory and a business inventory. The following is an outline; you may have additional information to include.

PERSONAL INVENTORY

Personal Information

Parents' names and addresses: _____

Siblings' names and addresses: _____

Descendants' names and addresses: _____

Name of former spouse, if any: _____

Date of divorce: _____

Location of divorce papers: _____

Date and place of death, if deceased: _____

Professional Advisers

	Name	Address	Telephone Number
Accountant:	_____	_____	_____
Attorney:	_____	_____	_____
Financial planner:	_____	_____	_____
Stockbroker:	_____	_____	_____

Social Security Number

Husband: _____ Wife: _____

Life Insurance

Policy Number	Company	Face Value	Location	Beneficiary
_____	_____	_____	_____	_____
_____	_____	_____	_____	_____
_____	_____	_____	_____	_____

(*continued on next page*)

WORKSHEET: PERSONAL AND BUSINESS INVENTORIES (*continued*)

Bank Accounts

Institution	Account Number	Location of Passbook	Location of Canceled Checks
_____	_____	_____	_____
_____	_____	_____	_____
_____	_____	_____	_____

Certificates of Deposit

Institution	Account Number	Amount	Maturity Date
_____	_____	_____	_____
_____	_____	_____	_____
_____	_____	_____	_____

Securities

Location of securities: _____

List of specific securities (stocks, bonds, mutual funds)

Company	Account/ Certificate Number	Number of Units
_____	_____	_____
_____	_____	_____
_____	_____	_____

Safe-Deposit Box

In whose name: _____

Location of box: _____ Of key: _____

List of contents: _____

Pension and Profit-Sharing Plans

	Husband	Wife
Name and address of employer:	_____	_____
Company and account number:	_____	_____
Beneficiary:	_____	_____

Keogh Plan/Ira

Location (bank? mutual fund?): _____

Account number: _____

Beneficiary: _____

Real Estate

Location	Mortgagor	Location of Documents	Insurer
_____	_____	_____	_____
_____	_____	_____	_____
_____	_____	_____	_____

Personal Property

Automobile(s): _____

Jewelry: _____

Collectibles: _____

Health Insurance

Company	Agent	Policy Number	Location of Policy
_____	_____	_____	_____
_____	_____	_____	_____
_____	_____	_____	_____

Tax Records

Location: _____

Credit Cards

Issuer	Account Number	Location of Card
_____	_____	_____
_____	_____	_____
_____	_____	_____

(*continued on next page*)

WORKSHEET: PERSONAL AND BUSINESS INVENTORIES (*continued*)

Creditors

Name	Type of Loan	Amount Due	Maturity
_____	_____	_____	_____
_____	_____	_____	_____
_____	_____	_____	_____

Will

Location of original: _____

Location of copy: _____

Name, address, telephone number of attorney: _____

Power of attorney: _____

   Location of document: _____

   Name of designated agent: _____

BUSINESS INVENTORY

Prepare a similar detailed list for your business. Pay special attention to creditors, financial advisers, and retirement plans.

Business Name: _____

Business Structure: _____

Partners: _____

Shareholders: _____

Bank Accounts

Institution	Account Number	Location of Canceled Checks
_____	_____	_____
_____	_____	_____
_____	_____	_____

Retirement Plans

Location? (bank? mutual fund?): _____

Account number: _____

Beneficiary: _____

Tax Records

Location: _____

Name, address, telephone number of accountant: _____

Credit Cards

Issuer	Account Number	Location of Card
_____	_____	_____
_____	_____	_____
_____	_____	_____

Creditors

Name	Type of Loan	Amount Due	Maturity
_____	_____	_____	_____
_____	_____	_____	_____
_____	_____	_____	_____

Business Advisers

	Name	Address	Telephone Number
Accountant:	_____	_____	_____
Attorney:	_____	_____	_____
Banker:	_____	_____	_____
Investment adviser:	_____	_____	_____
Technical adviser:	_____	_____	_____

You *do* need to write a will. Without one, state law will determine who gets everything you've worked so hard to build. Don't assume that your spouse will inherit everything. If you have children, the laws of most states will protect them by putting a portion of your estate into their names; if they are minors the state will also name a guardian to protect their rights, leaving your spouse unable to tap the money without that guardian's permission. If your spouse was counting on that money to keep your business going, the business that would in turn provide income to support your spouse and children, he or she may be out of luck. The business may even have to be sold.

If you are unmarried, the people you consider closest may very possibly not be the people the state would name to receive your assets. If you want your business to continue and your personal property distributed to the people you choose, you must make plans.

It isn't good enough to put assets in joint ownership, create a living trust, or designate beneficiaries for life insurance policies and pension plans. While these techniques can ensure that much of your property passes automatically, bypassing probate procedures, you still need a will, for the following reasons:

- To dispose of your business, if it is a business that can continue after you, in tandem with the buy-sell agreements or other contractual arrangements discussed on page 267. According to Alex Soled, "In most states, unless there are specific instructions or authority in the will, any unincorporated business may not be continued for any lengthy period of time."
- To make special provisions for a disabled child or an aged parent or a dear friend.
- To name a guardian, if you have minor children.
- To make specific charitable bequests.
- To distribute property that is not in joint ownership, passed to a named beneficiary (as life insurance or pension benefits can be), or that comes your way after

death, such as a financial settlement if you die in an accident.

- To select your executor, the person who will follow your instructions in distributing the property that passes through your will, and eliminate the necessity of a court-appointed—and expensive—administrator of your estate.

Will Basics

Yes, you can write your own will. Computer software is available that lets you fill in the blanks and produce a simple, valid will. Handwritten ("holographic") wills are even legal in some states, if you follow the rules of those states (which may mean *not* having witnesses, in some jurisdictions). But you are self-employed. Your financial affairs and your estate are more complicated than most people's. You should consult an attorney.

That doesn't mean you should leave decisions to the attorney. You must know what you want. And it always helps to be armed with knowledge when you consult a professional. Here are some of the things you should know:

TIP

If you own a business that will survive you, you should mention something about its operation in your will. This specific authorization to continue a business is required in most states, according to the American Institute of CPAs; without it your executor could run into trouble.

"As a general rule," attorney Stephan R. Leimberg writes in the AICPA's useful booklet *Understanding Probate and Estate Administration*, "an executor must liquidate a business as quickly as reasonable or continue to run the business at the executor's own risk. . . . An executor must *personally run* the business, an onerous task that cannot be delegated."

TIP

Joint ownership, sometimes called "the poor man's will," does ensure that assets pass directly to the surviving owner. But joint ownership is not the answer to every question. Look at some of the drawbacks:

• If you own property jointly with rights of survivorship, you have nothing more to say about its future ownership. You may not leave your share of the property to anyone other than the joint owner, and that owner may dispose of the property later as he or she sees fit.

• Jointly held assets do pass directly to the survivor, but directly does not necessarily mean immediately. Joint bank accounts, for example, may be temporarily blocked by state tax authorities.

• When you put assets into joint ownership with someone other than a spouse, you may incur a gift tax liability. You may also incur a sizable estate tax liability when each of you dies.

• You and your spouse, even if you are in business together, should have separate wills. A joint will, unless it is exceedingly carefully drafted, may restrict the ability of the surviving spouse to make any changes, no matter how circumstances may change. Your wills may be mirror images of each other or they may be different, but they should be separate legal documents.

• You will need either two or three witnesses to the signing of your will, depending on the state in which you live. A beneficiary of the will should not be a witness, or the legacy may be disallowed.

• Spell out what happens should a beneficiary die before you do, or simultaneously, and name secondary ("contingent") beneficiaries.

• Name an executor who is both able and willing to carry out the time-consuming chores associated with settling your estate. These chores include preparing an inventory of your estate;

collecting money owed to you and paying any money you owe at the time of your death; filing all income tax, estate tax, and inheritance tax returns and paying any taxes that may be due; distributing your estate in accordance with your wishes; and making an accounting to the court and to the beneficiaries. Name an alternate as well, in case your first choice is unable to serve when the time comes. How to decide on the best person? Leimberg suggests, "Select a person who has the most to lose from a sloppy job and the most to gain from an efficient estate settlement." Typically this is a major beneficiary under your will.

• Leave the original of your will with the attorney who drafted it (although you may want to tell your executors that they are not obligated to use that attorney), in a fireproof box at home, or in your spouse's safe-deposit box. Your own safe-deposit box may be sealed by tax authorities at your death, and while the box usually can be opened to look for a will, the process is time-consuming. Keep an unsigned copy of the will at home or in your office for ready reference. And be sure to tell someone where the original is located.

• Review your will every few years, and be sure to do so if you sell or expand your business, move to another state, marry or divorce or remarry, become a parent or a grandparent, or do anything that could affect the distribution of your estate and the validity of your existing will. Review it, too, every time there is a major change in the tax laws.

TIP

Some estate-planning advisers suggest naming a bank trust department as coexecutor with a family member. This way the institution can handle the paperwork chores while your family member makes the decisions. My suggestion: stick to a reliable relative or friend; that person can always hire an institution to do the work but will have more control if he or she makes the choice and does the hiring.

Estate Taxes

More has probably been written about minimizing federal estate taxes than about any other area of estate planning—and for good reason. Federal estate taxes now start at 37 percent on taxable estates over $600,000 and end at a nominal 55 percent on taxable estates over $3 million (nominal, because phaseouts make rates higher still on estates over $10 million). Table 9.1 shows federal estate tax rates. State taxes are another story.

The fifty states do not necessarily conform to federal rules. Some do not have a full marital exemption and therefore tax property owned jointly by spouses. Some have their own limits, lower than the federal $10,000 a year per person, on how much may be given without taxation. And some states have death taxes on estates too small to be taxed by Uncle Sam. Although many high-tax states are moderating death taxes, after realizing that affluent residents were being driven away, about half of the states still levy estate or inheritance taxes.

There is a difference. An *estate tax* is a tax on the right to dispose of property; it is assessed against the estate (after allowable deductions) and typically paid by the estate before assets are distributed. There is usually a credit against the federal estate tax, so that no tax is actually due on the state level, but a few states have tax rates exceeding the credit. An *inheritance tax* is a tax on the right to receive property and is paid by the recipient. In many states the inheritance tax is graduated so that close relatives may receive larger amounts without paying tax. Find out the death tax rules in your state. If you plan to establish a business in or move your business to another state, be sure you know that state's tax rules before your decision is final.

The $600,000 federal exemption was meant to exclude most estates from federal tax, but the amount was never indexed for inflation, and $600,000 just isn't what it used to be. Add up the value of your house, life insurance, retirement plan death benefits, and business, and you may be surprised at how much you're worth. What's more, under the unified gift and estate tax rules, giving large sums away during life may be—but isn't always—the

Table 9.1: Federal Tax Rates on Gifts and Estates

TAXABLE ESTATE AFTER DEDUCTIONS	TAX	MARGINAL TAX RATE (TAX ON NEXT DOLLAR)
$ 600,000 or less	$ 0	37%
750,000	55,500	39
1,000,000	153,000	41
1,250,000	255,500	43
1,500,000	363,000	45
2,000,000	588,000	49
2,500,000	833,000	53
3,000,000	1,098,000	55

NOTE: The benefits of the graduated estate and gift tax rates and $600,000 exemption are phased out for gifts and estates over $10 million, producing an effective marginal tax rate of 60 percent.

solution to avoiding taxes after death. Consult a competent attorney who specializes in estate planning and is familiar with the particular problems of your business. Here is a brief overview of estate-planning facts and issues:

First, no federal estate tax return need be filed under current law for most estates under $600,000. (Under legislation currently before Congress, the exclusion may be raised to $750,000.) This is your gross estate. Your *taxable* estate is your gross estate less outstanding debts, funeral expenses, executor's and legal fees, and other allowable deductions.

Second, with the unlimited marital exemption, any amount of money and property may be left to your spouse without any tax liability. (If your spouse is not a citizen of the United States, however, the $600,000 threshold applies unless you establish a special trust to obtain the marital deduction.) The unlimited marital exemption doesn't eliminate the need to plan, however, since the assets you leave to your spouse will be subject to tax when your spouse dies.

If you are married and your joint assets—business, investments, real estate, life insurance, pension plans, and so on—add up to more than $600,000, you should title your assets so that you each own approximately half of the total. This basic step makes it possible to plan for the disposition of assets after the first and then the second death without excessive taxation. If you are in this category, of course, you should consult an attorney who specializes in estate planning. You may also need to consult your business advisers, particularly if your business makes up a sizable portion of your assets.

Minimizing Estate Taxes

There are some legitimate ways to reduce the estate tax burden. You can give money away during your lifetime, thereby reducing the taxable estate itself, and you can establish trusts to funnel money to the next generation.

Giving Gifts. Money you give away during your lifetime is counted toward the $600,000 you are allowed to give without tax either before or after death. But there is an exception: you are allowed to give $10,000 apiece to as many people as you like in any one year, without paying gift tax or filing a gift tax return. If you are married, your joint gifts may be $20,000 to each recipient (if the funds come from just one of you, a gift tax return indicating the consent of the other spouse should be filed, even though no tax is due). Some business owners use this exemption to transfer partial ownership in the business to their intended beneficiaries; more on this later.

Note, though, that there is serious talk about limiting this privilege. While many tax professionals think the $600,000 estate tax threshold is safe for the foreseeable future, despite periodic rumblings for change, most also think that the provision for unlimited gifts of $10,000 may be curtailed in the near future. No one knows exactly what the Congress will do, if anything, but there appear to be two strong possibilities: either per-person gifts may be limited to immediate family or total gifts may be capped at $30,000.

You may also give away additional sums, free of gift tax, if the money is paid directly to a medical or educational institution for medical or educational purposes. In other words, you might pay your granddaughter's law school tuition or pick up hospital bills for a grandparent. You can't take an income tax deduction for these payments, but no gift tax is due.

Otherwise you may give as much as you like, so long as you file a gift tax return. No tax is due when the gift is made. Instead, amounts given during life are combined with amounts left to your heirs after death; together, all of your gifts and bequests are then subject to tax.

Note, however, that although the federal gift and estate tax is unified, and the tax rates are the same on gifts and estates, it can actually save your heirs money to give them assets during your lifetime (subject to capital gains considerations; see below). That's because the estate tax is levied on the entire amount, while the gift tax is levied on the gift. As Anita Rosenbloom, an estate-planning attorney with Stroock & Stroock & Lavan in New York City, puts it: "The estate tax system is tax-inclusive while the gift tax system is tax-exclusive."

As an example: You leave your children $1 million in your will. At a 50 percent estate tax rate, they actually receive $500,000, while Uncle Sam collects $500,000. Give away the same million dollars while you live and the tax is levied on the gift rather than on the total; the children receive roughly $667,000 with a gift tax of $333,000, or 50 percent of the gifted amount. So your children get more, while the amount of the gift tax itself reduces your taxable estate. Again, there's an exception (no one ever said tax rules were designed to be simple): if you make a gift, pay gift tax, and die within three years, the amount of the gift tax is added back into your estate for the purpose of calculating how much estate tax is due.

An advantage of lifetime taxes is that if you give property that then appreciates in value, the amount of the appreciation will escape estate taxes. But don't forget capital gains. Before you give away appreciated assets while you're living, bear in mind that the cost basis for measuring capital gains on the sale of inherited assets is fixed at the time of death, while the cost basis for gifted assets is generally fixed at what you paid. Let's say you have shares of stock for which you paid twenty dollars. The stock is now worth sixty dollars a share. If you give the stock to your daughter and she sells it, she will owe capital gains tax on the forty-dollars-per-share gain. If you leave the stock to your daughter in your will and she sells it right away, she will owe no capital gains tax at all. This "stepped-up basis" for inherited wealth (the cost is stepped up to its value at the owner's death) may tempt you to leave appreciated assets in your will rather than giving them away during your lifetime.

Never give away assets during your lifetime if you need the income those assets throw off. If you don't need current income from these assets, you'll have to weigh the relative merits of the stepped-up basis of those assets at your death against the lower estate-and-gift tax during your lifetime.

If you do decide to make lifetime gifts, think about giving (a) *appreciating* assets, such as common stock, to keep any increase in value out of your taxable estate and in the hands of the next generation, or (b) pieces of your business, to take advantage of discounted values.

Gifts and Your Business. If you want your family to continue your business, you can utilize gift giving just as you can for your personal assets. In the simplest version of gift giving, the same $10,000-per-person-per-year rule holds. Over a period of years you could give your children a majority interest in your business via these $10,000 gifts that are totally without tax. But it's also possible to give considerably more, under the unified gift-and-estate tax formula. In fact, it's now possible to benefit from giving sizable portions of your business to your family, either all at once or in increments, in your lifetime. As Frank Rainaldi, a director of the American Society of Chartered Life Underwriters (CLU) and Chartered Financial Consultants (ChFC), notes, under a recent IRS ruling, "it's basically cheaper to give away a business than to die owning it." That's because the IRS now lets you utilize "minority discounts" in giving pieces of a family business to family members.

The concept behind a minority discount is this: a small piece of a business is worth less than its proportion of the whole because that piece is not marketable and its owner has no say in

TIP

Estate taxes are normally due within nine months after death, but the due date may be deferred with respect to taxes due on a closely held business interest if the value of that business exceeds 35 percent of the adjusted gross estate. A sole proprietorship is automatically defined as closely held; partnerships and corporations are typically considered closely held if 20 percent or more of the entity's assets are in the estate.

When this is the case, while the balance of estate taxes due must be paid on schedule, no payment (except interest) need be made until five years after the normal due date for taxes owed on the value of the business. Thereafter the tax related to the closely held business interest may be paid in ten annual installments. This deferral provision may allow your family to keep the business intact and not be forced to sell to raise money in order to pay estate taxes.

Interest is due on the deferred payments, but at what Jerome Manning calls a "bargain" rate on small-business interests: only 4 percent on the first $153,000 of tax. If the tax exceeds $153,000, interest is at the then-current IRS rate for underpayment, adjusted quarterly and compounded daily. In mid-1994 the rate was 7 percent. You may want to consider less expensive financing.

running the business. The concept is well established for arm's-length transactions; only recently has the IRS agreed that it may also be applied to businesses owned entirely by family members. Until it lost several court rulings, the IRS position was that the family as a whole still controlled the business. Now it recognizes what families have long known: family members can disagree just as strangers do.

Thus, says Rainaldi, if you die owning a business worth $1 million, your estate could be taxed on that much. If you give each of your four children 25 percent of the business before you die, the minority discount could mean that each gift is worth $150,000 instead of the $250,000 at which it would otherwise be valued; you would have given a total of $600,000 instead of $1 million, thereby saving the tax on $400,000.

But you don't have to give away the entire business in order to qualify for the discount. You can give your children ownership up to a total of, say, 48 percent and retain control yourself. It isn't a bad idea to retain control of your business, and to ensure your own financial security. Never let a desire to save on taxes override other considerations. Anita Rosenbloom points out, however, that the IRS may then try to exact a premium when you die. As always, if your affairs are complicated or you're thinking of complicated maneuvers, get competent advice.

The IRS doesn't specify how much of a discount may be taken, but 30 to 40 percent appears to be reasonable. You do, however, have to have the business appraised to determine its value.

Trusts. Another way to reduce estate taxes is to put assets in trust. A trust is simply a three-part agreement in which the owner of property (the grantor) transfers legal title to that property to someone else (the trustee) for the benefit of one or more third parties (the beneficiaries).

But all trusts are not created equal. Some do nothing at all toward minimizing estate taxes. Living trusts, so popular today that they are the subject of sales pitches and seminars across the country, actually do not save on taxes at all. The definition of a living trust is that it is revocable. That means that you retain control over the assets in the trust. As a result, those assets remain in your taxable estate.

Living trusts avoid *probate*, which is not the same thing as avoiding taxes. Probate is simply the procedure of "proving" a will; unfortunately, in some states, probate and the subsequent administration of the estate are very expensive. Putting assets in a living trust, if you live in such a state (California has been a prime example), may save money because the assets pass directly to the named beneficiaries without going through probate. But the tax consequences do not change. In any event, with or without a living trust, you still need a will. Only with a will can

> **TIP**
>
> Should you decide to set up a living trust, be sure you follow through and actually place your assets in the trust. Unless you retitle them so that the assets—your securities, bank accounts, and so on—are owned by the trust and not by you, the trust itself will remain an empty shell and will accomplish nothing.

you be sure that property not jointly owned, left to a named beneficiary or held in trust (jewelry, for example, or an after-death accident settlement), will pass to the people you choose.

Irrevocable trusts, on the other hand, do remove the assets they contain from your taxable estate. But irrevocable means just that. Once you put assets into an irrevocable trust, you have no more control over those assets. Don't do so unless you are absolutely sure you won't need the money. And don't do so without seeking professional advice. There are a number of trust types, for most of which John and Jane Doe need an interpreter; before you enter the world of GRITs, GRATs and GRUTs—just three examples of trust alphabet soup—be sure you have a trustworthy guide.

One type of irrevocable trust you may want to consider, if you are using life insurance in your estate planning, is a life insurance trust. Trust or not, as a business owner, life insurance may be important.

Life Insurance

Life insurance can provide essential liquidity—the cash needed to keep your family comfortable and your business alive. Life insurance provides an "instant estate," for example, for young parents who have not yet amassed other significant assets. Life insurance may also be useful where there are other assets, but those assets (such as real estate or a small business) are difficult to convert to cash. Life insurance can provide immediate cash to run a business, a cushion to keep things going until decisions can be made. Life insurance can provide buy-out money for a successor (see page 267). And it can provide the funds to pay Uncle Sam his due.

If you need life insurance, having it owned by a trust can be a means of removing the policy proceeds from your taxable estate. You can accomplish the same purpose at less cost by having your life insurance owned by an adult child. Just be sure you understand the rules:

- If you retain any incidents of ownership in the policy—if you can change the beneficiary, for example, or borrow against the policy—the IRS will consider you the owner.
- If you transfer an existing policy, you must relinquish all incidents of ownership at least three years before your death or you will be considered the owner for estate tax purposes. Your best bet is to have your trust, or your child, buy a new policy.
- If you transfer an existing cash value policy, you may also incur considerable gift tax liability. Again, the best course is to buy a new policy. Using the gift tax rules, you may give up to $10,000 per person per year ($20,000 if you and your spouse agree) to pay the premiums. If you spend more, the balance will be applied against your unified estate and gift tax exclusion of $600,000 ($1.2 million for a married couple).

What kind of life insurance should you buy?

Term insurance is pure insurance, with a death benefit but no cash value. It is very inexpensive for young people and is a good way for young parents, for example, to acquire large amounts of insurance to protect their family. Term insurance becomes more expensive with each passing year, however, and is rarely kept throughout life. Life insurance agents rarely recommend term insurance, both because it seldom provides lifetime protection and because they earn considerably less than they do in selling more permanent protection.

Nonetheless, term insurance can serve a useful purpose. In addition to letting you buy far more insurance for the same premium dollars until you reach age fifty or so, term insurance can be a good way to get started. Ray Silva of the Guardian Life Insurance Company, and president of the American Society of CLU and ChFC, says, "We often utilize term initially just to get insurance in place, preserve the client's insurability. We can always convert to whole life downstream, but the important thing is to get the death benefit in place."

Declining balance term insurance, sometimes called decreasing term, works a bit differently. It has a level premium for a specified period of years, while the face amount of the policy declines. This kind of policy is most often purchased to cover a declining mortgage balance. It can also be used to protect a family while children are young, or to provide additional death benefits during the income-short start-up years of a new business.

Whole life or *permanent insurance* has a level premium pegged to the insured's age when it is first purchased; it is more expensive for younger people to buy but does not become more expensive as the years go by. Whole life insurance also builds cash value, which can be tapped by borrowing against the policy. Whole life insurance, because it is more flexible and hence more likely to be kept for a lifetime, is better suited for estate-planning purposes. Don't buy whole life, however, unless you intend to keep it

---

TIP

If you want term insurance, it's easy to comparison shop by calling services that provide quotes from a number of insurers. Some of the services, those that also sell insurance, are free. Others charge a modest fee.

For example:

- **SelectQuote, 800-343-1985**
- **InsuranceQuote, 800-972-1104**
- **LifeQuote, 800-521-7873**
- **TermQuote, 800-444-8376**
- **Insurance Information, 800-472-5800**
- **Quotesmith, 800-556-9393**

in force; let most policies lapse in the early years and you will get little or nothing back.

There are also a number of variations of whole life. *Universal life* offers both flexible premiums and flexible face amounts, with a guaranteed minimum return. Universal life was very popular in the high-interest-rate environment of the mid-1980s and may become the product of choice if interest rates rise again. It is a lot less popular now, because premiums rise as interest rates fall and the policies lose their competitive advantage. Moreover, high initial charges, like the loads on some mutual funds, reduce your effective yield.

Variable life offers the opportunity for a policy to grow in value through the policyholder's choice of investment options. If you choose wrong, the policy may decline in value, although usually not below an amount fixed in the contract. If you choose wisely, both the death benefit and the cash value may increase. These policies are more expensive to administer, and you will pay for the privilege; don't go with variable life unless (a) you are prepared to hold the policy for a number of years, and (b) you are prepared to gamble with an investment in equities. It doesn't pay to use a variable life policy to stick to fixed-income investments.

Variable universal life is a hybrid that may be the most aggressive way to purchase life insurance. The death benefit usually cannot fall below the original face value of the policy, but there are virtually no other guarantees. The flexibility that may seem attractive also makes this policy a high-risk venture for someone whose family will depend on insurance proceeds.

First-to-die policies insure two lives but pay a death benefit only on the first to die. The policies are generally about 25 percent less expensive than two equivalent policies. You wouldn't want first-to-die if you have a spouse and dependent children, in which case each parent should carry insurance, but you might want it if you are a two-income childless couple where the survivor may need liquidity. You may also want it if you are in a business partnership, where the survivor will need cash to buy out your interest and keep the business going. First-to-die policies, in fact, are often used to fund buy-sell agreements (see page

267), but they can be worded so that, should you sever your partnership, the contract is split between you.

Second-to-die policies also insure two lives, but pay only on the second death. They are useful for married couples where no estate tax is due on money left by the first spouse but a hefty tax may be due when the second spouse dies. They may also be useful in some business situations. Talk to your insurance agent.

Comparison Shopping for Insurance

It can be tough to compare apples with apples when shopping for insurance. Policy illustrations are notoriously unreliable, so much so that regulators are moving in to curtail excesses by zealous salespeople. Illustrations—actually projections of what might happen in the future as dividends are paid under a particular policy—didn't become an issue until interest rates dropped sharply. Then many policyholders, particularly holders of universal life policies, found themselves having to pay more premiums over a longer period than the policy illustrations had "promised."

Under proposals by the National Association of Insurance Commissioners, projections may be allowed on the death benefit and the cash value, both guaranteed in the policy itself. Growth via dividends could be shown only in terms of past performance, much as mutual funds are required to indicate that past performance is no indication of future results. Until this proposal is adopted, take policy illustrations with a grain of salt and focus on the safety of the insurer.

A new measuring tool called the "risk-based capital ratio" shows how much capital an insurance company has to back its operations. The ratios are intended as an early warning signal to regulators that companies may be heading for trouble. A rating below 125 percent means that state insurance departments can ask for more information; a rating below 50 percent may lead to a state takeover; a rating below 35 percent means a mandatory state takeover. But there are two problems with this measuring rod. First, the number is only one indicator, and it is insufficient when it comes to picking a sound company.

Second, state regulators won't allow companies to disclose their rating, because they don't want it to be used competitively.

Some rating agencies plan to publish the risk-based ratings, sidestepping the regulators' prohibition on companies' doing so. But your best bet is to check the soundness of a specific company by checking its overall rating from A. M. Best, Standard & Poor's, and Moody's in your local library. You can also rely on a competent insurance agent or financial planner, particularly one who represents a number of highly rated companies rather than just one, to make recommendations and steer you toward the right policy for your estate-planning needs.

An alternative, if you know exactly what you want and don't need the assistance of a life insurance agent or planner, is low-load insurance. Commissions can make up as much as 165 percent of a first-year insurance premium; yes, that's more than you pay in. As a result, you pay a hefty premium and cash values are very slow to build. With a low-load policy (similar in concept to low-load mutual funds) you pay much less (underwriting and administrative costs run around 25 percent) and also have the advantage of immediate cash values that you can tap by borrowing against the policy or surrendering it.

Low-load policies are available directly from some insurers, through some fee-only financial planners, and (in most states) through the Wholesale Insurance Network. WIN represents ten insurers, selling most forms of life insurance, including second-to-die as well as annuities, and will provide free price quotes if you call 800-808-5810.

Business Succession Strategies

Many business exit and succession strategies are best suited to larger businesses that are incorporated as regular C corps. But the owner of any business with survival value—sole proprietorship, partnership, or corporation—needs to think through what will happen when it's time to move on.

Will your business survive your retirement or your death? Is anyone in the family interested in carrying on? If not, the business (if it has ongoing value) may have to be sold. As Jerome Manning notes, "The cost of hiring someone to run the business, keeping them interested and keeping them honest, is probably too high a cost for the family to bear." If the business is not run well, income will diminish and your family will suffer. If there is no family member to carry on, it may therefore be wiser to sell the business yourself; if it must be sold after your death, Manning says, "the executors may take a licking."

The first step, even if you're only beginning to think about exiting gracefully, is to put a value on your business. But be realistic. Value is not necessarily the same as price. Your business may be potentially valuable in terms of future sales, but its current price is what a willing buyer agrees to pay. If you run a small service business, you may assume that it has no value to anyone but you. But satisfied customers, and the client list holding those names, may be very valuable to someone else. Whatever type of business you have, put all of your documents in order—income statements, accounts receivable, balance sheets, contracts, leases, income tax returns—and then turn to an impartial appraiser to set a value. Your best bet is an appraiser specializing in your business niche.

Then, if you are not selling right away, you should adjust that value periodically as the years go by. That's the ideal. But many owners are too busy to bother. As an alternative, when the time comes to sell, you can adjust the agreed-upon value upward for each year that has gone by; the consumer price index might be an appropriate inflation factor.

If value is being set at the time of death, for the purpose of estate taxes, it may be more difficult. As Manning points out, "The taxpayer and the IRS almost certainly won't see eye to eye on valuation." What's more, he writes, "The government is in the enviable position of requiring the taxpayer to make the first move." Once you set a value for your business on either a gift tax return or an estate tax return, the government can challenge your calculation. (In fact, the government can, and frequently does, challenge the valuation of all kinds of property, not just a family business—Oriental art collections, real estate investments, and so on.) What you need, therefore, is adequate documentation to support the declared valuation.

What is adequate documentation? For a home, says Manning, it could be comparable sales. For commercial real estate it could be comparable sales or a multiple of cash flow. For your collection of Oriental art it could be prices at a recent auction. For your business, according to Manning, "it could be asset value or a multiple of earnings or, in some cases, a reflection of market value for a comparable business that is a public company." Whichever path you choose, don't create the numbers yourself; although your financial data will form the basis of the valuation and must be available to the IRS, the opinion of a qualified professional such as an appraiser or an accountant will carry far more weight with the IRS.

Once you have put a value on your business, you can consider specific succession strategies. You should enlist an experienced accountant and attorney before embarking on any strategy, but the following pages discuss some of the possibilities you may want to consider.

TIP

Don't lowball a valuation figure in the hopes that it will pass IRS scrutiny. First, the IRS examines every estate tax return. Second, there are tough penalties to pay on valuations that the IRS successfully challenges. The penalties are based on the amount of the discrepancy. If a business valuation is raised by the IRS from $100,000 to $200,000, for example, your estate will owe a penalty of 20 percent of the tax on the $100,000 increase in value. If the IRS concludes that the value of your business interest is actually $400,000, the penalty could be 40 percent of the tax on the $300,000 increase in value.

Buy-Sell Agreements

Buy-sell agreements can be used between family members or between unrelated business partners. Let's say you and your daughter work together in the business. You would like her to succeed you eventually, but she is not yet a full partner. Your agreement states that your daughter will buy out the business upon your retirement, death, or disability.

The triggering event must be defined if the agreement is mandatory; some agreements are voluntary and do not require that you sell your share of the business at any given time. Either way, the agreement should specify a purchase price formula and the terms and means of payment. If you use insurance to fund the agreement, your daughter will have the necessary cash to buy the business, your other children will have an equivalent inheritance, and your estate will have liquidity to cover estate taxes.

Where full-fledged partnerships use buy-sell agreements, Silva notes, they are more often funded by a cross-purchase arrangement. Each partner buys life insurance on the other, funded out of his or her own partnership earnings, to provide the cash to take over the business when the first partner dies. Buy-sell agreements may be particularly important in partnerships, since, unless there is a written agreement to the contrary, the death of a partner may automatically dissolve the business. Restructuring and a new partnership agreement may be necessary if the business is to continue. But just as businesses differ dramatically in their composition, buy-sell agreements must be tailored to suit specific needs.

TIP

The buy-sell agreement in a family business must be comparable to similar agreements between unrelated parties, structured as an arm's-length transaction. And the sales price must be the fair market value. If it is less, the IRS will insist that the full value be included in your estate tax return.

Split-Dollar Life Insurance

"Split dollar" is not a type of life insurance but an arrangement under which company dollars are used to buy life insurance on an individual. It works best when those "company dollars" come from a regular C corporation, because taxes on C corporations are lower than taxes on high-income individuals.

Let's say you have a key employee, one you would like to take over when you are gone. The employee doesn't have the cash to purchase the business or even to purchase life insurance to fund a buy-sell agreement. With a split-dollar arrangement the employer can put up most of the money with the employee as the owner and beneficiary of the life insurance policy. The insurance company repays the corporation for the cumulative premiums upon the death of the owner, then pays the remaining death benefit to the employee.

An S corporation could make the same arrangement but, says Silva, an S corp has no retained earnings, no surplus, so premiums would have to be paid with money on which the owner has already paid tax.

Family Limited Partnerships

If transferring assets within the gift tax limitations would quickly put your children and grandchildren in control of your

---

TIP

A cautionary note: if you are the majority shareholder and want the proceeds of a split-dollar policy to remain outside your estate, the policy must restrict your right to borrow against its cash value. If you can tap the policy to meet the corporation's cash needs, the IRS will probably assume that you own the policy and its proceeds will wind up in your taxable estate. This prohibition does not apply if there is no majority shareholder.

business, you may want to consider setting up a family limited partnership (legal in most states). You are the general partner, making management decisions. Your children and/or grandchildren (or a trust on their behalf) can receive limited partnership units; this transfers partial ownership without giving the younger generation immediate control over the enterprise. Alternatively, if you are ready to bow out, a family partnership for your children could make those actively involved in the business managing partners while the others are limited partners. What's more, those limited-partnership units may qualify for the minority discounts discussed earlier. Properly constructed—and that means expert legal advice—family limited partnerships can keep the business intact while reducing estate tax and minimizing dissension among family members.

There are many other succession techniques, most of them more applicable to larger businesses. The important thing for you, as a self-employed individual, is to look ahead and, if your business can survive you, do the advance planning that will make that possible.

Additional Considerations

Whatever plans you make for disposing of your business, there are additional estate-planning steps that you should take to protect yourself and your family. Most important are a durable power of attorney for financial matters and an advance directive in the form of a living will and/or health-care proxy for medical decision making.

Durable Power of Attorney

In addition to a will, you need a durable power of attorney. This is the document that will let someone act for you if you cannot, in both personal and business financial affairs. It can be limited, dealing only with a particular piece of property or investment account, or it can be broad, so that your agent can act for you in every kind of financial transaction. It can be immediate or (if you don't quite trust your agent to wait until it actually needs to be implemented) it can be "springing," so that it takes effect only when you are actually incapacitated; a springing power can be worded so that two doctors, for example, must agree. The one thing it must be is durable, or it will not be usable in the event of incapacity, exactly when you need it most.

Note: if you want your agent to be able to make gifts on your behalf, be sure to include appropriate language in the power of attorney. Even then some states do not permit agents to make gifts to themselves.

Advance Directives

With an advance directive you can have some say about the kind of medical care you will receive if you are unable to speak for yourself. There are two types. A *living will* specifically describes the type of health care you do or do not want if you become terminally ill. A *health care proxy*, sometimes called a durable power of attorney for health care, designates someone to act on your behalf if you are unable to do so. A proxy is more flexible than a living will, but you may want to have both. Some states accept one or the other; some accept both.

TIP
While you should execute an all-purpose durable power of attorney, some banks and brokerage firms insist on their own documents; you can avoid later hassle if you execute those as well. While you're at it, sign several originals of your all-purpose general power and have them notarized; some institutions will insist on keeping an original document.

Chapter Highlights

- Your business is probably a significant portion of your total assets; a first step in estate planning is determining whether that business can live on after you or will have to be liquidated.
- A family member is generally the best choice to carry on a small business, but family issues (such as divorce and sibling rivalry) may make planning difficult.
- A will is an essential first step in disposing of both personal and business property.
- Federal and state death taxes can consume sizable sums; lifetime gifts and trusts are two ways to minimize the impact.
- Life insurance can provide the funds to buy out the business or to pay estate taxes.
- A value should be put on your business, and periodically updated, whether you plan to sell your business or hope to leave it to your family.
- Specific succession strategies include buy-sell agreements, split-dollar life insurance, and family-limited partnerships.
- A durable power of attorney and advance health directives round out the process.

Part V

Growing Your Business

10 Finding Help as Your Business Grows

As a self-employed person, you are very likely to be chief cook and bottle washer for your business as well as its bookkeeper, marketing expert, typist, file clerk, and strategic planner. Eventually you may be able to delegate some of these tasks to other people. Even at the outset, however, you would be well advised to seek professional guidance in a number of key areas. This chapter deals first with finding and evaluating that professional guidance, then with other ways to share the work of making your business grow.

Professional Advisers

Many people can be of help to the struggling entrepreneur— and to the successful one as well. Note, though, that you shouldn't underestimate your own abilities. There are a number of things that you can and probably should do for yourself, especially in the early stages of a business when you may have more time than money. Go to your local library and ask the librarian for help. Consult the nearest Small Business Development Center and make full use of the help available there. Even if you then decide to use outside professional help, you'll save money by knowing exactly what to ask and what you want. You'll also be far more certain that the adviser is doing the job you need done.

When you do seek help, the two key people are probably an accountant and an attorney. Other members of your team—and your advisers should function as a team—include a banker and an insurance agent. As business improves, you may also want to consult a financial planner, a stockbroker, and/or an investment adviser or money manager. In addition you may want to seek technical help that is directly related to your business, perhaps from a marketing consultant, a computer guru, or a graphic designer.

Let's look at exactly what each can do.

Accountants

An accountant can help with year-round tax planning and the preparation of both business and personal tax returns. But a good accountant can do far more: he or she can help you develop your business plan, determine what business structure will work best for you, set up your business books, analyze the tax consequences of business decisions, suggest helpful computer software, and manage cash flow. Accountants can also help with the kind of personal financial planning that overlaps business planning, including tailoring succession and estate plans to suit you and your family.

Anticipate expending a bit more effort to find this kind of accountant, and paying a bit more for his or her services, than you would if all you want is the preparation of tax returns. Ask other small-business owners, as well as other advisers (such as your lawyer or banker), for recommendations. Take financial statements along with prior tax returns to an introductory meeting and see what suggestions the accountant makes. Ask for specific examples of recommendations the firm has made to other clients, preferably those in similar business situations.

You may want to steer clear of one-person accounting firms; some fine accountants practice this way, but what will happen to

> ### TIP
> Don't confuse the functions of an accountant and a book-keeper. An accountant can provide valuable insight and analysis of your business problems. A bookkeeper might be used on a regular basis to enter business transactions into the appropriate ledgers or as a onetime consultant to help you get started.

your business if the accountant becomes ill or is unavailable because of some other personal emergency? You want some backup. Furthermore, in most midsize and larger firms, returns are subject to review by a second person. That review can pick up anything from a typographical error to a more serious mistake; a good reviewer may even note something you should be doing differently to improve your tax picture.

But you don't necessarily want the biggest firm around. Some small-business owners believe that it's worth paying the price for the expertise backing an individual practitioner at a very large firm and many believe that it's easier to secure a business loan if your accounting firm has a recognizable name. But it's also generally true that the Big Six, the giants of the accounting industry, aren't interested in the smallest of small businesses. If someone at a huge firm is interested, that person probably has very little experience with the practical day-to-day problems you face. What's more, you probably couldn't afford their services.

My recommendation: find an accountant with at least one partner or with solid arrangements for backup support; find an accountant who works with businesses like yours and people like you.

Attorneys

Attorneys who specialize in estate planning can help you organize your business and personal financial affairs to provide maximum benefit to your family. Attorneys can also draw up papers for the business structure you choose, if you decide on a form other than sole proprietorship, so that you will be legally incorporated or protected by a proper partnership agreement. Note, though, that in many states it's possible to prepare and file these papers on your own, with a nominal filing fee; it's not hard to do, especially if you enlist the help of experts at a Small Business Development Center.

Nonetheless, there will almost certainly be times when you need an attorney to handle special business situations, from reviewing a lease to determining product liability. To find one who will meet your needs, ask your other professional advisers and other small-business owners. You can also consult a referral service at a nearby Small Business Development Center, chamber of commerce, or bar association. If you use a referral service, bear in mind that you may simply be given names; it will be up to you to make sure that the attorney's experience matches your needs and to ask for the names of clients you can call. And, as with any important adviser, it's up to you to be sure that you are comfortable with this person and on the same wavelength.

If you do use an attorney, be sure you understand exactly how you will be billed and what extra expenses may be incurred. If an attorney is vague about billing practices, find another attorney.

Ask as many hard questions of your lawyer as you do of your accountant and other professional advisers. Don't take anything for granted, or you may wind up in the sad shoes of a New York consultant. Savvy about her business, using her time to market her services, she let her attorney file incorporation papers without full discussion. Then tax time arrived. Certain that her business was an S corporation, as she had requested, she took business losses on her personal return. First came the bad news from New York State, then from the IRS. S corp status must be elected with both the state (where it recognizes S corps; not all do) and the IRS; in this case, neither New York State nor the IRS had any record of the business's S corp status. Tax returns had to be amended, interest and penalties paid, and enormous time and effort expended in resolving the mess.

BILLING METHODS

Professional advisers may bill for their services in a variety of ways:

- By the hour
- By the day
- By the project
- On a contingency basis; they get a percentage of what they win for you (lawyers) or save for you (certain management consultants)
- On a retainer (a monthly fee covering specified services)
- Through a commission (as insurance agents and some financial planners are paid for products they sell)

Bankers

Bankers may come to mind first as the providers of business loans; as we've seen, however, fledgling businesses typically have a hard time establishing credit with a bank. But you will still want to build a cordial relationship with a bank officer, because banks offer a wide assortment of useful products, from checking accounts to mutual funds, and can be very helpful to your business as it grows.

Insurance Agents

An insurance agent, particularly one familiar with the specific type of business you own, can help you secure the business coverage you need. If you run a home-based business, in fact, your choice of an agent and a company is critical; as noted in chapter 5, there are vast differences in the coverage of so-called incidental businesses at home. Wherever your business is located, though, you need competent advice on property and liability coverages as well as health and disability insurance.

Insurance agents can play an important role in estate planning as well as help you select the policies best suited to protect you, your family, and your property. (Note, though, that while an insurance agent is essential in selecting property coverages for home and business, it is possible to save money on life insurance—assuming that you know what you need—by buying "low-load" policies, as described in chapter 9.)

Stockbrokers

Stockbrokers execute your orders to buy and sell securities. Full-service stockbrokers also provide research and recommendations on investments that can meet your personal and business needs. You can save money on commissions by doing your own research (assuming that you have time to do so while running your business), then using a discount broker, or investing directly in no-load mutual funds. Full-service brokerage firms and a number of the larger discount firms also have money market mutual funds that can be used to hold business income before it is invested or plowed back into the business; checks can usually be written on these funds as well, although often in a minimum amount of $500.

TIP

Be sure you understand exactly what you're being advised to do. I was asked in mid-1994 to comment on a "financial adviser's" recommendation to a small-business owner to deposit his salary (the checks he wrote to himself each week) into a money market fund paying 9 percent, so that he could make money on his money before he transferred it to his checking account to pay bills. As I told the caller, there was only one problem with this scheme: in mid-1994 there was no such thing as a money market mutual fund paying 9 percent. The fund had to be a high-yield, otherwise known as "junk," bond fund. This meant that there was considerable risk of losing money. Furthermore, checks written on a bond fund, unlike checks written on a money market fund, are a sale of shares and hence a taxable event.

Money Managers

Investment advisers, or money managers, manage investment portfolios for a fee that is typically a percentage of the assets under management. This fee arrangement removes the incentive that commission-based stockbrokers have to buy and sell whether or not doing so is appropriate for you at a given time. But most money managers will work only with sizable portfolios of at least $250,000 and often more. When you qualify, if you decide to take this route, shop carefully before you entrust your money to anyone. Remember: expertise can be learned, but no one, ever, will care as much about your money as you do.

Financial Planners

Often working as part of a team with your accountant, lawyer, and insurance agent, financial planners can make suggestions and help you develop and implement an overall financial plan for both your family and your business. Again, if you want business planning you should seek someone familiar with your type of business. You should also be aware that financial planners are unregulated; anyone can hang out a shingle. Be sure you deal with a reputable planner (see the box on page 282). And be sure you understand how planners are compensated.

TIP

"Wrap accounts" at brokerage houses are being billed as money managers for the middle class. These accounts have one distinct advantage: because they have a fixed fee, including commissions, there is little incentive for a broker to push purchases and sales. The disadvantage, however, is that this fee tends to be high. At a typical 3 percent of assets (sometimes including money market funds, which require no management at all), you could do better obtaining professional management through a no-load mutual fund.

Some financial planners work on commission, charging you little or nothing directly but earning their compensation in the form of commissions on the products they sell you to implement the plan they recommend. Commission-based planners can serve you well, but they also face an inherent conflict of interest, since the financial products paying the highest commission may not be the products best suited for you. Fee-based planners do not earn commissions; instead they charge flat fees, either for the entire plan or on an hourly basis. There is no conflict of interest here, but since fees are their only source of income, fee-based planners can be expensive. Some planners operate on a combination of commission and fees, charging a nominal fee for the plan itself and then commissions on the products that help to meet the agreed-upon goals.

FINDING A FINANCIAL PLANNER

For information about financial planners and referrals to planners near you, contact:

- National Association of Personal Financial Advisors (NAPFA) 800-366-2732—fee-only planners.
- American Institute of Certified Public Accountants (AICPA) 800-862-4272—CPAs who have specialized in personal financial planning; typically fee-only.
- Institute of Certified Financial Planners (ICFP) 800-282-7526—planners who have earned the CFP designation; may be fee-based or commission-based.
- International Association for Financial Planning (IAFP) 800-945-4237—planners who have qualified for IAFP's Registry; may be fee-based or commission-based.
- American Society of CLU and ChFC 800-392-6900—insurance agents and planners; typically commission-based.

As you select advisers of all kinds, get referrals from friends and colleagues and other professional advisers, placing particular weight on recommendations from people in similar business situations. Then interview several people, asking each:

• What is your professional training? How do you stay up-to-date? (Appropriate answers include seminars, continuing education, in-service training, reading professional literature, belonging to professional organizations.)

• What licenses, certifications, and registrations do you have? (The appropriate answer will vary with the specialty of the adviser you are interviewing; most, however, will have the official sanction of either the federal or state government.)

• Have you ever been censured, suspended, or reprimanded for your business practices? (While the financial adviser should disclose this information, do not hesitate to contact the regulatory agency in the specific field for further information.)

• Will you provide me with names of current and past clients I can talk to? (An adviser may wish to check with clients before releasing their names—indeed, he or she should do so—but should be able to get back to you with the names of several people willing to talk to you.)

• May I see a sample of work you've done for other clients? (This could be a financial plan from a planner, a business plan from an accountant, an estate plan from an attorney. Names and identifying details should be concealed, of course, to preserve client confidentiality.)

• Will your bills be itemized so that they can be clearly understood? (If you are paying by the hour, ask that bills show hours worked and hourly fees for the adviser and for any lower-paid assistants; ask, too, for a breakdown of such expenses as photocopying and messenger services and not just a lump sum.)

• What is your attitude toward risk? (It's reasonable to argue that you can reap more rewards by taking more risk, but advisers should not push you into taking risks that you can ill afford or that you are uncomfortable taking.)

• Do you sell financial products as well as financial services? If I buy a particular product that you recommend, will you tell me exactly how you will be compensated for that purchase? Will you put our fee arrangement in writing, including exactly what services are provided for the specified fee and when the fee is to be paid? (Steer clear of anyone who won't give you a straight answer to these questions.)

• Do your clients earn an income similar to mine? (A financial adviser may pay little attention to you if most other clients have far more to spend.)

• Do you belong to any professional organizations? (Most such organizations—whether the AICPA, the American Bar Association, or one of the financial-planning associations—have codes of ethics and require continuing education for their members.)

• Do you keep in touch with clients and make recommendations as appropriate? (You don't want someone breathing down your neck, constantly urging you to buy or try something new. You do want advisers who will keep you informed of new developments and new products that might be of interest. Your state, for example, might decide to recognize subchapter S corporations or limited liability companies. Your insurance company may come out with a new policy specifically for small businesses. Your investment goals might mesh with a newly offered investment product. Work out an arrangement with your adviser whereby you'll be kept informed.)

Then, based on the experience of the New York consultant who thought she had an S corporation when she did not: Ask open-ended questions. Ask for a checklist of what a small business should know or do. Keep asking questions until you're sure every avenue has been explored.

Technical Help

Technical help is another ball game. You can market your own product or service, learn your own computer program, design your own stationery or product brochures. But there may come a time when you would be better served by turning to professionals in some or all of these areas while you concentrate your efforts on doing what you do best. If you are spending undue amounts of time mastering accounting software, consider using a computer expert to get you started or a bookkeeper to maintain your accounts. If you should be out calling on clients instead of laying out your marketing brochure, call on a graphics firm to do the layout and production for you. "Outsourcing" to find specialized help, on a short-term or project basis, makes a lot more sense than hiring employees.

If you can't afford high-priced technical help, consider bartering, a money-saving technique discussed at greater length in chapter 2. Consult colleagues and offer to swap services. Perhaps you can write advertising copy for the graphic designer who, in turn, will lay out your marketing brochure.

Or go beyond simple bartering to form what's called a *strategic alliance* or *virtual corporation.* These are new terms, says Paramus, New Jersey, attorney Fred Nicoll, for the old-fashioned joint venture. Whatever you call it, the concept is this: as a one-person operation (or two- or three-person, or whatever), you can vastly expand the expertise you offer your customers by drawing on the skills of colleagues in related fields. All it means, really, is that you form a loose network of colleagues with complementary skills (and client lists), so that you can help one another as needed. The key is to form the network before the need arises, and to establish both clear lines of communication and a clear understanding of how you will split fees.

The understanding is crucial. Nicoll suggests drawing up an agreement covering these key points: the duration and purpose of the enterprise, who will contribute what, who will be in control and manage the operation, and the allocation of profits or losses. Be sure to address what happens when the venture is over—when it's time, as Nicoll says, "to unscramble the omelet."

TIP

Need help writing a business plan? Securing a loan? Figuring out whether it's time to expand your business into larger quarters? If you contact the nearest business school and your project poses an interesting challenge, it could become a class assignment for which students earn credit.

If you lay the groundwork for working together, you'll be ready to respond to new business opportunities. As an example, when a potential client says, "I'd be glad to have you write my brochure copy, but I need someone with graphics capability so that I can have the complete package in my hands by next week," you can respond, "My firm can do that." Large corporations are forming strategic alliances these days, by the way, as they keep in-house staffing to a minimum. It's an accepted way of doing business. As Terri Lonier points out in her book *Working Solo* (Portico Press, 1993), Hollywood provides a model: "When it's time to create a film, a producer gathers the best talent available and assembles a top-notch team. Each member contributes his or her expertise, and once the film is completed, the group dissolves and the individuals move on to other projects."

It can also be useful to make an arrangement with a colleague who does the same kind of work that you do, both for the times that one of you has more work than you can handle—you would never want to turn a client away—and for projects you can develop together. Chicago marketing communications consultant Annie Moldafsky has such an arrangement with a colleague. "We work together on the proposal and the pricing, then whoever makes the contact and brings in the account gets 60 percent of the fee and the other person gets 40 percent, over and above expenses. We also continue to pursue our individual assignments."

Moldafsky's partner happens to be nearby, in Chicago. But

TIP

An alternative to a joint venture, especially if you anticipate working together for a while, might be a limited liability company. Under the laws of most states, this relatively new organizational structure (described more fully in chapter 1) offers a great deal of flexibility with many of the benefits of both corporations and partnerships.

partners can be anywhere, thanks to computers, fax machines, and overnight delivery services. A colleague in another city, in fact, can give your business the prestige of two office locations.

PROS AND CONS OF THE VIRTUAL CORPORATION

Benefits include:

- Leverage, through meshing the participants' skills and experience;
- Lower taxes than you would have as a real corporation;
- Spontaneity, giving you the ability to respond quickly to market opportunities.

Potential disadvantages include:

- Liability, because your personal assets could be vulnerable to claims against the joint venture if your business is not incorporated;
- Lack of control, because your partners in the venture may speak for you and make commitments you would not have made;
- Lack of quality control, because you are not performing all of the work your name is associated with and thus you may be disappointed in the end result;
- Dissension, if the allocation of profits and losses is not clearly spelled out in advance.

SOURCE: Fred Nicoll, telephone interview with author, April 29, 1994.

In-House Help

You've drawn on your professional advisers, networked with colleagues, outsourced what you can . . . yet you still need help. Is it time to hire employees? Maybe. But hiring employees is costly in many ways. In addition to salaries, you may have to consider providing benefits. And, most definitely, you will take on a time-consuming paperwork burden as you collect payroll taxes and pass them on to Uncle Sam.

Before you take on payroll obligations, consider using interns, temps, independent contractors, or leased employees. Then, in order of cost and complexity, consider hiring your own family, part-timers, or full-time employees.

Interns

Interns are available through many colleges. Generally they are young people eager to gain career experience—and to have that experience to show on their resumes. While many interns prefer the prestige of big-name companies, smart ones recognize that they can get much broader hands-on experience in a small company like yours. At Lerner Duane Communications in Milburn, New Jersey, for example, Deborah Lerner uses interns to do everything from drafting press releases to media research, from developing press kits to making follow-up telephone calls to reporters. "Even something like setting up labels on the computer," Lerner notes, "shows them who we want to get in touch with and why."

Interns can be a practical solution to the problem of needing additional staff when you're not quite sure you can make a commitment to salary and benefits for a full-time person. Undergraduate interns generally don't have to be paid (some get college credit for the experience), although you may want to provide a stipend to cover transportation and lunch.

You may even find an agency able to make a match for you. Robin Sidwa started her Intern Placement Service as her own venture into small business when she left an advertising agency a few years ago. She screens resumes and preinterviews potential interns, then puts together a job description based on client needs and narrows the field to two or three likely candidates, all for a flat fee of $750. This may seem high (in fact, the fee is probably higher by now), but, as she notes, it is a labor-intensive business.

Alternatively, of course, you can find an intern yourself. Get in touch with the relevant department at local colleges and universities—accounting, journalism, and marketing might be examples—and be as specific as you can about the work you can provide (will it be very routine, or will there be at least an occasional challenge?), the hours you need, and the qualifications (such as computer skills) that the intern must have. And be prepared to fulfill the role of teacher, with more patience than might be required for a regular employee.

Temporary Workers

Temporary workers, available through agencies, can fill a wide variety of slots. Don't think only of clerical help when you think of temps. With the downsizing of American corporations, workers with varied technical and professional skills can now be obtained through temporary agencies. According to surveys by the National Association of Temporary Services, the office/clerical segment is still the largest, although it makes up less than 45 percent of the temporary payroll; this group includes secretaries, file clerks, receptionists, word-processing operators, cashiers, and others. The technical category, slightly more than 10 percent of the temporary worker pool, includes computer programmers and systems analysts, designers, editors, and engineers. Professional temporaries include accountants, sales and marketing professionals, and management. If you need a worker to fill just about any short-term assignment, consider a temporary worker.

There are two big advantages to using temporary workers: the agency pays the employee and does all of the paperwork, and you have no obligation to keep the worker beyond your actual need. The disadvantage, of course, is that temporary workers may never really learn your business or care about its success.

Independent Contractors

Independent contractors—you may be one yourself—can allow small businesses to stay lean and mean while tapping a wide array of skills. They offer the advantage of being on hand when you need them, with no ongoing obligation. The time frame of the assignment may be established up front. Or it may be as long as it takes to complete a specific job; *you* decide when the task is done, and you have no further responsibility for the worker. The problem, as noted in chapter 6, is that the IRS does not look kindly on independent contractors. It prefers to classify most workers as employees so that employers will have to collect taxes and pass them on. Court cases have revolved around workers as diverse as nurses, carpenters, sales representatives, and carpet installers. Some have been resolved one way, some another.

But there certainly are legitimate independent contractors out there. If you use computer or marketing or editorial consultants, for example, those consultants are truly independent contractors if they work for a number of companies (not just for you), set their own work schedules (you don't care if they work at two o'clock in the morning instead of two in the afternoon, so long as the work gets done), work on their own premises (although a computer consultant, clearly, must visit your office), use their own equipment and supplies, and stand to profit from the services they provide.

To be on the safe side, draw up an agreement with any independent contractor you engage. Spell out the terms of the assignment, including the contractor's understanding that he or she will not file unemployment or workers' compensation claims. These claims, filed by some consultants when the assignment is completed, have triggered IRS audits for many small businesses, along with an obligation to pay back taxes, interest, and penalties. Then be sure to provide 1099 forms at year-end for any subcontractor you've paid more than $600.

Don't expect independent contractors to be inexpensive. After all, the flip side of the fact that you don't have to provide benefits for them is that they must provide those benefits for themselves. But independent contractors can definitely be a cost-effective way of securing help as it is needed.

To find independent contractors, contact professional or trade associations, either job-specific (such as a local chapter of the Public Relations Society of America) or general (such as a local chapter of the National Association of Women Business Owners), or try an outplacement service—many displaced corporate employees have skills they would be happy to put to use on a project basis. If you advertise for help, try the business opportunities section of the newspaper rather than the help-wanted ads; as author-attorney James Urquhart III points out, independent contractors tend to respond to the first, employees to the second.

Leased Employees

Leased employees actually work for a leasing company (there are almost fifteen hundred nationwide) that, in turn, puts them on your premises. These are generally full-time employees who, for all intents and purposes, are working for your company. The advantage is that the leasing company carries workers' compensation and liability insurance on the employees, pays their salaries, and provides them with health insurance. Urquhart cautions, however, that long-term leasing may not work. Employees leased for two or three years may under the law be your employees, making you responsible for workers' compensation, unemployment compensation, and benefit plans. Even if your intent is to lease employees for a short period, you should investigate leasing arrangements very carefully; some are on the up and up while others are not all they seem.

TIP

Worried that an independent contractor will move in on your clients and push you out of the picture? Two solutions: Either keep the subcontractor in the background, while you handle all of the direct client contact. Or have the subcontractor sign a noncompete agreement, prohibiting similar work for the same client within a year.

TIP

Finding help without actually hiring employees saves both money and hassle. As CPA Bernard Kamoroff writes in *Small-Time Operator*, "It's been estimated that the employer's taxes, workers' comp insurance and paperwork will cost you an additional thirty percent of your payroll"— to say nothing of the time it will take to fill out all of the necessary forms and the increased government regulation you'll face.

Family Members

Your family has probably pitched in when you urgently needed to put address labels on a mailing or to get out from under unfiled correspondence. You can formalize the arrangement, if you choose to do so, with some advantages to both parties. Hire your kids, for example, and you can deduct their salaries as a business expense, while they can start putting money away in a tax-sheltered IRA.

The arrangement is completely legitimate, so long as you pay them a reasonable wage and they actually perform the work. Each child must fill out a W-4 form, and you will have to withhold income tax; you will also have to file a W-2 for wages earned during the year. But so long as your business is a sole proprietorship or a partnership made up solely of you and your spouse, you don't have to withhold your child's share or pay the employer's share of Social Security or federal unemployment taxes. Social Security tax becomes due only when a parent employs a child who is at least eighteen years old, and federal unemployment tax is due only when a parent employs a child who is at least twenty-one.

Part-time Workers

Part-time workers may be paid a salary or an hourly fee. Either way they represent a smaller financial outlay for your growing business than a full-time worker would, and generally without the obligation to provide fringe benefits. Under current law, you must include an employee in your pension plan once that employee meets certain requirements: With a Keogh plan, you must include (and make contributions for) any employee who is over twenty-one years old, who has worked for you two or more years, and who works for you at least one thousand hours a year. This rule effectively excludes part-timers. If you have a Simplified Employee Pension, or SEP, however, you must include any employee over age twenty-one who has worked for you for three of the last five years, *no matter how few hours the employee puts in.*

Note, though, that the field of labor law is constantly undergoing change; before assuming that you must provide or need not provide health insurance or a pension plan for your part-time worker, consult a knowledgeable adviser—accountant, lawyer, financial planner, or pension consultant.

Where to find qualified part-timers? Don't overlook young people; college or even high school students can do research, stuff envelopes, enter data into the computer, make trips to the post office. Another potential source of employees: young parents who want to be home with children but have time during school hours. If you can be flexible, willing to skip a day if an employee's child is sick or on school vacation, you may find very capable workers. Still another source is retirees. Older men and women who no longer want to work full time but have skills and energy they'd like to put to use part time may be perfect for your business needs.

To reach one or more of these groups, try an ad in your local weekly "shopper" or in the PTA newsletter. Post your job with the high school guidance office or college placement office. Or contact local organizations, from chapters of the American Association of Retired Persons to the League of Women Voters, to ask for referrals to capable people.

Full-time Employees

It may be easier to find full-time employees through newspaper advertisements (placed by you or by them) or through employment agencies. The most important thing you can do, however, long before you start the actual search, is to identify the job you want done. Write a job description, so that both you and the employee understand what's expected. Try to define the work in terms of goals rather than play-by-play activities— "prepare products for shipping to customers within two days of receipt of orders," for example, would be better than "enter orders in computer, wrap packages, take to post office." You want employees to do what needs to be done to fulfill a certain objective rather than being locked into narrowly defined tasks.

Be prepared for your own responsibilities as an employer, too. You'll need to apply for a federal employer identification number if you don't already have one. And you'll need to give employees W-4 forms and then withhold income tax in line with the number of deductions they claim; the IRS provides the necessary tables. You must pay federal and state unemployment tax. You must also withhold the employee's share of the tax for Social Security and for Medicare and pay your own share on behalf of each employee.

Federal payroll tax returns are due quarterly and *must* be filed promptly; Uncle Sam frowns—and levies severe penalties— when returns, and the accompanying money, are submitted late. What's more, once your payroll taxes for any quarter exceed $500, you must deposit the amount in a bank each month and then pass it on to the government each quarter. Then, instead of the 1099 forms you would supply to independent contractors or freelancers, you must supply W-2 forms before the end of January each year, with copies to the Social Security Administration and to each employee. Your state will also have requirements that must be followed; many states, as one example, require employers to provide disability coverage for employees.

Insurance may become more expensive; ask your insurance agent whether you need to add more coverage or higher limits once you have employees. Bookkeeping also becomes more of a headache, because simple ledgers will no longer do the job. Once you have employees, you need a separate payroll ledger to

---

TIP

A payroll-processing company can absorb many of the headaches associated with hiring full-time employees, leaving you more time to run your business. As an example: for less than ten dollars per week, PayChex (800-322-7292) will take care of all of the paperwork for two employees—drawing checks, providing documentation for your records, and preparing signature-ready tax forms to file with federal, state, and local tax authorities. For a small additional charge, the company will actually file the returns and assume full responsibility for accuracy.

---

record all of the details of wages and taxes. You'll need to keep these ledgers indefinitely. As Kamoroff says, "Long-gone employees can come back to haunt you years later, usually when there's some problem with social security retirement."

Moving from solo entrepreneur to full-fledged business by hiring help is truly a giant step both financially and psychologically. Once you conquer the logistics, however, you can expect to derive great pleasure and equally great practical rewards from seeing your business grow. Good luck!

Chapter Highlights

- Key professional advisers include an accountant and an attorney; other members of your team include a banker, an insurance agent, and a financial planner or investment adviser. Choose each with an eye to their experience in your kind of business.
- Technical help can be found by hiring consultants, bartering services, or forming a "virtual corporation."
- Sources of in-house help include interns, temporary workers, independent contractors, leased employees, and family members.

- Part-time workers may be paid a salary or an hourly fee, will mean some paperwork for you, but may not require fringe benefits.
- When you hire full-time employees, you assume major responsibility for taxes and paperwork; a payroll service can ease some of that burden.

Resources

General

Abarbanel, Karin. *How to Succeed on Your Own*. New York: Henry Holt, 1994.

Applegate, Jane. *Succeeding in Small Business*. New York: Plume, 1992.

Attard, Janet. *The Home Office and Small Business Answer Book*. New York: Henry Holt, 1993.

Brabec, Barbara. *Homemade Money: How to Select, Start, Manage, Market, and Multiply the Profits of a Business at Home*. Cincinnati: Betterway Books, 1994.

Edwards, Paul, and Sarah Edwards. *Working from Home*. New York: Jeremy P. Tarcher/Putnam, 1994.

Fleury, Robert. *The Small Business Survival Guide*. Naperville, Ill.: Sourcebooks Trade, 1992.

Kamoroff, Bernard. *Small-Time Operator*. Laytonville, Calif.: Bell Springs Publishing, 1992. This manual for the self-employed, revised every year or two, is indispensable.

Lonier, Terri. *Working Solo*. New Paltz, N.Y.: Portico Press, 1993.

Maul, Lyle, and Dianne Mayfield. *The Entrepreneur's Road Map to Business Success*. Alexandria, Va.: Saxtons River Publications, 1992.

Weinstein, Grace W. *The Lifetime Book of Money Management*. Detroit: Visible Ink Press, 1993.

Whitmyer, Claude, and Salli Rasberry. *Running a One-Person Business*. Berkeley, Calif.: Ten Speed Press, 1994.

Williams, Bruce, and Warren Sloat. *In Business for Yourself*. Chelsea, Mich.: Scarborough House, 1991.

Getting Started

Alarid, William, and Gustav Berle. *Free Help from Uncle Sam to Start Your Own Business*. Santa Maria, Calif.: Puma Publishing, 1992.

Berle, Gustav, and Paul Kirschner. *The Instant Business Plan*. Santa Maria, Calif.: Puma Publishing, 1994.

Clifford, Denis. *The Partnership Book*, 4th ed. Berkeley, Calif.: Nolo Press, 1991.

Davidson, Jeffrey P., and Charles W. Dean. *Cash Traps: Small Business Secrets for Reducing Costs and Improving Cash Flow*. New York: Wiley, 1992.

Gumpert, David E. *How to Really Start Your Own Business*. Boston: Inc. Publishing, Goldhirsh Group, 1991.

McKeever, Mike. *How to Write a Business Plan*. Berkeley, Calif.: Nolo Press, 1992.

McQuown, Judith H. *Inc. Yourself*. New York: HarperCollins, 1992.

Office of Advocacy, Small Business Administration. *The States and Small Business: A Directory of Programs and Activities*. Washington, D.C.: Government Printing Office, 1993.

Borrowing

Alarid, William. *Money Sources for Small Business*. Santa Maria, Calif.: Puma Publishing, 1991.

Blechman, Bruce, and Jay Conrad Levinson. *Guerrilla Financing: Alternative Techniques to Finance Any Small Business*. Boston: Houghton Mifflin, 1992.

Blum, Laurie. *Free Money for Small Business and Entrepreneurs*. New York: Wiley, 1992.

The Credit Process: A Guide for Small Business Owners. New York: Federal Reserve Bank of New York, 1994. (Available from the Federal Reserve Bank of New York, Public Information Department, 33 Liberty Street, New York, NY 10045.)

Dawson, George M. *Borrowing for Your Business*. Dover, N.H.: Upstart Publishing, 1991.

Legal

Department of Labor. *Small Business Handbook: Laws, Regulations and Technical Assistance Services*. Washington, D.C.: Government Printing Office, 1993.

Munna, Raymond J. *Legal Power for Small Business Owners and Managers*. Kenner, La.: A*Granite Publishers, 1991.

Steingold, Fred S. *The Legal Guide for Starting and Running a Small Business*. Berkeley, Calif.: Nolo Press, 1992.

Insurance

Burkett, Barbara Taylor. *How to Get Your Money's Worth in Home and Auto Insurance*. New York: McGraw-Hill, 1991.

Mooney, Sean. *Insuring Your Business*. New York: Insurance Information Institute Press, 1992.

O'Donnell, Jeff. *Insurance Smart: How to Buy the Right Insurance at the Right Price*. New York: Wiley, 1991.

Benefits

Keher, Daniel. *Kiplinger's 12 Steps to a Worry-free Retirement*. Washington, D.C.: Kiplinger Books, 1993.

Lesko, Matthew. *What to Do when You Can't Afford Health Care*. Kensington, Md.: Information USA, 1993.

White, Jane and Bruce Pyenson. *J. K. Lasser's Employee Benefits for Small Business*. New York: Prentice Hall, 1993.

Tax Planning

Internal Revenue Service publications, revised each year, available by calling 800-829-3676:

Publication 334, "Tax Guide for Small Business"

Publication 587, "Business Use of Your Home"

Publication 583, "Taxpayers Starting a Business"

The Price Waterhouse Investor's Tax Adviser. New York: Prentice Hall, 1993.

The Price Waterhouse Personal Tax Adviser. New York: Prentice Hall, 1993.

Urquhart, James R. III. *The IRS, Independent Contractors and You!* Irvine, Calif.: Fidelity Publishing Company of America, 1993.

Taxes and the Home Office

Block, Julian. *The Homeowner's Tax Guide.* Northbrook, Ill.: Runzheimer International, 1991.

Home Office Deductions: Tax Tips for Individuals. Chicago: Commerce Clearing House, 1993. ($6.50 from Commerce Clearing House; 800-248-3248.)

Succession Planning

Jaffe, Dennis T. *Working with the Ones You Love.* Berkeley, Calif.: Conari Press, 1990.

Lea, James W. *Keeping It in the Family.* New York: Wiley, 1991.

Manning, Jerome A. *Estate Planning: How to Preserve Your Estate for Your Loved Ones.* New York: Practicing Law Institute, 1992.

Organizations and Associations

American Women's Economic Development Corporation (AWED), 60 East Forty-second Street, New York, NY 10165; 800-222-AWED.

National Association for the Cottage Industry, P.O. Box 14850, Chicago, IL 60614; 312-472-8116.

National Association for the Self-Employed, P.O. Box 612067, Dallas, TX 75261; 800-232-6273.

National Association of Home-Based Businesses, 10451 Mill Run Circle, Suite 400, Owings Mills, MD 21117; 410-363-3698.

National Association of Small Business Investment Companies, P.O. Box 2039, Merrifield, VA 22116; 703-683-1601. A trade group of venture capital firms.

National Association of Women Business Owners, 1377 K Street, N.W., Suite 637, Washington, DC 20005; 800-222-3838 or 301-608-2590.

National Business Incubation Association, One President Street, Athens, OH 45701; 614-593-4331. Members provide low-cost services and, sometimes, loans to small businesses.

National Federation of Independent Business, 600 Maryland Ave., S.W., Suite 700, Washington, DC 20024; 202-554-9000.

National Staff Leasing Association, 1735 North Lynn Street, Suite 950, Arlington, VA 22209, 703-524-3636.

Self-Employment Survival Letter (formerly the *National Home Business Report*), published bimonthly by Barbara Brabec, P.O. Box 2137, Naperville, IL 60567-2137.

Service Corps of Retired Executives (SCORE). Check your local telephone directory under Small Business Administration or call 800-634-0245 or 202-653-6279.

Small Business Administration (SBA). Check your local telephone directory or call 800-8-ASK-SBA.

Small Business Development Centers are in every state, with more than seven hundred service locations. Check your local telephone directory under Small Business Administration or call 800-634-0245.

Index